Attack of the Leading Ladies

Film and Culture
A series of Columbia University Press
Edited by John Belton

Attack of the Leading Ladies

Gender, Sexuality,

and Spectatorship in

Classic Horror Cinema

Rhona J. Berenstein

Columbia University Press
New York

Columbia University Press
New York   Chichester, West Sussex
Copyright © 1996 Columbia University Press

Cover photo: Elsa Lanchester as The Bride in James Whale's *Bride of Frankenstein*.
Photo courtesy of Ronald V. Borst/Hollywood Movie Posters. Copyright © by
Universal City Studios, Inc. Courtesy of MCA Publishing Rights, a Division of MCA, Inc.

Cataloging-in-Publication Data

Berenstein, Rhona J.
    Attack of the leading ladies : gender, sexuality, and
  spectatorship in classic horror cinema / Rhona J. Berenstein.
        p.   cm. — (Film and culture)
      Filmography: p.
      Includes bibliographical references and index.
      ISBN 0–231–08462–5— ISBN 0–231–08463–3 (pbk.)
      1. Horror films—History and criticism.   2. Sex roles in motion
  pictures. 3. Motion picture audiences.   I. Title. II. Series.
  PN 1995.9.H6B48 1995
  791.43'616—dc20   95–31390

Casebound editions of Columbia University Press books are printed on permanent and durable acid-free paper.

Printed in the United States of America

c 10 9 8 7 6 5 4 3 2 1
p 10 9 8 7 6 5 4 3 2 1

For Ann

and in memory of Yitzchak Berenstein (1922–1994)

The Spine Chillers

How spooky the movies are getting!
Their patrons are gasping for breath.
The morgue is the usual setting
For thrillers that scare you to death.
We shudder at Frankenstein's creature,
And maidens transformed to wax,
There isn't one hideous feature
The present-day cinema lacks.

—Norman R. Jaffray,
Saturday Evening Post (1933)

Contents

Preface

When I began to think about writing this preface a year or so ago, I conceived of the following pages as a textual roadmap of sorts, a guide to the reader as to how to traverse the main axioms that underlie *Attack of the Leading Ladies*. I had expected to write about the ambiguous gender traits of monsters in 1930s films, the complex relationships between heroines and usually male-coded fiends in the genre's classic movies, the multiple sexualities expressed by horror's monsters in the 1930s, and the gender performances that are enacted both on- and offscreen by male and female characters and spectators who confront monstrous figures in both the dark of the movie theater and the night-time settings of cinematic space.

Upon reflection, however, I have decided to offer this preface as a guide of a rather different sort. It is written as a roadmap not to the textual specificities of *Attack of the Leading Ladies*, which I address in some detail in chapter 1, but rather to the emotional nuances and ambivalences that led me, in part, to write this work and to spend the last many years immersed in the world of monsters and screaming heroines.

Like all moments of significance, the publication of a first book marks time—it not only indicates something about where I am now, it also speaks volumes about where I have been in the past. In that sense, both the starting point and moment of completion of this book can be understood not only as blips along a scholarly timeline but also as markers of two significant life events. In keeping with this personal view of the creative process, I believe that writers, whether academic or otherwise, write from experience. Such experience includes writing out of, or in opposition to, family history, identity, fantasy, and other elements of our lives that are far too easily relegated to the distanced perspectives couched behind the phrase "academic research." *Attack of the Leading Ladies* is, no doubt, the result of my academic research into 1930s classic horror films. From that perspective, it is a book that offers new insights into the classic era of horror cinema in this country, as well as into the gender dynamics of the films under consideration here.

But this book is also part of my personal history, for I began *Attack of the Leading Ladies* at the same time that I came out as a lesbian—in fact, I could not begin this book, which was then a dissertation, without coming out. My interest in gender identity and sexuality in classic horror cinema could only be spoken aloud once I began putting into words my own sense of identity and sexuality. So, at the simplest of levels, my moment of coming out is where this book began. Where it ends is much more complex—for it ends, as do so many horror films, with a death—in this case the death of my father in December 1994.

Whereas my coming out process and a book about the amorphous qualities of identity and sexuality can be aligned easily with each other, the relevance of my father to a work about horror seems, at first glance, considerably less direct. Yet my interest in writing about primarily male-coded monsters that are objects of both female fascination and terror is most assuredly linked to my father. For my father was a severe and mostly untreated manic-depressive throughout my life—in short, he was the first monster I ever feared and loved. Though my father was capable of great kindness, he often counterbalanced his affection with angry and violent outbursts, emotional eruptions that were relentless and ruthless. My dual responses to my father—love and fear—were matched by his dual responses to me—love and the tormenting of those whom he loved. My relationship with him was—like all parent-child rapports—ambivalent, only ours was an ambivalence shepherded by his extreme emotional moodswings.

The simultaneity of fear and love in my relationship with my father, the coexistence of those emotions throughout my childhood and adulthood, and their perseverance beyond his death, not only signify my very complicated emotional journey with him, they also link that journey to this book—a book that traces the complexity of the heroine-monster rapport, a rapport marked by contradictory responses on the part of the woman to her would-be attacker. While the heroine-monster alliance of classic horror cinema is in some ways quite different from my relationship with my father, *Attack of the Leading Ladies* is, in a preliminary fashion, indebted to my bond with him. The coincidence of his death with the completion of this book is, then, not only a bittersweet moment of loss and accomplishment for me; more than that, it is a time of letting go.

In writing all of this at the start of my book, I run the risk of reducing the following chapters to the level of personal predilection, to the specificities of my own history and psyche. My intent is neither to privilege my personal history as the primary signifier in this book nor to reduce my arguments in the forthcoming chapters to that history. Rather, my hope is that what I have just written and revealed about myself will be understood by the reader as but one conceptual framework, among many, with which to approach *Attack of the Leading Ladies*, a framework as fraught with ambivalence and ambiguity as are the monsters, heroines, heroes, and films that I consider in the pages that follow.

Los Angeles, California
April 1995

Acknowledgments

*Although I am tempted to blame them on
television, the shortcomings of this book are
my own. Although I am tempted to take full
credit for them, the insights of this book
would not have been possible without the
support and companionship and ideas of
many others.*

—Joshua Gramson,
Claims to Fame

While it might seem like an odd gesture to quote someone else's acknowledgments at the start of my own, Joshua Gramson's remarks strike me as the kind that I would like to have written, had I thought of them first. I want to open my acknowledgments, then, with Gramson's words of wisdom and offer thanks, first, to the people who gave me access to films and other research materials: William K. Everson screened his collection of classic horror films for me on a rainy afternoon in New York City and, as an unexpected bonus, told me Erich Von Stroheim anecdotes; Ronald V. Borst invited me to his home in "the valley" and methodically pulled out file after file of photographs, Pressbooks, and other 1930s memorabilia so that I might have my pick of his best materials; Madeline Matz coordinated my screenings and research at the Library of Congress on two separate occasions and went above and beyond the call of duty to make sure that my stay in Washington, D.C., was pleasant; Ned Comstock at the University of Southern California Special Collections Cinema Archives photocopied all of the 1930s horror reviews in the *Los Angeles Examiner* to save me precious time; Stuart Ng at the Warner Bros. Archives at the University of Southern California gave me easy access to the Fay Wray Collection; Sam Gill responded efficiently to my panicked calls to the Margaret Herrick Library when I believed that I just had to look at an MPAA file immediately; Eric Schaefer at Emerson College generously provided me with frame enlargements for a number of jungle films; Michael Friend at the Margaret Herrick Library steered me in the right direction for copyright permissions; Kathy Lendech at Turner Entertainment kindly offered an educational discount for reproducing stills, as did Nancy Cushing-Jones and Annie Auerbach at MCA/Universal; Andrea Kalas and Steve Ricci of the Archive Research and Study Center gave me access to horror and jungle films at the University of California, Los Angeles's Film and Television Archive at a time when screening multiple titles was a strain on the staff; and David Russell lent me numerous books and videos from his horror collection when—in the midst of our dissertations—a less generous graduate student would have hesitated to share resources.

Next, I would like to express my thanks to my dissertation committee—Janet Bergstrom, Teshome Gabriel, Steve Mamber, Anne Mellor, Fran Olsen, and Linda Williams. They were kind enough to sign off on my dissertation, upon which this book is based, in the nick of time. I think they knew that I would have crumbled under the pressure of still more revisions. So, I thank them for their faith that whatever major deficiencies existed in that project would be worked through to the best of my ability in this one.

Various people read significant portions of this book and offered valuable suggestions and to them I owe a great deal of thanks: John Belton approved this project for his Film and Culture series at Columbia University Press very early on; Jennifer Crewe has been a kind and, especially, patient editor from the start; Adam Tibbs, Jennifer's assistant, has been very helpful; Susan Heath and Anne McCoy copyedited and supervised the publication of this manuscript with great care; Carol J. Clover suggested important revisions for chapter 3; Mary Desjardins read and reread this work at various points and proposed important changes that substantially improved all chapters; and Lauren Rabinovitz and the anonymous reader for Rutgers University Press provided detailed critiques of my dissertation, which compelled me to rewrite most of what follows.

Special thanks are also due to Ellen Broidy, Andrea Kalas, and Patty White, who read the next-to-final draft of this book with great care and whose criticisms, insights, and comments greatly improved this project.

For Lia Hotchkiss, my research assistant, I have nothing but respect and appreciation—she braved the freeways between Irvine and Los xv

Acknowledgments

Angeles to check and double-check historical data on more than one occasion. Her efforts greatly enhanced what follows. Thanks also to Vikki Duncan, department manager of the program in film studies at the University of California, Irvine, who made her way through bureaucratic channels to gather research and travel funds on my behalf. Thanks also to the University of California, Irvine committee on travel and research, whose generosity funded research outings and some of the photographic stills in this book.

Thanks also to a number of friends with whom I jumped through the hoops of graduate school: David Gardner, Dan Harries, Alison McKee, David Pendleton, Britta Sjogren, and Justin Wyatt. Colleagues at the University of California, Irvine who supported me in important ways during the writing of this book include Joan Ariel, Barbara Friedrichsen, and Susan Klein. Other pals and family members who provided encouragement and were kind enough to *not* ask me too often how my book was coming along are Varda and Isidore Berenstein, Dan Bucatinsky and Don Roos, Pam Cohen and Ann Epstein, Paula Fleisher, Mark Halman, Ilan Levy and Gay Gooderham, Debbie Lillis, Tommy and Lori Klein, Grazyna Krupa, Amy Roos, Julia Salazar, Megan Siler, Naomi Wise, Leylâ Vural, Cyndi Zale, and Shandiz Zandi.

My colleagues at the University of California, Irvine deserve special mention. Anne Friedberg, Eric Rentschler, and Linda Williams were always generous with their time, willing to discuss book-related concerns ranging from anxieties about writing to the minutiae of format. Los Angeles-to-Irvine commuting conversations with Anne greatly improved chapters 2 and 3. Rick's preparations for his "Gone Primitive" course helped me work through some ideas for chapter 6. More than any other person, Linda was a source of constant intellectual support and critical clarity from the early dissertation through the book publication stages. If every doctoral student were to have someone like Linda on his or her committee and, then, as a colleague and friend, scholarly confidence would come with relative ease and much professional angst would be avoided.

I am not sure how to thank Alison McKee adequately. She read numerous versions of the chapters that follow at various points in their development and made detailed comments that have substantially improved this book. But most of all she offered her invaluable friendship during and since our time spent at the University of California, Los Angeles. I will always appreciate her efforts to calm my hysteria during a theory seminar when I did not quite understand Roland Barthes's symbolic code (to be quite honest, I am still not sure if I do) and her unfailing ability to put academic (and other) anxieties into much-needed and always humorous perspective.

Finally, a huge thank you to Ann Donahue, who not only put up with me during the research and writing stages of both my dissertation and this book but was kind enough to serve as my personal editor both then and now. Ann made numerous and important suggestions that greatly improved the content and style of this study. She also managed to remain patient and enthusiastic each time I discovered a new marketing ploy or review that seemed pivotal to my arguments. That those discoveries were often not nearly as momentous as I originally thought is a testament to her unfailing love and support.

Attack of the Leading Ladies

Figure 1.1. As the prototypical heroine in distress, Fay Wray gazes offscreen at an unseen threat in this publicity still from *King Kong*. Photo courtesy of the Academy of Motion Picture Arts and Sciences. *Copyright © 1933 RKO Pictures, Inc. Used by permission of Turner Entertainment Co. All rights reserved.*

Introduction: Horror of Classic Horrors

A woman in the shape of a monster
A monster in the shape of a woman,
The skies are full of them.

—Adrienne Rich

I

Picture a woman's face—her mouth is open as if in midscream, her eyes stare at an offscreen terror, and fear is chiseled into her features. One of the fascinations of this image, aside from the ease with which it can be conjured, is the references it brings to mind. For this face, with its promise of an offscreen fiend, succinctly signifies the American horror film. No matter what the generic complexities of Hollywood's horror cinema, the cropped image of a woman gazing at an unseen threat has the kind of cultural and marketing clout that streamlines analysis and affirms the simplicity of visual symbols. This image, then, both signifies a genre that came into its own in Hollywood during the first half of the 1930s and places gender at the center of a marketing system and iconographic repertoire used to this very day (figure 1.1).

Attack of the Leading Ladies is a study of classic horror's terrified women—an analysis of the on- and offscreen incarnations of female fear in Hollywood horror movies made between 1931 and 1936. But it is also a book devoted to interrogating popular assumptions about horror's representations of gender. Horror's gender dynamics are usually described in simple terms. The genre's primary participants include a hideous monster, often identified as male,[1] and a heroine who turned silent displays of terror into blood-curdling screams upon the arrival of sound. Here, sound technology had an important role. The female scream, and other sound cues such as creaking doors, heightened and transformed the visual effects of the silent era.

This book looks at classic horror through the lenses of gender and sexuality. Given this focus, *Attack of the Leading Ladies* is neither a seamless narrative of all classic horror movies, a task achieved by other critics,[2] nor a comprehensive philosophy of horror, which would have to account for a range of antinomies that structure the genre, such as dead/living, animal/human, polluted/pure, and inside/outside. Instead, *Attack of the Leading Ladies* offers a number of interventions into key aspects of horror criticism pertaining to gender issues. It examines (1) the assumption that the sadistic male viewer is the genre's ideal imputed spectator; (2) the belief that the historical spectator for classic horror was male and that the female patron (rarely present at a horror movie, according to more recent accounts) cowered in fear whenever in attendance; (3) the presumption that the textual dynamics of classic horror are structured around a sadistic male gaze, which echoes the imputed and historical male spectator's point of view and terrorizes passive heroines in the process; and (4) the assertion that classic horror's stories center upon heterosexual, albeit monstrous, desire. The chapters that follow argue against these assumptions or, at the very least, for a more subtle reading of them.

Classic horror narratives are fairly straightforward: a monster is made or arrives in a village/town/city, wreaks havoc on its inhabitants, especially the heroine, and is destroyed by a bold and impressive hero, with the aid of an older man. The relationship between the monster and hero plays out a number of oppositions, such as inhuman versus human, uncivilized versus civilized, sexual versus asexual, and monstrous versus normal. Convention holds that males perform both the civilized and uncivilized parts, and that their status as fiend or hero is determined via a woman. Attack a woman and you are a monster; save a woman and you are a chivalrous man. This sexual division of labor reappears in assumptions about horror spectatorship. Men are thought to be brave viewers who enjoy and remain unshaken by on-screen terrors, while women clutch the shoulders of dates for comfort, cover their eyes in response to images too evil to view, and scream uncontrollably at the hideous exploits depicted.[3]

This model of the genre posed a dilemma when I first began to study classic horror. Perhaps, I told myself, my fascination with the genre and my sense that there is more than conventional gender dynamics at work in classic films, are functions of historical hindsight. Gazing at 1930s chillers, as some movies were called, from the vantage point of the 1990s might merely be an act of rewriting what was then in terms of here and now. But contemporary horror fared no better with critics until recently, at least in terms of gender. The genre, I was told, was off-limits to women spectators, unless they are masochists, while it remained fair game for men, assuming they are sadists.

Although these generic elements are indeed tenacious, they are also exaggerated. True, horror is filled with the torture and suffering of women, but as Carol J. Clover has claimed of contemporary films, in horror "gender is less a wall than a permeable membrane."[4] Although heroines may be female and most monsters male, characters repeatedly exhibit qualities associated with the opposite sex. This sliding of gender traits drew me to the classic films of the genre and sparked my interest in studying more closely the lures of fiends that terrorize men and women alike and threaten to dislodge some of American culture's most treasured possessions, including heterosexual matrimony, the law, medicine, and science.

Classic horror attacks assumptions regarding gender at both textual and extratextual levels. As Linda Williams notes in "When the Woman Looks," horror not only represents gender as a slippery element of identity but toys with conventional identifications as well. Williams claims that the monster, like women, exhibits a renegade sexuality—"the feared power and potency of a different kind of sexuality (the monster as double for the women)."[5] This doubling of woman and fiend is achieved through point-of-view structures:

> There is a sense in which the woman's look at the monster is more than simply a punishment for looking, or a narcissistic fascination with the distortion of her own image in the mirror that patriarchy holds up to her; it is also a recognition of their similar status as potent threats to a vulnerable male power. (90)

Williams's recognition of the monster-heroine affinity recasts the gender oversights performed by other critics. She suggests a much more complex and less rigidly patriarchal vision of horror cinema than is proffered by and large. Williams also describes classic horror as a generic space that might have something to offer the heroine and, by implication, the female spectator over and above masochistic identification with suffering—namely, identification with a powerful creature.

That my instincts were right about horror, and that Williams is on to something in her conceptualization of female spectatorship, was reinforced recently when I discussed this book with a graduating senior. When I provided an overview of my arguments, she looked up, paused for a moment, and blurted out that she had spent her high school years fascinated by horror movies and loves them to this day. There was something of a confession in what she said and how she said it, as if the admission were a betrayal of her sense of self or what she thought was my impression of her. I am not sure what our conversation meant to her—she is now graduated and traveling across the country—but it confirmed for me that horror's lures extend far beyond the sadistic male spectator. Her admission also made me wonder how many other closeted female horror aficionados are lurking out there, reveling in the dark side of the genre—the side that promises to toy with gender, destroy the traditional values that American society holds dear, and dislodge not only the propriety of human bonds but human identity itself.

Horror's threats to human identity, its propensity to play with gender roles and conventional mores, are linked directly to the monster. As Noël Carroll puts it, monsters "are beings or creatures that specialize in formlessness, incompleteness, categorical interstitiality, and categorical contradictoriness. . . . Horrific monsters often involve the mixture of what is normally distinct."[6] Although Carroll focuses on their movements across the boundaries that separate the pure from the impure, and the living from the dead, there is little doubt that monsters also throw into question the opposition between male and female. For the monster is an ontological oddity, a being whose membership in categories of biological sex is often unstable and a sham. After all, a monster may look like a man but, in most cases, it is not human.[7]

The question arises: how can *real* men be identified, especially if monsters can look so much like them? Classic horror's answer is that they cannot, at least not until the film's conclusion. Horror narratives always provide heroes of sorts, men who look as if they would be heroic if given half a chance. The only problem is they usually cannot figure out how to save the day. Over and over again heroes fail to dispatch the fiend—leaving that task to some other character—and are attacked and subdued by a creature. As Roy Huss asserts, "The horror film genre seems to reserve no place for the dashing young savior-hero."[8] Surprising as it may seem, given the genre's reputation, most of classic horror's heroes are feminized men. Yet the genre does not let all gender codes run amuck. In the final moments of most films, the hero gets the girl and clasps her to his chest or lips to make sure that she does not get away again. His prior failures are seemingly forgotten and he takes his place as a real man. The hope is that since the monster is believed to be dead, ontological and gender instability evaporate, and traditional roles are firmly in place.

Yet the hero's ineptitude throughout the bulk of horror's narratives suggests that the monster's categorical transgressions have a profound impact on other characters as well. Thus, while Carroll privileges interstitiality as a trait possessed by monsters, he overlooks the contagion of boundary crossings in the genre (crossings that include the transgression of the border between heterosexual and homosexual). It is as if the fiend's toying with, and mixture of, elements that usually remain separate, such as male and female gender traits, force or invite human characters to cross boundaries as well. As a result, classic horror is not only home to unsightly monsters created by mad scientists or devious creatures that invade London or New York from a foreign land. It is also a generic space in which human characters, male *and* female, behave monstrously and transgress the social rules and roles that usually confine them. That they do so for only ninety minutes, or however long it takes for the monster to be subdued, is both the promise and the letdown of horror's narrative contract.

Appearing near the end of sound horror's first cycle of motion pictures, Karl Freund's *Mad Love* (MGM), a 1935 mad-doctor movie that was Peter Lorre's American screen debut, opens with a sequence that looks like a short-hand version of horror's traditional generic tropes. Upon closer examination, however, Freund also offers an introduction to some of the genre's most insistent efforts to play with gender. The camera, editing, and dialogue cues are as follows: fade-up to a male mannequin hanging from rafters overhead. Pan to a theater marquee that reads: "Le Théâtre des Horreurs." Cut to a grotesque mask that rests beneath the sign and dissolve to another mask, while a female voice declares from offscreen: "No, I won't." Pull back to reveal that the mask is worn by a vendor who is selling theater tickets to a man and a woman. As the man begins to pay, the woman pleads:

"Let's get out of here." To which he responds: "There's nothing to be afraid of." But she does not agree and tells him in no uncertain terms: "You bring me to a place like this where they make you scream and faint." Unlike her date, she refuses to go to the play and rejects the man who enjoys such heinous entertainment. He acquiesces, tells her that she has "got it all wrong," and they depart from the theater. Pan to a publicity poster of a woman's face as she stares wide-eyed and frightened at some off-frame horror. Cut to the next scene.

In a matter of a few moments, Freund provides horror's key generic ingredients: a limp and possibly tortured body; the promise of a scary performance; a monstrous figure; a resistant and frightened woman;[9] and an eager male spectator. Moreover, the scene's closing image, a static frame of a terrified actress, situates *Mad Love* squarely within the vernacular of American horror. As Joe Kane noted in *Take One* in the early 1970s: "Women have been at the mercy of monsters and madmen bent upon mauling, molesting, mutilating and murdering them for the better part of a century now."[10] *Mad Love*'s opening reinforces Kane's point: the poster warns the female spectator, the woman who insists that she and her date seek their amusements elsewhere, that to enter the theater means witnessing a woman's suffering at the hands of a beast.

While this description of the scene reinforces traditional expectations in terms of gender, Freund also provides clues to suggest that horror's sexual division of labor is not so streamlined. For example, what about the first image: a *male* mannequin suspended by a noose from above? Granted, he is not a main character in the film nor, for that matter, is he animate, but this tale of horror begins with a male victim of sorts and not a female one. This point is reinforced by the woman's reaction in the sequence: "You bring me to a place like this where they make *you* scream and faint," she tells her date (emphasis added). Although women are assumed to be horror's primary screamers and fainters, *Mad Love* opens with the declaration that the Theater of Horrors makes *you*, her male companion, writhe in fear.

Although the woman's intended meaning is surely broader than my added inflection—she is probably referring to *all* horror spectators—her date is singled out grammatically. Thus, one of the underlying messages of this segment is that the genre makes *men* scream and faint, a point underscored by Carol J. Clover in her book, *Men, Women, and Chain Saws*. As she notes of the rapport between male spectators and the contemporary slasher film: "The willingness and

Figure 1.2. Dr. Gogol (Peter Lorre)—the mad doctor—and Yvonne Orlac (Frances Drake)—the heroine—stare at a pair of menacing hands in this still from *Mad Love*. While Yvonne appears distressed, Gogol's wide-eyed response suggests that he, too, is terrified. *Copyright © 1935 Turner Entertainment Co. All rights reserved.*

even eagerness of the male viewer to throw in his emotional lot, if only temporarily, with not only a woman but a woman in fear and pain . . . would seem to suggest he has a vicarious stake in that fear and pain" (60). In keeping with Clover's perspective, *Mad Love* may look like a film about the suffering experienced by a woman, but at a deeper, more sustained level it is dedicated to the unspeakable terrors endured by men (figure 1.2).

But what of the *appearance* of female fear in *Mad Love*'s prologue? There are two responses to this question and both coexist in horror cinema. On the one hand, the display of female fear is exactly what it looks like: an unwilling woman endures the advances of a man, whether he is the date who tries to lure her into watching a terrifying play or the offscreen suitor who taunts the actress on the poster. On the other hand, female fear and horror in general are linked directly with performance in this scene: there are two masks, one of which is suspended on a wall and the other worn by the vendor; the location is a theater in which a horror play is being staged; and the image of a frightened woman that closes the scene is marked explicitly as an advertisement, right down to the actress's name, which appears under her face. Horror may be home to sadistic men and masochistic women, according to *Mad Love*'s opening, but it also depicts role-playing, mask-wearing, and theatrical performances, and it requires women to act terrified.

Classic horror films are filled with performances of one sort or another: Dr. Jekyll plays the piano in *Dr. Jekyll and Mr. Hyde* (Paramount, 1932), as does Stephen Orlac, the hero, in *Mad Love*. King Kong is chained on a theater stage before an eager New York audience in RKO's 1933 production, and, in *Dracula* (Universal, 1931), the count first meets the hero and heroine in their box at the symphony, as they watch an offscreen concert.[11] This repeated inclusion of performances in classic horror films is by no means accidental. As a genre that trades in the masking and unmasking of creatures and celebrates the discovery that characters are not what they seem (consider Dracula's initial introduction as a suave aristocrat or Dr. Jekyll's kindness as a physician), the performance of roles is a crucial generic component.

Needless to say, the centrality of performance has a profound impact on gender roles. The heroine's fear, and her scream in particular, is not only the genre's most familiar trope, it is also a significant example of gender performance. The heroine's displays of terror are often coded so heavily, so theatrically in fact, that they underscore the degree to which gender behaviors are adopted in American culture, as opposed to being natural. Here, Marjorie Garber's work on cross-dressing frames the concept of gender as performance, a concept that underlies this book. Writing of the implied messages embedded in transvestite self-help magazines, Garber comments: "The social critique performed by these transvestite magazines for readers who are not themselves cross-dressers is to point out the degree to which *all* women cross-dress as women when they produce themselves as artifacts" (emphasis in original).[12] Thus, in order to construct the signifier "woman" via accoutrements such as clothing, jewelry, and makeup, Garber argues, women perform their sexual identities and adopt gender as a costumed role.

Gender as a form of role play, as a highly promoted cultural costume for women, was implied in a number of contemporary classic horror reviews. For example, *Time*'s reporter had the following to say about Helen Chandler's rendering of Mina in Tod Browning's 1931 production of *Dracula*: "Silliest sound: Helen Chandler's feeble soprano chirrup uttered repeatedly as an indication of superhuman fear."[13] A similar acknowledgment of the heavy-handed performance offered by an actress appeared two years later. For *King Kong*'s debut in 1933, *Variety* described Fay Wray's role as "a 96-minute screaming session for her, too much for any actress and any audience." Bige, *Variety*'s reporter, went so far as to link the film's lack of credibility to Wray's screams: "Another of the unbelievable facts is that Kong shouldn't drop her and look for a non-screamer—even if he has to settle for a brunet [sic]."[14]

Both examples suggest that the female scream was a generic staple by the early 1930s, a significant point given the recent introduction of sound. The reviews also indicate that the heroine's terror was sometimes unconvincing and silly, as in the case of *Dracula*, and an overwrought and literally incredible performance, as was suggested of *King Kong*. While the female scream and other displays of terror are generic staples indebted to the conventions of femininity, these reviewers suggested that they were heavily coded in classic horror (and, perhaps, in culture at large). This recognition of the performative dimension of female terror underscores the degree to which gender behaviors are *worn*, the degree to which they are taught as cultural lessons that men and women often learn remarkably well.

The question that arises is: Why are horror's female performances of gender traits so extreme? The response is that they must be extreme in order to maintain the genre's dual relationship with society at large: to destroy the status quo on the one hand, to confirm it on the other. The representation of gender traits as overwrought performances covers, or at least buffers, the genre's depiction of behaviors that push the parameters of patriarchal culture—such as female independence, a will to power and monstrosity, male fear and effeminacy, and male and female homosexuality. Here, I am indebted to Clover's writing on the occult film. Noting that the subgenre appears to be the most female and feminine of contemporary horror's offerings, Clover argues that the focus on orifices and the ease of inter-character transfusions offer narrative spaces in which gender crossings occur. Those crossings are, however, constrained by tradition to the degree that male forays into femininity must be accompanied by portrayals of women in greater distress. As she notes: "Crudely put, for a space to be created in which men can weep without being labeled feminine, women must be relocated to a space where they will be made to wail uncontrollably" (105). The frightened heroine—and the female scream in particular—serves this function in classic horror. Films are filled with women engaged in histrionic displays, terror that is coded so theatrically that it deflects attention away from the other horrors taking place, such as male anxiety, while it also insists that female fear be marked *as* a performance.

Despite my belief in the fluidity of female gender performances in classic horror, I do not want to stake a claim for the genre as home to a radical ideological critique. Gender-bending on-screen does little to unhinge the everyday workings of American patriarchy outside the theater. Thus, when I write of classic horror's transgressions in this and other chapters, I am referring first to a disruption of the bulk of genre criticism,[15] and second to the provision of a monstrous but fictional alternative to a culture that calls for rigid and highly differentiated sex roles for women and men. What I do not argue is that classic horror is transgressive from a larger ideological perspective. While the efforts of critics to plot the political efficacy or failure of genres have produced some fascinating studies, such as Robin Wood's work on horror,[16] to claim that the genre is *either* politically progressive *or* conservative oversimplifies one of its most important qualities; namely, its function as a site of ideological contradiction and negotiation.

Thus one of the fascinations of horror is that it is a venue for the dual operations of convention and transgression. Horror is committed to the maintenance of the status quo, in terms not only of gender roles but also of social structures, institutions, and belief systems in general. Yet, at the same time, it engages in full-throttle efforts to destroy those systems or at least loosen them from their stable foundations. Horror accommodates these dueling motives remarkably well, and trying to narrow its overall ideological project reduces the ability to understand the genre as a whole and, further, to account for its power to both frighten and mesmerize spectators.

II

In order to tease out horror's gender dynamics, this book focuses on three principal subgenres: hypnosis films, which include vampires, zombies, and mummies; mad-doctor movies, such as *Mad Love*; and jungle-horror pictures like *King Kong*, which cross into the generic category of jungle-adventure cinema. Each of classic horror's sub-genres both toys with and confirms conventional gender roles, yet each subgenre, and in some instances each film, does so in its own unique fashion. Given my belief that classic horror is built upon competing meaning systems—such as a battle between ideologically progressive and conservative forces—I approach the genre from multiple perspectives: the analysis of publicity campaigns, censorship files, and reviews is combined with close readings of individual films. In combining diverse approaches, my aim is to avoid a simplistic reflection study of classic horror movies and to posit, instead, the dynamic and contradictory relationships among social, institutional, economic, and creative discourses and contexts.

Before moving on to a more specific discussion of the genre's gender dynamics, I want to explore the importance of the early 1930s in the development of classic horror, as well as to suggest the crucial role of cross-generic analysis in a study of this particular era. The decision to widen my generic lens to include jungle-adventure cinema near the end of this book is based on two considerations. First, horror and jungle films share a number of crucial similarities, such as a focus on monstrosity. In classic horror, as I have suggested thus far, the monster is often a supernatural creature that invades or is born into the Western world and attacks its value systems, as well as its young men and women. Jungle movies, too, construct fiends of sorts, although monstrosity is usually equated with black Africans and, sometimes, Asians who live in the wilds of Third World jungles. Thus, monstrosity is the result of racial difference from whites in this genre, and not a by-product of scientific experiments gone awry or supernatural beings on a rampage.

Second, I believe that in studying films from the 1930s it is important to respect some of the generic looseness practiced by reviewers at the time and, therefore, to consider horror films in cross-generic terms. For example, *Dracula's Daughter*, Universal's 1936 sequel to the Bela Lugosi classic, was referred to as a melodrama in one review, a chiller in another, and a "cute little horror picture" in a third.[17] *Island of Lost Souls* (Paramount, 1933), a mad-doctor movie starring Charles Laughton, was categorized by James Wingate, assistant to Will Hays of the Motion Picture Producers and Distributors of America (MPPDA), as a "horror thrill." Yet Wingate described jungle-adventure films with no hint of a supernatural monster, such as *Nagana* (Universal, 1933), as horror thrills as well.[18]

The combination of genres was also common practice, accounting for *Film Daily*'s description of *Mad Love* as "strong horror melodrama."[19] This combination may have had something to do with gender for, as I will argue in chapter 3, women were assumed to be drawn to love stories and films were often marketed with diverse genres and, hence, spectators in mind. Cultural historian David J. Skal goes so far as to claim that the phrase "horror movies" was in "many ways an invention of 1931."[20] Support for Skal's claim can be found in reviews of Tod Browning's *Dracula*, in which the term *horror* was used, but not as a generic label.[21]

The significance of Browning's film in the history of horror should not be underestimated. His adaptation of *Dracula* marks the beginning of a brief foray into big-budget sound productions, adaptations, and original scenarios that were often huge box-office successes. It also marks the central role of women in Hollywood's approach to the genre. For as a cinematic transformation of the Gothic novel, horror movies cast women as screaming victims in the early 1930s, figures faced with insecure environments and threatening males. Unlike the Gothic novel, however, heroines are not confronted by the men closest to them—such as husbands, fathers, and suitors.[22] Instead, women are attacked or seduced by foreign male (and, sometimes, female) fiends.

But there is even more at stake in the gender ploys of horror cinema in the early 1930s and in *Dracula* in particular. For like the monsters that threaten them, the women, too, are suspected of becoming monstrous and of being drawn to an alien force, usually coded as male. "HERE'S HOW TO SELL . . . DRACULA," was the phrase used to open one section of Universal's Pressbook in 1931. Although the fine print goes on to note that "little stress is placed on the love story," the Pressbook posters tell another tale. One Pressbook advertisement, in particular, details the extent to which the film combines the figure of the foreign male seducer (who was so well represented by Erich Von Stroheim in Universal's *Foolish Wives* in 1922) with the heroine's own monstrous transformation. Here, an image of Dracula is separated from a drawing of a sleeping Mina by the following cutline: "WHILE SHE SLEPT THIS CREATURE OF THE NIGHT..THIS THING..THAT HAD DIED..FIVE HUNDRED YEARS AGO..RETURNED..TO FEAST ON HER BEAUTY..TO DRINK OF HER BLOOD..TO MAKE OF HER..ANOTHER CREATURE..LIKE HIMSELF."[23] The heroine's dual roles are put into words in the Pressbook advertisement—she is the monster's vulnerable victim who will become his fiendish partner (figure 1.3).

Figure 1.3. In this one-sheet for *Dracula*, "THE STORY OF THE STRANGEST PASSION THE WORLD HAS EVER KNOWN" is used as a selling ploy. Instead of holding Mina Seward (Helen Chandler) in his arms, as in the Pressbook poster, however, the count (Bela Lugosi) ensnares her along with his vampire-wives, just as he too appears caught in the spider's web. Photo courtesy of Ronald V. Borst/ Hollywood Movie Posters. *Copyright © by Universal City Studios, Inc. Courtesy of* MCA *Publishing Rights, a Division of* MCA, *Inc.*

Hollywood's most prolific era of horror films was, then, launched with both terror and romance in mind—cutlines often combined connotations in compelling ways. "THE STORY OF THE STRANGEST PASSION THE WORLD HAS EVER KNOWN," is how one Pressbook poster put it, while a drawing of Mina swooning in Dracula's embrace fills the advertisement.[24] In fact, the promise of *Dracula*'s appeal to female viewers preceded Browning's film and was, by all accounts, precipitated by Bela Lugosi's stage success in the eponymous role. His female fans, so the rumors go, swooned in their seats and wrote him love letters detailing their attraction to the Transylvanian vampire.[25]

Thus, while German expressionist films of the 1920s contributed significantly to the visual style of Hollywood horror, in part because of the importation of creative personnel such as Karl Freund from Germany,[26] it was in the early 1930s that horror became a significant American sound film phenomenon. It spanned studios, spawned series, achieved monetary success, and attained enough financial stability and international recognition to have a lengthy A-picture run. The recognition, at least for *Dracula*, was foreshadowed on the New York stage when Hamilton Deane and John L. Balderston's play opened in October 1927 starring Bela Lugosi as the lady-killer. *Dracula* was a Broadway hit, and its thirty-three week run was joined by two touring companies the following year. *Frankenstein*, too, was revived theatrically—Peggy Webling's stage adaptation debuted in London's West End and toured the United States in 1930.

Universal acquired the rights to both *Dracula* and *Frankenstein* early on, which helped seal the genre's on-screen fate. In fact, horror's A-movie stature in the early 1930s is often attributed to Universal, the first and only studio to rely primarily on horror to pull it out of the Depression's economic woes. While other studios, such as Paramount, produced a few big-budget horror movies at the time, only Universal devoted itself to horror on a large scale, releasing the bulk of the genre's output during the cycle's heyday, a heyday remarked upon by critics starting in 1931.[27] The cycle was still going strong as late as 1935 when F. S. N. commented in a *New York Times* review of MGM's *Mark of the Vampire* (1935) that horror is a "precious commodity and a potent lure to the box-office."[28]

While the start of the first sound horror cycle can be traced with relative ease to *Dracula*, the end point is less clear. For example, Skal maintains that *Son of Frankenstein* (Universal, 1939) marked the conclusion, although he notes that the film is "sometimes considered part of a new cycle" (206).[29] I prefer 1936 as the end point, the year in which the A-budget devotion to horror concluded (B-productions, however, continued). The Laemmles' control of Universal was compromised in the spring of that year when Standard Capital Corporation took over the studio.[30] Although B-grade horror continued at Universal and elsewhere and was on an upswing at the end of the decade (after the phenomenal success of the double-bill reissue of *Dracula* and *Frankenstein* in 1938), horror's A-picture fame was a thing of the past.

Another factor contributing to the end of the horror cycle was the increasing resistance of foreign censors to accepting horror films. Britain, a popular market for Hollywood motion pictures, was a significant case. The British Board of Film Censors was approving fewer horror movies each year until, as Skal reports, "On August 23, 1935, the Associated Press finally ran a headline the studios had been dreading: 'HORROR FILMS TABOO IN BRITAIN—"THE RAVEN" LAST'" (195). Since many of the genre's most acclaimed films debuted before 1934—before foreign censors were thoroughly disgruntled with the genre, and before Joseph Breen took over the Production Code Administration at the MPPDA—they evaded post-1934 domestic and foreign censorship boards, which were far more ruthless than their predecessors. Breen's more enthusiastic enforcement of the industry's Production Code, which I will discuss later in this chapter, was combined with growing international disdain for horror, especially its denigration of Christianity and its perverse representations of sex. This trend was accompanied by an upsurge in domestic commitment to high-budget prestige pictures. The result was a decrease in horror's popularity, particularly in terms of studio rosters for big-money productions.

The reasons for horror's acclaim in the early 1930s are multifold, some owing to the economic and cultural climate of the time, while others are linked to an historical legacy that dates back to the English Gothic novel, the German *schauer-roman*, and the French *roman noir*.[31] Certainly, the Depression, which wrought havoc on the financial and emotional well-being of the nation, fostered a climate in which the destruction of the social fabric by monsters was greeted by spectators with a sense of familiarity if not relief.

Furthermore, the era's shifts in gender roles may have had some link to on-screen representations. For example, "New Woman" was the turn-of-the-century name given to women who believed they had a right to both education and independence from conventional ties such as matrimony. By the late 1920s and early 1930s, however, New Women were described in a range of popular discourses as vixens intent on overturning social mores. In an effort to save modern womanhood from ruin, educated women were urged to return to the safety of marriage and maternity lest their independence (from men) destroy the traditional fabric of American culture.

Horror's heroines were lured away from convention by devious but seductive fiends only to be returned to the arms of their appropriate male mates by the closing moments of the films, thus providing a parallel saga to the New Woman's initial refusal of traditional choices and her eventual return, in many cases, to conventional ties. A similar parallel can be drawn between the genre's representations of Otherness, in the form of the monster, and the spate of racial conflicts—between whites and African Americans, as well as Asians—during the 1920s and 1930s. Each of these historical factors contributed, in some degree, to horror's popular reception.

But to characterize the early 1930s as an historical vacuum in which horror reigned solely because of socioeconomic conditions, as some have done,[32] is also to overlook the genre's continuum with Gothic and other artistic sources. Mary Shelley's *Frankenstein* (1816), for example, was adapted for the stage a number of times during the 1800s and early 1900s, and Robert Louis Stevenson's *The Strange Case of Dr. Jekyll and Mr. Hyde* (1886) and Bram Stoker's *Dracula* (1897) were likewise turned into theatrical performances from the turn of the century onward. Furthermore, German expressionist horror debuted after World War I, as did some American movies such as *Phantom of the Opera* (Universal, 1925) and *London After Midnight* (MGM, 1927). Thus, while Hollywood's first cycle of sound horror was significant in terms of audiences and generous budgets, as well as in its ability to endure in the popular imagination for decades, it did not spring forth out of the Depression but was linked to literary and artistic precursors. *Dracula*'s Broadway and touring successes, remember, took place in 1927 and 1928, prior to the stock market's plummet. What did spring forth in a significant manner in the early 1930s were horror's representations of female fear, especially the genre's blood-curdling renditions of the female scream. Sound gave film directors and producers a new medium of expression, one they used to give voice to the heroine's relationship with the monster and to frame the genre's portrayals of gender dynamics in very spectacular terms.

III

What characteristics of horror seem most engaging to spectators? What elements are the most salient in terms of viewer concerns? For me, these are not merely questions of why people watch horror but of how they watch it as well. Like other critics, I think horror's draw is akin to the thrills offered by a roller coaster. As James B. Twitchell notes, "on the downward ride there is ample time for the boys to practice bravery by biting their nether lip, while squealing girls perfect their own control by surrender."[33] While the roller-coaster analogy is compelling, Twitchell's insistence on a traditional model of gender difference is also confining. Granted, in this culture men and boys are taught to act bravely, while women and girls are given freer rein in terms of emotions. Yet horror's affective enticements are so numerous and shifting that a wider spectrum of gendered responses most certainly occurs.

Twitchell's own wording allows for this interpretation. Although some boys may, as he says, practice bravery, they may also fail in their efforts to perfect it. Furthermore, Twitchell overlooks the strong possibility that how male and female spectators behave in an audience— with silence or screams—may not tell all in terms of how they *feel* while watching a film. A roller-coaster ride is filled with ups and downs, moments in which there is a lull in tension, others when riders are giddy with anticipation, still other times in which they scream to their hearts' content, while simultaneously giggling. Terror, anxiety, nausea, anticipation, disappointment, surprise, delight, and a desire for more are all states often experienced on a roller coaster; the emotions oscillate depending on where the rider is in the course of the ride.

In fact, roller coasters offer riders an outlet for emotional performances. Both female and male riders at the top of an incline know they are supposed to scream or act bravely (depending on gender mandates) once they plunge down the hill. Their responses, then, are part of a social ritual, fulfillments of cultural expectations, and may not be precise indices of their feelings. Given that a roller-coaster ride, like the spectator's journey through classic horror, is filled with moments in which the rider/spectator knows what is coming—a quick turn or a monster's attack—male and female spectatorship needs to be viewed as flexible, an experience in which a range of affective states, some prescribed and others not, are induced and adopted.

Despite my call for flexibility, the bulk of horror criticism is fairly rigid and attempts to account for the genre's appeal in a formulaic manner. In his book-length study of horror, for example, Twitchell draws a detailed picture of the genre's lures, again invoking the amusement park ride: "First, horror is like a roller-coaster, pleasurable because it lets you be frightened without being hurt; second, horror 'pulls the pop-top' off repressed urges to let them escape via the fizz of fantasy; and third, the horror art plays out the 'do's' and 'don'ts' of adolescent sexuality explaining to the soon-to-be-reproductive audience exactly how to avoid making horrible mistakes—namely monsters."[34] Given the popularity of the genre among adults in the early 1930s, Twitchell's third point needs to be rephrased. Horror is not only instructive in terms of what should and should not be done by adolescents, it is illustrative of what cannot be stopped among adults, such as homosexuality and the failure to conform to conventional gender roles. This last concept is neither about repression, Twitchell's second point, nor reproductive sexuality, his third, but is a significant concern in terms of society's failure to enforce its own rules of conduct.

As the following excerpt suggests, Twitchell shuts down horror's play of signifiers by looking for an ultimate terror. Twitchell asks: "What is the sexual act that must be feared . . . lest real horror result?" The response: "I think it is incest. I think that . . . the fear of incest underlies all horror myths in our culture that are repeatedly told for more than one generation" (DP 93).

I disagree. For while incest is certainly a popular horror motif, it is not the genre's primary, underlying theme as Twitchell would have it. Unlike Twitchell, I think the genre is so troubling to conventional assumptions regarding gender, for example, because its terrors cannot be reduced to one prima facie theme or generative cause. As Tzvetan Todorov notes, in line with Noël Carroll's thinking on monsters, "the fantastic permits us to cross certain frontiers that are inaccessible so long as we have no recourse to it."[35] Horror's ability to trade simultaneously in more than one forbidden or culturally marginalized theme, including those that are not explicitly or even implicitly sexual—such as dirt, dissection, and digestion—makes it amorphous in generic terms, and insures that its terrors and fascinations are grounded, in large part, in its celebration of multiple and shifting forbidden themes.

In a sense, horror is about the failure or absence of meaning at two levels. The first is narrative construction: a fantastic story is told, which cannot be explained in any logical fashion. The second level is personal identity: plots focus on a creature that looks more or less like a human being, but is not a human being. The monster is simultaneously repulsive and desirable, and it manages to overturn a slew of social mores, at least for the span of a movie. Cause-effect structures are broken down, characters do not behave as expected or as they are supposed to in a well-functioning society (monsters are seductive, romantic suitors are ineffectual, and heroines are drawn away from propriety and marriage), and what you see is not necessarily what you get. These attributes make horror terrifying to characters and spectators alike. They also make the genre alluring. As Carroll notes, monsters are anomalous beings that are "repelling because they violate standing categories. But for the self-same reason, they are also compelling of our attention" (PH 188).

Horror's signifying complexity and commitment to the underside of humanity form part of its links to psychoanalytic interpretation. Horror is full of hidden meanings, latent messages that can be mined from manifest images and emotions. But that complexity also precludes psychoanalysis from providing a comprehensive model for the genre's machinations. Reducing horror to a libidinal economy, stages of psychic and social development, unconscious urges, and the mapping of sexual difference, disregards those attributes of the genre that cannot be accounted for by psychoanalytic constructs. For example, horror's representations are often linked to a particular culture's anxieties about racial differences and the possibility of miscegenation, generic elements that remain outside the purview of psychoanalysis. That psychoanalysis is a useful paradigm with which to address horror goes without saying. That it can capture fully the complex twists and turns of a genre that is constantly in flux, toying with boundaries, identities, and feelings at will, is not so absolute.

The range of horror's affective lures is Noël Carroll's focus in *The Philosophy of Horror*. For him, horror's uniqueness rests neither upon the presence of a monster nor upon an underlying incest taboo, but on characters' responses to the fiend. Fear and disgust on the part of heroes and heroines, according to Carroll, signify the genre and, moreover, cue the audience as to how to react to the stories and images. As Carroll remarks, "horror appears to be one of those gen-

Figure 1.4. Despite the terror that the overgrown ape inspires in everyone who gazes at him in this one-sheet from *King Kong*, his plunge from the Empire State Building also inspires pity and empathy in characters and spectators alike. *Copyright © 1933* RKO *Pictures, Inc. Used by permission of Turner Entertainment Co. All rights reserved.*

res in which the emotive responses of the audience, ideally, run parallel to the emotions of characters. . . . The emotional reactions of characters, then, provide a set of instructions or, rather, examples about the way in which the audience is to respond to the monsters in the fiction" (PH 17) (figure 1.4).

Carroll's ideas are a good starting point for conceptualizing horror's affective force both on- and offscreen. But, given the unlikelihood that audience and character affect are always a perfect match, his model has to be expanded. This is true especially considering that Carroll leaves little room for viewers to parallel monsters' affective states, reject the emotional climate depicted on-screen, or respond to creatures on their own. Take, for example, the finale of *King Kong* in which Denham (Robert Armstrong), the film director who heads the expedition to the creature's island and brings Kong back to New York for a brief but memorable stint on stage, recites an epitaph about beauty killing the beast. Denham is a far from sympathetic character and his summation of the proceedings is rendered without emotion or sensitivity. Despite Denham's distanced mediation, however, spectators may well sympathize and identify with Kong's tragic fate, a point argued recently by James Snead regarding the differential responses of a black versus white audience to the film's conclusion.[36]

There is every indication that viewers' feelings toward monsters were more expansive than those of heroes or heroines in the 1930s, as Jerry Hoffman of the *Los Angeles Examiner* expressed in 1935. In his review of *Bride of Frankenstein*, Hoffman remarked: "The monster himself is made a more sympathetic figure; at times the audience being touched with pity for him."[37] Yet the film's characters are remarkably lacking in empathy for the fiend. Dr. Pretorius (Ernest Thesiger), an evil scientist who urges Dr. Frankenstein (Colin Clive) to continue his experiments, comes the closest of the main characters to showing kindness to the creature (Boris Karloff). But his reactions are marked more by greed than generosity, pity, or empathy. Frankenstein, the hero, usually responds with revulsion, and his wife is a locus of fear throughout the movie. According to Carroll's affective schema, repulsion and fear are the examples set for audiences. Yet Hoffman's review of the film suggests that spectator reactions may have run counter to, or been more complicated than, character affect.

The roller-coaster analogy works well here insofar as horror viewers experience a range of thrills while strapped safely to their seats. The genre's allure involves the admixture of danger and security, surprise and knowledge, and terror and delight. Horror elicits a variety of often contradictory emotional responses. Not surprisingly, those contradictions surfaced in contemporary film reviews. For example, while a *Variety* reporter claimed that *The Crime of Dr. Crespi*, a mad-doctor B-movie starring Erich von Stroheim, brought "laughs where none were sought," *Film Daily*'s reviewer thought it was a "sordid story, with no elements of relief, too gruesome for general entertainment."[38]

Thus, while reviews are instructive as to the ways in which some spectators responded during the 1930s, they may also tell as much about reporter biases as about audience reactions. For example, Mordaunt Hall of the *New York Times* relied on a fairly straightforward psychological profile to explain spectator behavior. Here, gender was not an issue. Instead, Hall theorized horror's affective draw for the audience as a whole. He believed that, when it came to horror films, laughter signaled audience discomfort. This assumption surfaced in at least three of his reviews. Of *Frankenstein*'s reception in a New York theater, he wrote that it "aroused so much excitement at the Mayfair yesterday that many in the audience laughed to cover their true feelings."[39] The following year, *Doctor X* (Warner Bros., 1931) received similar treatment: "That the audience which filled the theatre was duly impressed was obvious from the nervous giggles and the sudden explosions of relieved laughter."[40] The responses of *King Kong*'s audience in 1933 were interpreted according to the same approach: "Needless to say that this picture was received by many a giggle to cover up fright."[41]

While Hall treated horror as a genre that elicited nervous laughter from male and female viewers intent upon hiding their true feelings, other reporters assumed that audiences were not hiding anything at all. In fact, having a good time and *not* believing the content of films were assumed to be elements of classic horror spectatorship. Here is what *Variety* noted of *Doctor X*, the same film Hall believed elicited laughter as a cover for anxiety: "The laughs might indicate that hardened film-goers, including women are getting used to seeing some of these things overdone. Nothing could be more unwelcome-looking than the makeup of Preston Foster, murder maniac, yet the Strand's audience accepted it humorously."[42] In addition to the welcome reference to women becoming acclimated to horror only one year after the release of *Dracula* and *Frankenstein*, the reporter assumed that laughter did not so much cover viewer feelings as express them directly. Slightly later in the decade, F.S.N. of the *New York Times* departed from Hall's earlier assessment of the genre and went so far as to classify horror spectatorship as full-fledged fun. Unlike Hall, F.S.N. approached spectatorship with a light touch in a 1935 review of *Mark of the Vampire*: "Like most good ghost stories, it's a lot of fun, even though you don't believe a word of it."[43] Mordaunt Hall, then, might have been convinced that laughter was a sign of affective displacement for horror spectators, but his opinion was not shared by all reporters at the time.

IV

As with any other genre, writing on classic horror gets filtered through the interpretive lenses of reviewers, whether they wrote about films in the 1930s or are writing about them now. My own lenses—gender and sexuality—lead me to revise previous critical oversights that either streamline the genre's sexual division of labor or underplay the force of border crossings at the narrative level. For example, Carroll quotes a passage from Bram Stoker's *Dracula* to illustrate the parallels between character and, in this case, reader affect. In the selection from "Jonathan Harker's Journal," the hero describes his response to the vampire thus: "As the Count leaned over me and his hands touched me I could not repress a shudder. It may have been that his breath was rank, but a horrible feeling of nausea came over me, which do what I would, I could not conceal" (Stoker, quoted in PH 17). For Carroll, the entry confirms that Harker is thoroughly revolted by the Count's proximity, and that nausea "structure[s] our emotional reception of the ensuing descriptions of Dracula" (PH 17). But were Carroll to admit the possibility that Harker's shudder connotes less revulsion than an unintended sexual response, the vampire's effect on Harker and, potentially, on the novel's readers, would be as much an expression of sexual desire as terror.[44] From this perspective, Harker's nauseated feeling might be (1) a response having nothing to do with his shudder, for the two sentences can be read as completely distinct; (2) a sincere reaction to the vampire's closeness; or (3) a shill, a deflection away from Dracula's erotic aura and Harker's response to it.

Given the vampire's sexual mobility, its conflation of male and female qualities (it penetrates victims but also feeds them from its breast), and its seduction of men and women alike, fear *and* desire, disgust *and* fascination, are often combined in character and, by extension, reader and spectator responses. This conflation of divergent reactions to horror's fiends reinforces the notion that the genre is founded on the breaking of boundaries, with the monster leading the way. As the Harker example suggests, one of the numerous boundaries broken has to do with sexual desire.

Yet most critics argue that fiends are decidedly heterosexual and that horror movies focus on the battles between men (monstrous and human) for the affections of a woman. But what of the fiend's precarious sexual membership? Dracula looks like a man but, as a monster, the count is not human. Thus, although most monsters are coded male, they are also more-than-male and different-from-male. Their erotic interactions with heroines, then, are more-than- or different-from-heterosexual. Given that their encounters with humans are usually depicted as seductive attacks, the sexual aura usually read into those assaults is connotative, a meaning attached to the monster's aggressive advances. While I firmly believe in the power and applicability of those connotative sexual meanings when it comes to classic horror, the traditional names given to sexual orientations among humans—heterosexual, homosexual, and bisexual—do not convey fully the contours of the fiend's attachment to its victims.

The claims to the primacy of heterosexuality in the genre are a misreading of classic horror. For the genre is not only home to representations that depict the breakdown of heterosexuality; it also portrays a wide spectrum of sexualities in the process. Lambert Hillyer's *Dracula's Daughter* (Universal, 1936) is a useful illustration of the genre's play with sexuality. Not only does *Dracula's Daughter* suggest that classic horror movies sometimes starred female-coded fiends, it also represents sexuality as a slippery matter (figure 1.5).

The film focuses on the trials and tribulations faced by a beautiful bloodsucker that perceives her vampirism as a malady. At her wit's end, Countess Marya Zaleska (Gloria Holden) appeals to Dr. Jeffrey Garth (Otto Kruger), a London psychiatrist, to cure what ails her. Without revealing her true identity to him until the film's conclusion, she describes her symptoms in veiled terms. Disheartened by Garth's prognosis and ineffective cure—she is supposed to seek out the evil to which she is most drawn and overcome her desire for it—Zaleska learns that Garth's medical advice pales in comparison to the bloody urges that run through her veins. Not only does she mesmerize and attack a young girl named Lili, in spite of Garth's prescription, but she also abducts Garth's secretary and leans seductively over her supine body until the final moments of the film, when Zaleska is killed by her own assistant.

At the most superficial level, *Dracula's Daughter* is a tale of heterosexual desire doomed to fail—the countess is drawn to the doctor, he is enamored of her, but her monstrosity prevents the consummation of their attraction, leaving Garth to turn his attentions from the perished Zaleska to his savvy and spunky secretary, Janet (Marguerite Churchill). The film's heterosexual surface plot was apparent to critics in 1936. As Douglas Gilbert noted of Zaleska's feelings in his review for the *New York World Telegram:* "At a dinner party, she meets Garth, London's leading psychiatrist, and goes for him in a big way."[45] But even Gilbert knew there was more going on than a simple tale of boy meets vampire. First, he criticized Garth's performance in the film: "Otto Kruger, usually a capable actor, seems to muff his role as the doctor, who is a phony all through the film." Assuming that Gilbert was not alone in his poor opinion of Kruger's thespian efforts, the actor's bad performance probably compromised his status as hero and object of desire for a good number of spectators as well.

Second, Gilbert was quite explicit about Zaleska's favorite hobbies: "She is not a nice person; goes around at night giving the eye to sweet young girls through her hypnotic power aided by the magic of a jeweled ring. After she taps their jugular veins for a couple of quarts she calls it a night and goes back to her studio."[46] Zaleska is a vampire unconstrained by conventional mores: she both eyes young girls and goes for Garth in a big way. Here, Gilbert inverts the usual presumption that monsters are heterosexual by drawing out the lesbian implications of Zaleska's urges. Even more striking is that he fails to mention that Zaleska's first victim in the movie is male.

Figure 1.5. In this one-sheet for *Dracula's Daughter,* Jeffrey Garth (Otto Kruger) and Countess Marya Zaleska (Gloria Holden) embrace in the bottom right corner. Yet the poster's cutline—"SHE GIVES YOU THAT WEIRD FEELING"—confirms that the codes of normativity, heterosexual or otherwise, are not the female fiend's primary concern.   *Copyright © by Universal City Studios, Inc. Courtesy of* MCA *Publishing Rights, a Division of* MCA, *Inc.*

Variety's reviewer, named Scho, also noted Zaleska's predilection for females. As she or he remarked, "Marguerite Churchill is Kruger's [Dr. Garth's] impish secretary and sweetheart, as well as a near-victim of the femme killer."[47] I cannot help but wonder if Scho's double-entendre was intentional. Did the phrase "femme killer" refer to Zaleska's status as a female fiend—she is a killer who is a femme—or to her favorite prey—she kills femmes? Either way, Zaleska is described as a female monster drawn to female victims.

The original story for the sequel to *Dracula* was quite different from Lambert Hillyer's final product. So much so, in fact, that it focused on an army of female vampires still under Dracula's sway. In the fall of 1935, Joseph Breen, head of the Production Code Administration (PCA), reviewed John L. Balderston's original script for the sequel and had the following to say: "The story in its present form is not quite acceptable under the provisions of our Production Code and is, like-wise, dangerous material from the standpoint of political censorship. This is because there remains in the script a flavor suggestive of a com-bination of sex and horror." Breen advised that instead of having Dracula gather an army of girls to spread vampirism across the world, the women should be dance partners for male vampires. Scenes in which young girls were to be shown lying down in Dracula's chambers were to be replaced, Breen advised, with them sitting upright, and the word *lover* was to be deleted wherever it appeared.[48]

The film's producer E. M. Asher was, according to correspondence with Breen, so disappointed with the original script, as well as its reception at the PCA, that he threw it out.[49] Countess Zaleska, then, arose from the ashes of that abandoned project. But she, too, had to pass through a censorship ritual to make it to the screen. In his letter to Universal executive Harry Zehner, Breen had the following com-ments about the new story outline: "We would like to mention in par-ticular the scene on pages 13 and 14 between the Countess and the girl Lili. This will need very careful handling to avoid any question-able flavor."[50] In a PCA file memo dated a month later, a reviewer iden-tified as "GS" had a number of suggestions to make about the new script: "The present suggestion that the girl Lili poses in the nude will be changed. She will be posing her neck and shoulders, and there will be no suggestion that she undresses, and no exposure of her person. . . . The whole sequence will be treated in such a way as to avoid any suggestion of perverse sexual desire on the part of Marya [Zaleska] or of an attempted sexual attack by her upon Lili."[51]

The PCA's failure to curb the film's illicit connotations is evident in its popularity among critics as an early representation of lesbianism in Hollywood cinema, as well as in the post-release censorship problems the movie encountered in at least one Canadian province and in Sweden. In a file memo authored by Breen in the fall of 1936, the following scenes were to be deleted from Swedish prints: "Dracula's daughter hypnotizing the girl who tried to commit suicide" and "Dracula's daughter and cooperator at Janet's bed."[52] Both sequences are the most explicit of the film in terms of lesbian desire (figure 1.6).

Dracula's Daughter is instructive for a number of reasons. First, it emerged within a censorship climate in which any combination of sex and horror, be it heterosexual as in the case of the first draft of the sequel, or lesbian as in the final movie, was unacceptable to the PCA and local censor boards. Second, the film suggests the degree to which the PCA's censorship endeavors may have curbed perverse meanings under Breen's tutelage but failed to fully expunge them. In fact, Universal marketed the film with the lesbian connotations intact, as one popular cutline suggests: "Save the women of London from Dracula's daughter." Finally, the PCA correspondence and the remarks by reviewers attest to the genre's fondness for sexually amorphous scenarios, storylines that portray monsters as hungry for and desirous of victims of both sexes.

But to characterize Zaleska as lesbian or bisexual in a conventional sense is to misread the transgressions performed by monsters. Monsters do not fit neatly with a model of human sexuality. Instead, they propose a paradigm of sexuality in which eros and danger, sensuality and destruction, human and inhuman, and male and female blur, overlap, and coalesce. In this schema, sexuality and identity remain murky matters, steeped in border crossings and marked by fuzzy boundaries. Thus classic horror may invoke existing definitions of sexuality, but the genre embellishes them with perversions that defy and exceed traditional categories of human desire.

Carol J. Clover's discussion of the one-sex nature of contemporary horror illustrates the genre's conundrum when it comes to sexuality and sexual identity. Drawing on the work of Thomas Laqueur, Clover notes of possession films: "If the project of these films is to update the binaries, the upshot is a sex/gender swamp—of male and female bodies collapsing into one another, of homo- and heterosexual stories tangled to the point of inextricability" (107). But how to account for this swamp in a world marked by sexual incommensurability?

Figure 1.6. Zaleska (Gloria Holden) uses her ring to hypnotize her favorite prey, Lili (Nan Grey), in this publicity still from *Dracula's Daughter*. Photo courtesy of Ronald V. Borst/Hollywood Movie Posters. *Copyright © by Universal City Studios, Inc. Courtesy of* MCA *Publishing Rights, a Division of* MCA, *Inc.*

Clover's response is to combine the dominant model of sexual difference so heavily promoted by Sigmund Freud with the one-sex system that, Laqueur argues, guided Western thought on biological sex until the Enlightenment.

In the one-sex model, notes Laqueur, "women had the same genitals as men except that [women's were inside and men's outside the body]. . . . In this world the vagina is imagined as an interior penis, the labia as foreskin, the uterus as scrotum, and the ovaries as testicles."[53] And he continues, "Women in other words, are inverted, and hence less perfect men" (26). According to Clover, the one-sex model provides a means with which to describe horror's confusion of gender roles. "Horror may in fact be the premier repository of one-sex reasoning in our time," notes Clover. "The world of horror is in any case one that knows very well that men and women are profoundly different (and that the former are vastly superior to the latter) but one that at the same time repeatedly contemplates mutations and slidings whereby women begin to look a lot like men (slasher films), men are pressured to become like women (possession films), and some people are impossible to tell apart" (15).

Horror, in Clover's view, is a throwback to one-sex thinking, but it is also firmly embedded in a two-sex world. The monster, then, both *is* and *is not* male or female. Yet if Clover is correct, the one-sex model still confines horror to a framework based on physical comparability and inferiority (women are inverted and, therefore, lesser men) and, thus, absolute difference—in this case, physical inversion. While that inversion may not have been absolute for all women, according to Laqueur, it was absolute and unalterable for men. Like the psycho-analytic model of sexual difference, therefore, the one-sex system still favors men and keeps them safely on the side of superior physical traits. Yet most classic monsters are coded as males that access conventionally feminine behaviors and female narrative positions. Thus, the movement of monsters toward femininity and femaleness transgresses not only the mandates of sexual difference but the rules of the one-sex model as well.

Clover is, then, correct to note that some contemporary horror cinema is marked by one-sex thinking, but that thinking needs to be taken a step further. The one-sex model as applied to classic horror is even more inverted than the Enlightenment paradigm. For in horror, male-coded monsters are not pressured to become like women, as are the possession film's heroes; instead they are quite willing to assume female narrative positions. Like women in states of extreme emotional upheaval, monsters are visually fascinating. And like heroines in distress at the monsters' advances, the hypnosis film's fiends often suffer as much as their victims. The genre, therefore, sends a troubling ripple through contemporary thought. It suggests, quite literally in the figure of the monster, that presumptions of sexual difference on the basis of biology are as fraught with ambiguities and are as historically constructed as are those based on gender attributes.

The latter point is an abbreviated version of Judith Butler's arguments in *Gender Trouble.* "The notion that there might be a 'truth' of sex, as Foucault ironically terms it," notes Butler, "is produced precisely through the regulatory practices that generate coherent identities through the matrix of coherent gender norms. The heterosexualization of desire requires and institutes the production of discrete and asymmetrical oppositions between 'feminine' and 'masculine,' where these are understood as expressive attributes of 'male' and 'female.'"[54] In a sense, therefore, classic horror overtly represents what theorists such as Butler, Laqueur, and Stephen Heath have noted recently—namely, designations of biological sex, like gender behaviors, are human constructs.[55]

V

This book is structured around six main chapters. The first three, including this one, address classic horror from broader theoretical and critical perspectives, while the last three apply those perspectives to the narrative level through close textual readings. As a result, the reader who is eager to study detailed analyses of specific classic horror films or subgenres may want to venture forward to chapters 4, 5, and 6, and leave chapters 2 and 3 for another time. That is, the reader's journey through *Attack of the Leading Ladies* need not be a linear one; this would, in fact, be rather fitting given that classic horror movies are often unconcerned with the sequential plotting of events.

In order to trace the border crossings in gender, sexual identity, and sexuality that occur in classic horror, chapter 2 is devoted to debates about spectatorship. Bridging the conventional gap between spectatorship as either sadistic or masochistic in quality, I argue for the convergence of those conditions in viewing patterns. I then offer a theory of classic horror spectatorship as a form of performance— what I call "spectatorship-as-drag." Basically, I assert that the gender-bending and border crossings that take place on-screen in classic horror films are also played out offscreen. As a follow-up to this theoretical model, chapter 3 focuses on the historical context in which films were made and introduces a range of marketing and publicity strategies that promoted the genre to male and female viewers. The notion of spectatorship-as-drag is addressed here in its incarnation at the site of reception.

Chapter 4 centers upon what I term the "hypnosis film"—movies in which victims are hypnotized by visually alluring and powerful monsters such as zombies, mummies, and vampires. In this chapter, I evaluate the gazes exchanged between monsters and heroines with a view to describing an economy of looks. Instead of aligning the heroine's gaze solely with masochism and passivity, I argue that beneath its vapid veneer rest intimations of power, desire, and monstrosity. In order to further examine the genre's gender play, chapter 5 concentrates on the homosocial dynamics of mad-doctor movies. The theatricalization of female fear is analyzed as a subgeneric staple in mad-doctor narratives, which is then used to disguise the terrors of male-on-male desire, masochism, helplessness, and the feminization of men. *Attack of the Leading Ladies* closes with chapter 6, which introduces the racial dynamics of the jungle-horror and jungle-adventure film. Here a fear of miscegenation is paramount, and white heroines serve as mediators between the white man's world and the dark monstrous domain of the jungle.

A final word on the monster. If monsters are the most compelling figures in these stories, and I believe they are, their destruction at the end of the films does little to quell the anxieties sparked during the bulk of the narrative action. Classic horror movies may close with the reunion of the heterosexual couple, but that conclusion is usually forced and inadequate. Narrative threads are often left hanging, and the promise of a sequel, which means the return of the monster or its brood, guarantees that happy endings and the stable gender roles they imply are temporary at best. These films highlight horror cinema's investment in playing with gender roles and its invitation to viewers to participate in that play. While classic horror films may trade in representations that are conventional, and although they instruct us over and over that girls will be girls and boys will be monsters, the genre also proclaims that all is not as it seems. Boundaries are made to be transgressed, and traditions, while protected at all costs, fall prey to creatures of the night. Classic horror cinema, like roller-coaster rides, pulls viewers into an alternate world in which fun and terror coexist, barriers are made to be broken, and monsters have to be embraced to get to the end of the ride.

2

Spectatorship-as-Drag: Re-Dressing Classic Horror Cinema

> *Heterosexuality, or male/female coupling,*
> *is as culturally imperative as masculine/feminine gender.*
> *Sexual role-playing, then,*
> *has implications for gender play;*
> *the way people perform their sexuality*
> *influences how they "wear" their gender.*
>
> —Jill Dolan

I

"BENEATH HER MASK OF BEAUTY . . . LURKS THE SPIRIT OF A DEMON . . . SHE'S A FEMALE 'JEKYLL & HYDE.'" This is the cutline that frames dual images of Carole Lombard in a striking poster from Paramount's Pressbook for *Supernatural* (1933).[1] Two shots of Lombard's head gaze at the reader/viewer. The first (background) image is of Lombard, who plays a heroine named Roma in the film, staring forward with a neutral expression. The second, slightly larger and foreground shot has Lombard gaze at the camera with a seductive and devious look on her face, signified by a raised eyebrow and the tilt of her head. Like Fredric March's dual eponymous roles in *Dr. Jekyll and Mr. Hyde* (Paramount, 1932) earlier in the decade, to which the advertisement refers, Lombard is split in two on the poster and in the movie. But whereas March's second self is given form in the figure of Hyde, whose monstrosity is depicted with the help of makeup, Lombard personifies a demon "beneath her mask of beauty." As the *Supernatural* poster notes in fine print: "What strange spirit controls the body of this innocent girl? . . . Using her living loveliness as an instrument of love and hate . . . to satisfy a craving for revenge."

The advertisement for Victor Halperin's *Supernatural* suggests that the heroine is not all that she seems to be. Beautiful surfaces are deceiving, they hide monsters beneath masks of loveliness. In its attention to deception as a selling ploy, *Supernatural* depicts classic horror's fondness for role-playing and disguise at both textual and extratextual levels. The movie traces Roma's travails after her twin brother, John (Lyman Williams), dies. Willing to believe anyone who promises her the chance to communicate with him, Roma is taken in by a fake spiritual guide named Paul Bavian (Allan Dinehart). In the midst of her psychic explorations, she is possessed by the spirit of Ruth Rogen (Vivienne Osborne), a convicted murderess executed at the film's start. Roma's possession is precipitated by the efforts of a psychologist (played by H. B. Warner) who tries to prevent Ruth's spirit from wreaking further havoc. Dr. Houston inadvertently sends the villain's soul into Roma's body when Roma is in a particularly vulnerable state. Roma's spiritual doubling does not cease here. Through metonymic devices like parallel editing, John's death is aligned with Ruth's demise, suggesting that it is no coincidence that Roma channels a dead woman's spirit, while trying to communicate with a dead man.

By the film's conclusion, Roma's internalization of Ruth is profound: she is acting sexually aggressive and independent. Her fiendish exploits are compounded by the mystical appearance of John's face, which floats in midair late in the narrative. Like Ruth's migrating soul, John, too, travels among the living and stays close to Roma. While Ruth literally occupies Roma's body, John is not far behind—he is bonded to his twin in death as in life. In a sense, therefore, when Roma channels Ruth, John also participates in a transmigration of souls.

On the one hand, Roma is the movie's appealing and innocent heroine, an object of desire for the hero, Grant Wilson (Randolph Scott), a suitable focus of identification and, potentially, desire for viewers, and a prime victim in Ruth's vengeful postmortem plans. On the other hand, Roma is doubled with a man, in this case her male twin, and she internalizes a monstrous figure, a woman accused of the mass murder of a group of men who were found dead in her Greenwich Village apartment (figure 2.1).

The dualistic nature of Lombard's role can be found in a number of posters from the Pressbook. For example, a one-sheet begins with the word TRANSFORMED in capital letters and continues at the bottom of the page as follows: "THE SPIRIT OF A MURDERESS ENTERS THE BODY OF A LOVELY, INNOCENT GIRL . . . IT'S 'SUPERNATURAL.'" Like the mesmerized heroines of hypnosis films (who will be addressed in chapter 4), Roma's fiendish exploits change her in significant ways. But unlike hypnosis heroines, who are brought under the spell of a mesmerizing and, usually, male-coded creature, Roma's transformation occurs once she literally internalizes a dead woman—she both is under a monster's sway and *is* a monster.

But what impact does Ruth have on Roma? According to the Pressbook, the net result of Roma's transformation is contradictory. "ENSLAVED . . . BY CONFLICTING EMOTIONS. HER HEART CRIED FOR LOVE . . . YET HER HANDS REACHED OUT TO DESTROY," is how a one-sheet summed up the proceedings.[2] While the cutline notes that Roma is enslaved by Ruth and subject to conflicting desires, a drawing in the center of the poster offers a more complex portrait of her

Figure 2.1. Dr. Houston (H. B. Warner) pays close attention to Ruth Rogen (Vivienne Osborne), the murderess whose soul he transfers accidentally into the heroine's (Carole Lombard) body in *Supernatural*. *Copyright © by Universal City Studios, Inc. Courtesy of* MCA *Publishing Rights, a Division of* MCA*, Inc.*

travails. A circle appears directly beneath a shot of Lombard's upturned face. A series of "scenes" from the film are drawn within the sphere, six images in all. Read in a clockwise fashion, they are configured thus: a shot of Roma leaning seductively over Bavian's yielding body as if about to kiss or bite him; an image of Roma and Grant, the hero, listening intently to another man; Roma and Grant in an embrace; Bavian menacing Roma from behind; and a drawing of Grant holding a fainted Roma in his arms.

Taken as a road map to Lombard's part in the film, and a guide for audiences as to how to perceive the heroine, the images suggest multiple and contradictory roles: monster, romantic lead, object of desire, and passive victim. More explicit, perhaps, than other movies at the narrative level,[3] *Supernatural* and its advertising campaign are steeped in the adoption of disguises and the construction of men, women, and monsters as figures who enact multiple roles. The film articulates one of classic horror's most insistent promises—namely, to confront spectators with stories, publicity, and on-screen characters who embody role-play as a thematic and selling ploy intended to elicit complex and *contradictory* viewer responses (figure 2.2).

In what follows, I am interested in theorizing the ways in which those responses are adopted by spectators. Specifically, I want to suggest how classic horror films both figure and free audiences from traditional assumptions about gender. In a sense, the narrative ploys and generic elements that I summarized in chapter 1, and that suggest that classic horror's gender dynamics are less streamlined than previously believed, form the foundation of my arguments here. My basic line of thinking is that classic horror cinema both reinforces traditional patterns of gendered spectatorship and explodes them.

II

As Jill Dolan remarks in the epigraph to this chapter, heterosexuality and gender roles are culturally promoted. So much so, in fact, that men and women wear gender on their sleeves, in a manner of speaking, both when they abide by traditional mores and when they overturn them.[4] Dolan articulates one of the assumptions with which I began *Attack of the Leading Ladies*—namely, that gender is performed in this culture insofar as it is heavily coded, encouraged, adopted, and, in some instances, policed as a means of confirming the supremacy

Figure 2.2. In this poster for *Supernatural*, Roma (Carole Lombard) clutches the villain, Bavian's (Allan Dinehart), crystal ball. Lit by the globe's mysterious light, she gazes at the spectator with a disconcerting look. Photo courtesy of Ronald V. Borst/Hollywood Movie Posters. *Copyright © by Universal City Studios, Inc. Courtesy of* MCA *Publishing Rights, a Division of* MCA, *Inc.*

and naturalness of heterosexuality.[5] I especially like Dolan's suggestion that sexuality is not mere performance but a sartorial display as well. Clothes make the man, or woman, as the case may be.

But what does all this have to do with classic horror? Traditional gender roles have been applied to the horror genre by critics with varying degrees of success, not only at the narrative level but also in terms of theories of viewing. As in film studies as a whole, the most popular models are sadistic male and passive female spectatorship (such as the model put forth by James B. Twitchell). Even less conventional paradigms, such as Carol J. Clover's assertion that contemporary horror elicits male masochism, reinforce gender conventions. Clover implies that female spectatorship is also primarily masochistic but does not address women viewers in any sustained fashion.[6] While these paradigms are suggestive, given the thematic focus on sadism and masochism in the genre, I want to realign the analytic lens in what follows. Instead of choosing between sadistic and masochistic models, I prefer Miriam Hansen's conceptualization of spectatorship as an oscillation between sadistic and masochistic poles.[7] My arguments in this chapter are indebted to Hansen's perspective, especially her assumption that spectatorship is a messy matter—slipping between identification and desire, between dominance and passivity.

What follows is a theory of spectatorship as a mode of performance, specifically, spectatorship-as-drag. I assume in this chapter that viewing is a social activity in which conventional gender roles get displayed. I also assume that cinema spectatorship is a cultural venue in which those roles are temporarily, unevenly, and alternately worn and discarded during the viewing experience. This is true especially of classic horror, which demands a more fluid theory of spectatorship, given its on-screen confusion of sexuality and gender traits and its affinity for representing sexual and monstrous identities as constantly in flux. Where drag proves useful is in offering a framework for addressing gender behaviors as performances, while throwing into question the notion of an authentic spectating self. From this perspective, identity politics remains a crucial mode of action in the political arena but becomes a less viable means of expression for spectators seated in a movie theater, especially those who watch classic horror. Thus, I take as a given that film patrons often engage in and exhibit a more mobile range of social behaviors and identifications than they would in the remainder of their everyday lives.

Studying imputed spectatorship is never a wholly theoretical task, as Judith Mayne points out: "The analysis of spectatorship is an analysis of one's *own* fascination and passion. Unless this is acknowledged, then we are left with a series of fuzzily defined 'ideal readers' in whom it is difficult to know how much of their responses are displaced representations of the critic's own."[8] So, here are the stakes of this chapter for me. As a lesbian film scholar and spectator living in a late twentieth-century culture in which heterosexuality is the norm, I delight in classic horror's transgressions of sexual difference and gender traits. While I may experience fear (although historical hindsight offers much in the way of critical distance), I also derive pleasure from viewing a monster that toys with the requisites of sexual identity as either male or female. Classic horror may do little to unhinge the workings of patriarchy outside the theater, but the genre plays with conventional identifications and roles behind closed doors, as the case of *Supernatural* suggests.

Marjorie Garber's work on cross-dressing lends a useful parallel to horror's machinations: "One of the most important aspects of cross-dressing is the way in which it offers a challenge to easy notions of binarity, putting into question the categories of 'female' and 'male,' whether they are considered essential or constructed, biological or cultural."[9] And she continues: "The transvestite . . . is both terrifying and seductive precisely because s/he incarnates and emblematizes the disruptive element that intervenes, signaling not just another category crisis, but . . . a crisis of 'category' itself" (32). Garber's description of the transvestite is similar to the role of monsters in horror. Like transvestites, fiends are interstitial; they transgress conventional categories of sexual and human identity and incite fear and desire in those whom they encounter.

While classic horror spectatorship is not entirely equivalent to the role-playing and disguise that are portrayed in storylines, it is unrealistic to assume that horror's investment in a multiplicity of roles does not resonate with spectators. Yet the specific impact on viewers may not be disruptive of the social sphere per se. Although classic horror movies depict gender-bending, it is unclear to what degree spectatorial identifications and desires are ideologically progressive outside of viewing practices. This is especially true regarding identity politics and spectator subjectivity. For what classic horror may offer is a temporary release from everyday identities, at the same time that it relies on those identities as a fall-back position.

Mayne introduces this possibility when she writes of cinema's "safe zone": "Film theory has been so bound by the heterosexual symmetry that supposedly governs Hollywood cinema that it has ignored the possibility, for instance, that one of the distinct pleasures of the cinema may well be a 'safe zone' in which homosexual as well as heterosexual desires can be fantasized and acted out" (97). In keeping with Mayne's thinking, classic horror is a genre in which spectators are invited to play it safe.

III

"Clothing typical of one sex worn by a person of the opposite sex." This is how Merriam Webster defines *drag*. It is a sartorial inversion, a reversal of the cultural relationship between assumptions about biological sex and gender displays. The transvestite is in drag whenever s/he wears men's or women's clothing, as the case may be. Here, by using the term *drag* as a model for classic horror spectatorship, I want to expand its meaning slightly. For my purposes, drag is not only a sartorial display, or a gender performance that engages and explodes the oppositions between male and female. Drag must also be understood as a more general performative paradigm, one that subsumes the terms *masquerade* and *transvestitism*, which I will address later in this chapter. From this perspective a woman may be in drag, as Garber suggests, whenever she produces herself as the signifier "woman." Thus, while drag is linked to classic horror via its transgression of gender roles and its connotations of terror and allure, it is also important as a more general performative model—one that, like monstrosity, poses a crisis of categories for those who perform and watch it.

As a practice that both relishes boundary crossings and questions the validity of boundaries themselves, drag offers a framework in which to situate classic horror's preoccupation with disguises and overwrought theatrical displays. Like the form of drag defined by Webster's dictionary, monsters often invoke both sexes at once. For example, when Ling Moy (Anna May Wong) agrees to continue her father's reign of terror in the Fu Manchu film, *Daughter of the Dragon* (Paramount, 1931), she tells the dying patriarch (played by Warner Oland) that she will become his son. This example served as a selling ploy in 1931. The Pressbook urged exhibitors to include the following paragraph in their promotional advertisements: " 'Daughter of the Dragon' is a fascinating account of a beautiful oriental stage actress, who turns from her London triumphs to become a true 'son' of the house of Fu Manchu."[10] Thus, while Ling Moy does not literally become a man, she alternately adopts narrative roles conventionally reserved for monstrous male figures, as well as those held by heroines. Fiends like Ling Moy personify a theoretical movement past the binaries of gender. In being like men *and* women, many monsters disrupt categories of sexual difference and humanness.[11] They also throw into question the concept of an essential identity, which is assumed to lie beneath the drag costume (figure 2.3).

Identity as a form of performance is a recurrent concept in recent gay and lesbian writing. Noting that the homo/heterosexual binary creates a tension between the original and its copy, Judith Butler

Figure 2.3. Dr. Fu Manchu (Warner Oland) asks Ling Moy (Anna May Wong) to become his son in this still from *Daughter of the Dragon*. Photo courtesy of Ronald V. Borst/Hollywood Movie Posters.   Copyright © by Universal City Studios, Inc. *Courtesy of* MCA *Publishing Rights, a Division of* MCA, *Inc.*

remarks: "If it were not for the notion of the homosexual *as* copy, there would be no construct of heterosexuality as *origin*. . . . The entire framework of copy and origin proves radically unstable as each position inverts into the other."[12] If sexual identities cannot be traced to a stable source, Butler argues, "*gender is a kind of imitation for which there is no original*" (emphasis in original; 21). Butler uses drag to focalize the constructed qualities of gender and identity. Although drag is best known as a gay male performance, Butler maintains that it is also a useful description of the degree to which gender behaviors are donned as costumes in more or less unconscious ways.[13]

Having staked a claim for the relationship between gender and role-playing, I do not want to suggest that gender and sexuality are always or only easily worn and discarded like pieces of clothing. Butler herself offers a corrective to some of the ways in which her notion of gender performativity has been deployed:

> For if I were to argue that genders are performative, that could mean that I thought that one woke in the morning, perused the

closet or some more open space for the gender of choice, donned that gender for the day, and then restored the garment to its place at night. Such a willful and instrumental subject, one who decides *on* its gender, is clearly not in gender from the start and fails to realize that its existence is already decided *by* gender. (emphasis in original) [14]

While Butler seems to shut down some of the gender play she introduces in *Gender Trouble* and elsewhere, she follows this discussion by posing an important question: "But if there is no subject who decides on its gender, and if, on the contrary, gender is part of what decides the subject, how might one formulate a project that preserves gender practices as sites of critical agency?" (x). How indeed? Butler's response is to note that public declarations of queerness are a discursive mode of performativity that transforms homosexuality as diseased cultural Other into a site of defiance and politicization. Such a process of discursive resignification is, while compelling, more elaborate than what is required at the level of cinema spectatorship (which is a far more circumscribed social activity than are the processes of subject-formation with which Butler grapples). For the performativity of gender, the practice of gender as a mode of cultural agency or commentary from within a preexistent gender system is possible in the sphere of spectatorship because that social space is itself, already, a performance space.

In *Mother Camp*, her book on female impersonators in the 1960s and 1970s, Esther Newton describes drag as a paradoxical performance:

> [Drag] symbolizes two somewhat conflicting statements concerning the sex-role system. The first statement is that the sex-role system is really natural: therefore homosexuals are unnatural.... The second symbolic statement of drag questions the "naturalness" of the sex-role system in toto; if sex-role behavior can be achieved by the "wrong" sex, it logically follows that it is in reality also achieved, not inherited, by the "right" sex. (emphasis in original; 103)

Newton's description of drag resonates for classic horror. For the monster poses the tension between Newton's symbolic statements: (1) as a figure that transgresses ontological classifications of humanness and sexual difference, the monster confirms the normalcy of those categories; and (2) the fiend is a reminder that monstrosity and normalcy are interdependent, that the unnatural resides within the natural and vice versa, and that both are constructed.

Newton argues that one of the most important aspects of female impersonators is that "they do not consider themselves to be females and neither do audiences. So if one is *really* male, it is even more of a feat to look like a glamorous and exciting woman" (emphasis in original; 57). A similar interaction between knowledge and disavowal gets played out by classic horror spectators. While viewers may, on one level, accept the male-coding of most monsters, and be convinced of their humanness, audiences also know that fiends defy ontological categories. Spectators trade in a process of disavowal by denying that fiends are inhuman and attributing stable identities to them. Yet horror always demands the acknowledgment of monstrosity. In a sense, viewers practice reverse fetishism. In lieu of devising elaborate means to disguise the creature's monstrosity—its *lack* of humanness—they encounter narrative and visual tropes designed to unmask monsters. Instead of revealing an inner core, however, unmasking offers more layers of drag.

Michael Curtiz's *The Mystery of the Wax Museum* (Warner Bros., 1933) trades in this masking/unmasking duality. Having been burned in a fire that destroyed his first wax museum and maimed his face in the process, Ivan (Lionel Atwill) traverses the film wearing and removing a mask that hides his molten features. Because a series of narrative cues builds toward the act of unmasking, that gesture is anticipated by the audience. Viewers already know that beneath the veneer of Ivan's costume lies a disfigured visage, a face with an artificial look. Yet the disguise Ivan wears to hide his burns is identical to his appearance before he was maimed, begging the question: which of the two faces is his real one? The answer proves elusive. Like Butler's arguments, it is difficult to determine the original Ivan from the copy. Instead of the "real" Ivan, the spectator is offered a series of appearances (figure 2.4).[15]

In addition to putting the concept of identity into question at the narrative level, Curtiz's film, and the publicity that surrounded it, suggests that monsters and heroines are aligned. As one poster in the Pressbook announced: "WOMEN OF FLESH BECOME WAX IN HIS HANDS. . . . WOMEN OF WAX BECOME FLESH!" The image that frames this cutline shows Lionel Atwill, as Ivan, smoking a cigarette with one hand, while he holds the wrist of the heroine, played by Fay Wray, with

Figure 2.4. In this French poster for *The Mystery of the Wax Museum*, Lionel Atwill's visage is rendered both alive and artificial. His face is expressive yet masklike, given the long stick that protrudes from behind his head. Fay Wray and Glenda Farrell also appear at once lifelike and manufactured. Photo courtesy of Ronald V. Borst/Hollywood Movie Posters. *Copyright © 1933 Turner Entertainment Co. All rights reserved.*

the other. To the left of Wray's head, the following question appears: "IS SHE WOMAN OR WAX?"[16] In addition to the connotations of sexual prowess attributed to Atwill/Ivan by the initial promotional line—he melts women with his hands—the poster also indicates that Ivan and the film's women are alike. For Ivan, too, is both wax and flesh, a monster whose ontological status is unclear.

So what effect do these textual forms of drag and role-playing have on spectators? As a sexually and ontologically ambiguous figure, the monster complicates a rigid one-to-one rapport with spectators; male viewers may identify with a male-coded monster, but not on the basis of a stable sexual or human identity. That is, classic horror's representations offer a schism between spectator (human) and monster (non-human) in viewing terms. That schism is compounded by the divide between character (monster) and role (man) that plays out at the diegetic level—meaning, Dracula seems to be a man, but he is an undead monster instead. The necessary theoretical leap, one that I make in the discussion that follows, is to assume that this schism can be transposed, in varying degrees, to viewers' responses to the genre. Just as horror's characters highlight both the strength and artificiality of conventional gender roles—e.g., Dracula's daughter looks like a woman, but is not one—so, too, do spectators behave according to traditional codes of gender behavior, while they also toy with, reject, and overact those roles.

Spectatorship-as-drag explains both the degree to which viewers act in line with traditional gender expectations, as well as the means by which they reject them. The first of these approaches is promoted by dominant culture. "Gender is *performative* in the sense that it constitutes as an effect the very subject it appears to express," writes Butler. "It is compulsory performance in the sense that acting out of line with heterosexual [and other] norms brings with it ostracism, punishment, and violence, not to mention the transgressive pleasures produced by those very prohibitions" ("IGI," emphasis in original; 24). As Butler suggests, the way one wears gender is often constrained by traditional cultural norms. Yet the viewing sphere, which is a locale aligned with fantasies, seems a likely place in which those norms may, if only temporarily, break down or oscillate. Thus, a female spectator who views a classic horror film may respond as culture dictates, with screams, but she may also aggressively identify with and desire the monster with whom the heroine is often doubled on-screen, as the publicity for *The Mystery of the Wax Museum* implies.

IV

Most feminist models of spectatorship, including more recent work, are built on familiar binaries—such as male/female and heterosexual/homosexual. Even those that propose the dissolution of oppositions, such as bisexual spectatorship or masochistic male viewing, rely either on bifurcated concepts (identification versus desire) or relegate female spectators to conventional roles (masochistic viewing pleasures). The endurance of binaries, then, indicates both the difficulty of, as well as the need to, theorize spectatorship differently—in this case, performatively.

In the introduction to her book, *The Women Who Knew Too Much*, Tania Modleski notes that Alfred Hitchcock's films portray a feminine ambivalence that undermines male mastery. Modleski asserts that one of her "intent[s] is to problematize *male* spectatorship and masculine identity in general" (emphasis in original); she explores the concept of double identification, in which men identify with characters of both sexes.[17] According to Modleski, male identification with and desire for Hitchcock's heroines align men with female bisexuality and remind "man of his *own* bisexuality . . . a bisexuality that threatens to subvert his 'proper' identity" (emphasis in original; 8).

Modleski makes an excellent effort to loosen male spectatorship from the sadistic, heterosexual confines of Laura Mulvey's 1975 model of the sadistic male gaze. However, Modleski's version of male bisexuality is tautological—according to her, women are bisexual and, therefore, men are bisexual because women are bisexual. One of the limitations of this concept, in addition to its equation of male with female spectatorship (a refreshing reversal of sexist claims that posit men as the norm), is that the brand of bisexuality alluded to by Modleski privileges identification over desire. Shared by a number of feminist critics, such as Mary Ann Doane and Linda Williams, the model depends on a female infant's identification with (and not desire for) her mother. It follows, then, that the male spectator's bisexuality is constrained—he may be "bi" in the realm of identification, but he remains heterosexual in terms of desire. The problem with this formulation for classic horror is that the genre invites all spectators to engage in processes of identification *and* desire for male, female, and monstrous characters. Bisexual spectatorship, then, leaves the complexities of classic horror at loose ends.

In an article on Hitchcock's *Strangers on a Train*, Robert J. Corber grapples with the heterosexist biases of much feminist film theory and confirms that Hitchcock's films are favored terrain for critics intent on questioning gender norms. In line with Modleski's approach, Corber appeals to psychoanalysis: "The male spectator's identification with the hero *always* involves the repression of a homosexual object-cathexis that recalls his pre-Oedipal attachment to the father" (emphasis added).[18] Like Modleski, Corber cites the pre-Oedipal to account for same-sex identification. Unlike female bisexuality, however, Corber eroticizes the male spectator's bond with onscreen heroes.

Yet Corber's article highlights the problems of theories of spectatorship that favor either Oedipal or pre-Oedipal configurations. As J. Laplanche and J.-B. Pontalis note of the pre-Oedipal/Oedipal division in Freud's work: "One may either accentuate the exclusiveness of the dual relationship [between the pre-Oedipal and the Oedipal] or else identify signs of the Oedipus complex so early on that it becomes impossible to isolate a strictly preoedipal [sic] phase."[19] If the pre-Oedipal and Oedipal are collapsed temporally, as Laplanche and Pontalis suggest they may very well be, then it is ill-advised for Corber and Modleski to privilege the earlier period in their theorizations of spectator subjectivity.

In fact, by relying on the pre-Oedipal phase, Corber treads close to what he critiques. He reduces the field of sexual identity to a pitched battle between homosexuality and heterosexuality. Although I sympathize with the lure of discussing homosexual desire as both central and preexistent to heterosexuality, reversing the hierarchy creates a whole new set of problems.[20] Surely Corber is wrong when he assumes that all male gazes are homosexual in form. Thus, despite Corber's efforts to provide an answer, the question remains: how to account for the specificities of male spectatorship?

Ellis Hanson offers an initial and inadvertent response in his article, "The Undead." Unlike Corber, when Hanson addresses male viewing patterns, he poses some important queries: "Is the gaze the gays'? What could it mean for a man to engage the gaze of another man? In psychoanalytic terms, such a gaze would be a form of madness. . . . The gay male gaze is the gaze of the male vampire: he with whom one is forbidden to identify."[21] Instead of beginning with a consideration of men in toto, as Corber does, Hanson focuses on gay men.

Hanson's belief that homosexual gazing is analogous to the look of a male vampire fits neatly with a consideration of classic horror. For Hanson not only invokes a monstrous figure, he also implies that viewing patterns are based on social and not just sexual categories. If a gay male gaze is horrifying, part of its horror resides in the recognition by gay man and monster of their similar status as outsiders to patriarchy. In other words, while not all male gazes are homosexual, some are and, in the realm of horror, homosexuality (a culturally monstrous identity) fosters desire for and identification with a socially marginalized fiend. Here, I am taking the meanings embedded in Hanson's original concept a step further and using the gay/vampire bond as a springboard for horror spectatorship.

Moving beyond the realm of homosexuality, Hanson's work suggests that viewer identification may be forged on the basis of shared social status. If a homosexual viewer's identifications exceed the traits of gender and sexual orientation by including social standing, then it follows that other groups may also identify via means other than biological sex. Thus, identification and desire formed on the basis of race, class, ethnicity, nationality, and so on may be as strong as those expressed on the basis of sexual identity.

The concept of viewing based on social categories raises an important question: to what degree do the sexual and social identities of spectators determine the identifications and desires deployed in viewing? Although recent gay and lesbian work has focused on homosexual subjectivity, the thorny question of the equivalence of a spectator's everyday identity with viewing positions has yet to be addressed fully. Having raised the issue, queries emerge: is it possible for a male homosexual viewer to identify with and desire a female character? Or, for that matter, is it possible for a heterosexual male to both identify with and desire a hero?[22] While it is important to theorize a cinematic and social space in which gays and lesbians access and are accorded the rights to express same-sex desire, doing so does not exhaust all possibilities for the viewer, gay or otherwise.

The theories that dominate the field describe viewing pleasures via similarities (e.g., women identify with heroines on the basis of shared biological sex), and sexual drives (e.g., straight women are romantically invested in heroes due to heterosexual desire). This scenario overlooks the possibility that spectators also identity *against* themselves. Viewing patterns depend as much upon the dissolution of a one-to-one viewer-character relationship as they do on its perpetuation, as Mayne notes of cinema's safe zone.[23] Identification-in-opposition may be one of the medium's primary pleasures—viewers may relish the ability to escape their everyday social, racial, sexual, and economic roles.[24] It is crucial to remember that narrative cinema is a fantasy scenario, a confirmation of, and temporary release from, the subjectivities engaged in by spectators in their everyday lives.

The ability to identify against one's everyday role, spectatorship as a form of drag, is invoked by Laura Mulvey in "Afterthoughts on 'Visual Pleasure and Narrative Cinema.'" Moving beyond the focus of her now-classic 1975 meditation on the sadistic male pleasures offered by narrative cinema, Mulvey argues that female spectators oscillate between passivity and transvestitism. In the first role they are allied with on-screen women. In the second they adopt a male point of view. While the latter approach includes cross-sex connotations, Mulvey views it as confining and, therefore, as conventional as passivity. Nowhere does she allow for the possibility that spectatorial transvestitism offers women the pleasures of identifying against their socially prescribed roles. Instead, she asserts that to give men what they want, and to access male powers, women imagine themselves in men's spectatorial positions.[25] Doing so offers female spectators the elusive and ultimately empty experience of wearing the emperor's clothes.

Mulvey, then, begins to unravel the complexities of female spectatorship, but she ultimately confines the viewing process to patriarchal mandates. As a response to Mulvey's limited perspective on female viewing, Mary Ann Doane offered an alternative paradigm in "Film and the Masquerade" in 1982. As she explained, Mulvey's passive female role constructs viewing as overidentification with women and images. Female overidentification is generated, according to Doane, by women's pre-Oedipal alignment with their sexually alike mothers—overidentification is a side effect of bisexuality. Lacking the ability to fetishize their mothers, argues Doane, women (unlike men) cannot assume a position of difference from the image and thereby engage in overidentification and masochism.[26] As an addition to, and departure from, Mulvey's spectatorial options, Doane suggests that female viewing may also be a masquerade, a performance in which the spectator creates distance from the image and plays her femininity as a role.[27]

Doane's notion, and critique, of female overidentification is based on the model of bisexuality I have already discussed. Female bi*sexuality* is, in a sense, a misnomer in that it articulates pre-Oedipal identifications between women and their mothers at the expense of addressing adult same-sex desire. Yet female bisexuality remains a staple in feminist theories of spectatorship, especially those written in the 1980s. As I have noted earlier, Modleski's work on Hitchcock is, like Doane's, based on a pre-Oedipal valorization of the maternal. Modleski, however, goes an important step further when she addresses lesbianism and asserts that "the desire of women for other women" sends a subversive ripple through culture (51). Yet in the final analysis, Modleski and Doane[28] explain the desire of one woman for another as a form of regression or an idealized mother-daughter relationship.

Linda Williams replicates this approach in her work on horror spectatorship. By noting that the monster and heroine are sexually alike in their shared difference from the male, Williams repeats the core argument of female bisexuality. She accentuates identification with the monster, while downplaying an attraction based on similarity: "The strange sympathy and affinity that often develops between the monster and the girl may thus be less an expression of sexual desire . . . and more a flash of sympathetic identification" (88). Desire based on sexual sameness is not only secondary for Williams, it is nearly effaced.

These feminist approaches use bisexuality, then, as a theoretical release from the dead end offered by heterosexual models of spectatorship. Despite good intentions, however, they confirm heterosexual desire. As Sue-Ellen Case argues: "This 'woman,' then, in Doane, Williams, and others, is really heterosexual woman. Though her desire is aroused vis-à-vis another woman (a monstrous occasion), and they are totally proximate, they identify with rather than desire one another. . . . What melds monster to woman is not lesbian desire . . . [but] daughter emulating mother in the Oedipal triangle with the absent male still at the apex."[29]

In an attempt to reconfigure the woman-monster bond, and to argue for the import of same-sex desire, Case introduces queers into the spectatorial mix. According to Case, queers (figures whose desires break down the boundaries of male/female and transgress the borders of heterosexual desire) occupy an ontological and social position between the living and the undead, a position that bonds woman to monster according to mutual desire. Case's queer, like Hanson's gay man, is a vampiric figure, a being who both is and desires a monster.

Despite her attempts to loosen feminist film theory from the chains of heterosexual desire, Case also falls prey to the lures of binary thinking. In addressing the vampire of folklore as a queer icon, she notes that "proximity is a central organizing principle—not only in the look, but also in the mise en scène" (13). While Case's invocation of the vampire is compelling, her valorization of proximity is troubling. For she fails to articulate how queer proximity is different from Doane, Modleski, and Williams's bisexual model. Queer proximity seems to be a departure only insofar as it insists on same-sex desire. While that difference is a crucial one, by aligning queer desire with proximity—with sameness and nearness—Case reproduces the core argument of theories of female bisexuality. It seems, then, that all women remain guided by proximity in Case's schema, although some express that nearness in terms of identification while others do so via desire. By insisting on proximity, Case creates a system in which sameness is to queerness what sexual difference is to heterosexuality. As a result, Case's model cannot allow differences *within* queer relationships, for difference remains heterosexual terrain.

Whereas some heterosexist theories of spectatorship privilege difference and distance or valorize bisexual identification over desire, "homosexist" accounts favor sameness as a means of *sexualizing* identification (Corber puts this into practice as forthrightly as Case). These approaches are all built on familiar and, I would argue, faulty binaries: male/female, difference/sameness, and heterosexual/homosexual. Thus, Case's version of proximity and sameness cuts out the play of differences in homosexual relationships. Like theories of overidentification, Case eliminates the role of similarity in heterosexual desire, as well as the potential play of sameness, difference, and distance in relationships that fall outside the hetero/homo divide.

In *Epistemology of the Closet*, Eve Kosofsky Sedgwick argues that the conflation of homosexual desire with identification has a long heritage: "The fact that 'homosexuality,' being . . . posited on definitional similarity, was the first modern piece of sexual definition that simply took as nugatory the distinction between relations of identification and relations of desire, meant that it posed a radical question to cross-gender relations and, in turn, to gender discourse in which a man's desire for a woman could not guarantee his difference from her—in which it might even, rather, suggest his likeness to her." [30] According to Sedgwick, one of the dangers of homosexuality is that its collapse of identification with desire throws the conventional separation of those responses into question in heterosexuality. But the reverse might also be true. The separation of identification and desire, the belief that heterosexual desire is based upon difference, also troubles the focus on sameness in homosexual rapports. There is every reason to believe that homosexual *and* heterosexual relations, as well as other relationships (e.g., bisexual and transsexual) engage processes of identification and desire based on differences as well as similarities. This possibility, however, risks shifting the balance of politics, and not only desire. For if both homosexual and heterosexual desires engage processes of similarity and difference, then their social and political separation is rather tenuous.

V

Theories of spectatorship that argue for the performative dimensions of viewing, such as masquerade and transvestitism, provide a first step in extricating film studies from favored binaries. Aligning viewing with performance, with the adoption of sexuality, gender, and, potentially, other performative identities (such as race), offers a starting point from which to expand classic horror spectatorship and allow for the simultaneity of similarity and difference.[31]

When Esther Newton argues that drag "implies *distance* between the actor and the role or 'act,'" she is in the same theoretical ballpark as Doane in "Film and the Masquerade" (emphasis in original; Newton 109). Doane uses masquerade to separate the woman from the screen and offers a more distanced and, according to Doane, liberating model of spectatorship than female overidentification and masochism. Relying on Joan Riviere's case study, Doane aligns female viewing with performance.

In her article "Womanliness as a Masquerade," written in 1929, Riviere describes the travails of a patient who performs femininity in response to her professional success with men. According to Riviere, when the patient displays her intellectual skills she reveals her possession of powers conventionally deemed masculine and male. (In psychoanalytic terms, Riviere phrases this as the patient's "exhibition of herself in possession of the father's penis, having castrated him."[32]) In order to compensate for her male attributes, womanliness is "assumed and worn as a mask, both to hide the possession of masculinity and to avert the reprisals expected if she was found to possess it" (38). In this schema, masculinity is dangerous both to the woman who displays it (she risks retribution from men) and to the men whom she encounters (they risk castration by her).

Masquerade is a reaction-formation that disguises a female threat to men under the veneer of a socially prescribed role. As a mask, femininity generates distance between the patient and the behavior she adopts. As a form of drag, the woman who masquerades is, through her performance of femininity, separated from the conventional female role. Doane utilizes the distance between actor and role in Riviere's case study to loosen female spectatorship from the trap of overidentification. She assumes that, like Riviere's patient, women in an audience can flaunt femininity as a role and can engage in spectatorial masquerade. While I think Doane is wrong to privilege distance as an organizing spectatorial principle, her work on masquerade remains crucial for its introduction of a performative trope into spectatorship. Whereas Doane relies on Riviere to analyze the heterosexual woman's masquerading options, however, I prefer to use the case study, and the concept of masquerade, to address a wider range of viewing possibilities.

In the context of classic horror, masquerade offers a productive means of explaining the popularity of conventional male and female responses to the genre. The traditional reactions of the female spectator, such as screams and eye-covering, can be explained, in part, as a function of masquerade. Although some women may be truly horrified by on-screen images, it is likely that others experience more than terror, as I will argue in greater detail. Here, Riviere's case study is instructive. The patient uses her femininity to mask threatening qualities: her accession to male roles; identification with masculinity and men; possible danger to men; and potential desire for women.[33] Each of these variables is fostered at the textual level in many classic horror films and, in a patriarchal culture, may demand a form of spectatorial masking that disguises gender-bending.

This is true especially in terms of sexual orientation. For Western patriarchy assumes that femininity and heterosexuality are synonymous for women. Again, Riviere provides an alternative lesson. Although Riviere's patient is said to be heterosexual (she is married), and while masquerade aids her in attaining male sexual interest, homosexuality persists as an undercurrent. In writing of research conducted by S. Ferenczi in 1916, Riviere notes: "homosexual men exaggerate their heterosexuality as a 'defence' [sic] against homosexuality." Riviere implies that heterosexuality is donned as a mask, a gendered disguise. For homosexual men, then, heterosexuality is mobilized under the guise of traditional masculinity. Riviere continues, "I shall attempt to show that women who wish for masculinity may put on a mask of womanliness to avert anxiety and the retribution feared from men" (35).

Whereas Riviere shifts easily from male sexual orientation to female gender behavior, her second comment literally follows the first, implying a rhetorical and logical connection between them. In other words, if homosexual men sometimes exaggerate their masculinity to pass as heterosexual, as Riviere claims, it follows that female exaggeration of femininity sometimes covers homosexuality. Riviere herself presents masquerade as a fluid performance, one that can be deployed as a means of disguising unconventional gender traits, as well as nontraditional sexual desires.

Masquerade's mobility is reinforced by Riviere when she addresses male homosexuality a second time. Unlike her first example, which privileges heterosexuality and masculinity as disguises, her second citation elevates femininity and femaleness. Riviere describes a homosexual man who is excited by his image in a mirror, in which his hair is parted and he wears a bow tie. As she notes: "These extraordinary 'fetishes' turned out to represent a *disguise of himself* as his sister; the hair and bow were taken from her. His conscious attitude was a desire to *be* a woman" (emphasis in original; 40). Whereas masquerade promotes the illusion of heterosexuality and masculinity in men in the first case, it simultaneously creates and masks the impression of femaleness in the second.

It is but a small leap from the examples of masquerade in Riviere's work to a consideration of heterosexual men. For if some heterosexual women use womanliness as a masquerade of their accession to male-coded prerogatives, it follows that some heterosexual men use "manliness" to disguise their investment in femininity. With this perspective in mind, classic horror offers a variety of potential applications of the masquerade. For example, at the beginning of *Dracula* (Universal, 1931), when the count (Bela Lugosi) tells his vampire-wives to leave Renfield (Dwight Frye) alone so that he can have him to himself, multiple identifications and desires are offered to heterosexual male spectators. Yet the invitation to identify with Renfield as a victim, with Dracula as an attacker, and with both as homosexual object-choices may take form in a straight male spectator's refusal to display fear.[34] In other words, a heterosexual male viewer of *Dracula* may identify with and desire feminine and nonheterosexual positions beneath a conventional and brave response. The scenario becomes more complex if a gay male viewer reacts in a similar fashion, that is, with a refusal to express fear. In both cases, identification with and desire for Dracula and Renfield circulate beneath society's expected and promoted spectatorial response.

But what of women? Writing of Doane's theorization of the masquerade, Teresa de Lauretis inquires: "The question remains . . . whether this distance [between the woman and the image] can in fact be assumed by the straight female spectator in relation to the image of woman on the screen: how would a spectator 'flaunt' her femininity, in the dark of the movie theatre?" (248). I would like to use de

Lauretis's question as a point of departure, not only to provide a tentative response but also to reconfigure masquerade as a model of spectatorship that takes the spectator on a journey that spans sexual orientations.

How might classic horror's heterosexual female viewers flaunt their femininity as they watch images of heroines and their monstrous doubles on-screen? Here, I need only reinvoke the conventional responses to classic horror described earlier—namely, a woman can scream bloody murder, cower behind the shoulder of her date, and alternately cover and uncover her eyes in a visual game of masking and unmasking not unlike that which often occurs on-screen. Thus, female spectators who watch horror films are assumed to flaunt their femininity all the time.

However, there may be a distinctly performative dimension to their display of terror, as a marketing ploy from 1935 suggests. During each screening of *Mark of the Vampire* (MGM, 1935) in Bridgeport, Connecticut, a female viewer was planted in the audience by the exhibitor. At predetermined moments, she began screaming and pretended to faint. Ushers then picked her up, rushed her from the theater, and whisked her away in an ambulance, which was stationed at the curb.[35] Traditionally feminine responses to horror were, in this instance, deployed as loaded cultural roles for theatrical and promotional purposes. While some women may, indeed, be frightened by the images they watch in classic films, the Bridgeport example begs an important revision when it comes to gendered spectatorship for horror: some women also exhibit extreme emotional affect as a gender *performance*.

In a 1989 study of viewers' affective responses to contemporary horror films, researchers made striking claims regarding gender: "It is assumed that the majority of young men and women in our society are socialized according to 'traditional' cultural gender roles, and that these rules of gender-specific conduct cover affect and its expression." And the authors continue: "Graphic horror films, in particular, appear to offer a unique, socially approved context in which gender specific roles can be enacted. At the horror movies, young men have a chance to show off their fearlessness. . . . Analogously, young women have a chance to display the 'appropriate' fear response, obtain 'protection' from men, and admire them for their 'heroics.'"[36]

The results of the study are remarkably consonant with conventional theories of horror spectatorship—men are brave viewers who protect their terrified female dates. Yet the research also suggests that horror cinema mobilizes social behavior as a means of *acting out* accepted cultural roles. Spectatorship is described as a socially sanctioned form of male/female bonding, as well as a vehicle for playing gendered parts as expected. The underlying message is that the gender performances described may not be comprehensive indicators of the emotions experienced by viewers while watching horror films. Instead, they are indices of the degree to which traditional gender roles and the rules of conduct for heterosexual coupling are promoted in patriarchal culture, not to mention the means with which they are practiced by men and women in a variety of settings and for various purposes. Those purposes include, but are not limited to, an attempt to garner social acceptance and, in the case of some women, to gain male attention.

Here, I want to return to de Lauretis's query and consider one of the questions it raises in terms of lesbian subjectivity: namely, how can lesbian spectators access the masquerade if they are not as concerned with masquerading for men as is Riviere's patient, or as are the subjects in the contemporary horror study cited? There are a number of ways in which to respond to this question. It can be argued that lesbian spectators cannot masquerade because that process is put into play for the benefit of men.[37] If, for argument's sake, lesbianism is a rejection of men as object-choices, lesbians would not need to masquerade. Their access to the female image is necessarily more direct than that of the masquerading heterosexual woman and is destined to replicate bisexual overidentification. Or, conversely, lesbians cannot masquerade precisely because they desire women, a fact that, according to enduring stereotypical assumptions, links them to masculinity. Lesbians cannot use womanliness as a masquerade because they exhibit signs of manliness instead.

Despite the fact that lesbians' objects of desire are usually not men (a contestable definition of sexual orientation), living in a patriarchal culture requires that some lesbians either must or choose to masquerade in order to access certain powers.[38] The masquerade is not solely a heterosexual woman's means of disguising independence and a will-to-power beneath a mask of womanliness or her opportunity to view an image of a woman at a greater distance, as Doane would have it. For masquerade also serves as some lesbians' and bisexual women's means of disguising their cinematic and everyday desires behind the same feminine mask.[39]

Asking how the heterosexual woman gazing at a female image can flaunt her femininity in a darkened theater is only part of the point. The more pressing question is how women *and* men either consciously or unconsciously access masquerade as a viewing position; meaning, how can their viewing responses be seen as both traditional and as a, more or less self-conscious, means of performing conventional social and sexual roles? And, furthermore, which movies and genres invite spectators to masquerade?

The most telling question for some lesbians may not be how do female spectators masquerade, but what happens when a lesbian or bisexual woman flaunts her femininity not only as a sign of her distance from the image, or as a means of protecting herself from patriarchal wrath, but as a disguise or display of her erotic investment in the image (an investment that is not equivalent to overidentification because it is motivated by same-sex desire)? In assuming a feminine position vis-à-vis the female image, or the image of her monstrous double, the lesbian or bisexual woman assumes a role that culture and psychoanalysis deem impossible: she surveys a female object of desire from a position of femininity. While this version of masquerade does not account for all types of viewing, it allows for the dual operations of distance (the lesbian flaunts femininity as a role) and proximity (one woman desires another).

A scene from Tod Browning's *Mark of the Vampire* provides a good example when it comes to the diverse possibilities of female masquerade. The most pronounced attack/seduction scene in this vampire tale occurs on a terrace outside the heroine's home. In a suggestive sequence, shots of the vampire Luna (Carol Borland) walking toward the camera are intercut with images of the heroine, Irena (Elizabeth Allan), who rises to meet the fiend. As she stares at Luna, Irena leaves her bedroom, moves across an outdoor terrace, and sits down in a trance-like state. Just before Luna bends over the heroine with a sweep of her capelike gown, Irena swoons (figure 2.5).

One type of lesbian spectator watching this scene may well flaunt her femininity by gasping at the horrifying sight of the monster's advances. But beneath that feminine veneer she may simultaneously harbor both a masculine identification with the aggressive fiend and a desire for the women engaged in an erotic embrace. In fact, a heterosexual woman may display and experience the same masquerading and illicit responses, thereby expanding the applicability of drag beyond the sexual orientations that spectators live out in their everyday lives. Here, Judith Mayne's characterization of cinema as a safe zone finds expression.

While I firmly believe that drag expands spectatorship in important ways, I do not want to lose sight of the fact that there are different stakes in the processes of identification and desire for different spectators, stakes that are sometimes either political or contextually politicized. Thus, for example, a self-identified lesbian spectator who enjoys the erotic lesbian vampire scenes in Lambert Hillyer's *Dracula's Daughter* (Universal, 1936) or Browning's *Mark of the Vampire* has a different desiring relationship to the on-screen images than, say, a straight woman, who may express similar desires. Part of the difference resides, though, not only in each woman's experience within the theater (although here, too, there could be variance in degrees of associative fantasies or memories inspired by on-screen images) but also in the relationship between what gets played out for spectators in a theater and their desiring experiences outside the movie context.

Figure 2.5. Luna (Carol Borland) leans menacingly over the fainting Irena (Elizabeth Allan) in this still from *Mark of the Vampire*. Photo courtesy of Ronald V. Borst/Hollywood Movie Posters. *Copyright © 1935 Turner Entertainment Co. All rights reserved.*

Whereas a heterosexual female spectator may have every reason to relinquish her homoerotic desires once she returns to her everyday life, a lesbian spectator may have every reason *not* to do so. There are untold pleasures in holding on to the sometimes-illicit identifications and desires that get played out at the movies for those whose everyday identities run contrary to dominant culture. This is true not only because movies, sometimes unintentionally, point to the existence and importance of those who exist at the margins of society—such as monsters and homosexuals—but also because the films that offer nontraditional identifications and desires are often lifelong touchstones for lesbians, gay men, and other gender outlaws, as Patricia White has recently argued.[40]

My main point in discussing drag is, then, not so much to level the playing field of spectatorship (by noting that *all* spectators share the same relationships to on-screen images and characters). Rather, I want to suggest that one pleasure offered by classic horror viewing is identifying against oneself. Of course, spectators do not always identify against themselves for the duration of films, and their investments in either doing or not doing so may well differ. What remains significant, however, is that classic horror cinema invites spectators to play out, temporarily and differentially, roles and responses that sometimes contrast with those they adopt or are asked to adopt on a day-to-day basis.

From this perspective, masquerade is a useful spectatorial position for classic horror. Not only does it allow for the simultaneity of multiple identifications and desires, it also accommodates an interplay between difference and similarity (e.g., gay male masquerade may involve identification with and/or against masculinity). As a genre that trades in patriarchal dicta (women are often victimized by monstrous males) and disrupts traditional expectations (women are aligned with monsters and fiends possess ambiguous gender traits), masquerade as a form of drag describes the genre's dual operations of convention and transgression.

Spectatorship-as-drag transposes classic horror's gender ambiguities from storylines and publicity campaigns to viewing. As a framework for spectatorship, drag suggests both that transgressive identifications and desires lurk beneath or on the surface of gender displays and that the lure of conventional roles does not counteract social expectations. Classic horror's spectatorial pleasures, whether they are the fulfillment of traditional expectations (the female scream) or a more performative approach to gender roles (the female scream planted in an audience), are intimately connected to the genre's appeal to the status quo.

Part of horror's draw is that the monster is repulsive and threatening to women, the obstacle heroes overcome to assume their proper places within patriarchy. Yet as I have argued thus far and will continue to argue in the remaining chapters, another part of the genre's appeal lies in the on- and offscreen malleability that classic horror celebrates: horror extends the invitation to identify with and desire against everyday behaviors as well as the invitation to play with the masks that Western culture treats as core identities—such as male and female, and homosexual and heterosexual. Amidst signifiers of fear and desire, loathing and longing, classic horror celebrates mobile spectatorial positions, the dissolution of conventional gender traits, the fragility of the heterosexual couple, and the precariousness of patriarchal institutions and values.

Alas, tradition wins out in the end. The straight couple usually parades away as the movie comes to a close. But many of these films invite viewers to witness temporarily an alternate world. There, in the company of monsters and dark jungle creatures, spectators oscillate between sadism and masochism and experience the pleasures of drag by screaming as expected or refusing to respond as culture dictates. No matter what they do, however, classic horror's patrons get to go home in their street clothes and leave the fiends that terrify and fascinate them in the dark of the movie theater. At least that is the hope.

3

Horror for Sale: The Marketing and Reception of Classic Horror Cinema

Take the girl friend and by the middle of the
first reel she'll have both arms around
your neck and holding on [sic] for dear life.

—James E. Mitchell
Review of *Doctor X* (Warner Bros., 1932)

I

What did a man have to do to be a good horror viewer in the 1930s? According to James E. Mitchell in his review of *Doctor X* for the *Los Angeles Examiner*, he had to take his girlfriend to the movies and subject himself to her hysterical clutches. Like the standard model of film and horror spectatorship, Mitchell casts men as the genre's brave patrons, while women cower in their seats and hold on to their dates as if their lives depend on it. In the dark of the theater, Mitchell seems to suggest, horror movies provide women with a socially sanctioned reason to grab on to their boyfriends, to hold tight with all their might.

But was holding a quivering woman the only thing a man had to do to be a horror viewer in the 1930s? Not quite. In an effort to open this chapter with the conventional version of spectatorship, I preempted Mitchell's words at a crucial moment: "Take the girl friend and by the middle of the first reel she'll have both arms around your neck and holding on [sic] for dear life. *And you'll be giggling hysterically, too, trying to convince her you are not scared to death, either*" (emphasis added).[1] Mitchell's direct address to horror's male viewer not only relies on traditional gender dynamics—women are terrified and men are called upon to be brave—but confirms that gender traits can be performed. Just as social mandates invited women in the 1930s to cling to men while screening horror movies, thus encouraging them to display conventionally feminine behavior as a means of garnering male attention, so, too, did the male viewer, at least according to Mitchell, use female fear, as well as his own traditional display of bravery, to disguise *his* terror behind a socially prescribed behavior.

Mitchell's recognition that male spectators perform traditional gender behaviors adds yet another element to horror viewing. For, according to Mitchell, not only is male courage acted out in the dark of the movie theater, so, too, are the traditional ground rules for heterosexual coupling performed by patrons. Mitchell's 1932 commentary reinforces the findings of Norbert Mundorf et al.'s recent study of horror spectatorship (discussed in chapter 2), which found that contemporary horror movies offer prime arenas for teenagers of both sexes to play out the conventional mandates of gender roles and heterosexual coupling. The socially prescribed behaviors that Mitchell details in his review of *Doctor X* are, then, markers of the degree to which traditional gender traits can be mobilized in a specific social setting—such as a movie theater, and for particular cultural purposes—such as abiding by gender expectations and performing heterosexual dating rituals as expected. Whether as gender play, dating ploy, or both, the performance of bravery on the part of the male spectator to whom Mitchell addresses his review underscores the degree to which traditional signs of masculinity and heterosexual coupling can be constructed.

What gender dynamics were played out in horror's reception during the 1930s? How were expectations about socially desirable gender traits mobilized in marketing the genre to exhibitors and viewers alike? How was gender portrayed in a manner that highlighted both the pervasiveness as well as the theatricality of conventional behaviors? And how did industry censorship manipulate the genre's address to spectators? This chapter is devoted to exploring these questions with a view to addressing the censorship, marketing, and reception of classic horror cinema as arenas for negotiation and contradiction. With that goal in mind, what follows is not a comprehensive study of classic horror's historical configurations. Instead, this chapter is a selective—primarily urban—analysis of the genre's appeal to audiences in the 1930s. While another scholar might be interested in 1930s attitudes regarding horror's impact on children,[2] a topic that was discussed at length in various venues, my focus is on the ways in which gender and sexuality were not only remarked upon in reviews and Production Code materials but also utilized as selling ploys for movies.

This chapter, then, is both a departure from and extension of the arguments offered in chapter 2. My intent is to present and situate original documents both as a means of tracing the historical twists and turns of classic horror reception—specifically, as it pertains to gender—as well as a vehicle for suggesting that theatrical role-play, which I have attributed to imputed spectators, was elicited by studio and theater marketing ploys, and in film reviews in the 1930s. Thus, the performative dimensions that I align with spectatorship in theoretical terms are framed here in historical terms.

My focus on the gender dynamics of Production Code reports, popular film reviews, and marketing tactics derives from my belief that the textual and extratextual levels of classic horror movies should be studied as parallel modes of expression, as meaning systems that toyed with gender repeatedly, yet also appealed to assumptions about appropriate gender behavior as a selling ploy. Whether the parallels between horror's on- and offscreen representations of gender were intended by those who produced them in the 1930s (such as publicity departments and directors) is of less interest to me than is tracing the genre's address to viewers on the basis of gender expectations. Offscreen mentions of horror's appeal to women or its ability to terrify them, for example, found parallel representations in movies that portrayed heroines who were positively transformed while under a monster's sway, or who swooned when faced with terrors too horrible to bear. Horror movies were sites of negotiation and contradiction when it came to their portrayals of and assumptions about gender, and similar efforts at negotiation and signs of contradiction were at work in the publicity ploys used to market them to male and female viewers in the 1930s.

Believing that the textual and extratextual levels are connected, however, is not the same as pinpointing the exact impact their convergence had on viewers. Much as I would like to claim that the gender behaviors that appear or are promoted on- and offscreen *fully* determine spectators' interpretations of classic horror, doing so would be an exercise in analytic projection, not precision. As Janet Staiger comments vis-à-vis notions of a coherent reader:

They derive from assuming something about texts (e.g., that texts are coherent), from confusing what might be "in" a text with what a reader might do with the details of a text, and from believing that the primary obligation of readers is creating a logical interpretation rather than, for instance, developing a coherent self in opposition to the text or finding pleasure in dispersion and contradiction.[3]

Staiger's points are well suited to classic horror, a genre whose films rarely offer coherent narratives. While viewers may try to make sense of storylines, they are often confronted with confusing plot twists, inconsistent character portrayals, sudden and unintended shifts of tone between horror and comedy, and narrative loose ends that go unexplained. As one *Variety* reviewer remarked of James Whale's *Old Dark House* (Universal, 1932) and of horror in general: "There are sundry inanities throughout, but as with the horror school the audience seemingly doesn't expect coherence, and so everything goes by the boards."[4] As the reporter's comments suggest, not only are horror movies filled with incoherent inanities but viewers expect those inconsistencies. Taking the opinion of the *Variety* reporter as a guide, classic horror's ideal is not a viewer who searches for coherence but one who accepts its absence.

Staiger's suggestion that readers respond to and find pleasure in dispersion and contradiction is a preferable model for cinematic spectatorship than one that relies on an ideal/coherent viewer. By the same token, however, assuming that viewing is entirely free-form, and owes nothing to textual and extratextual meanings, is to locate *all* signification in the act of spectatorship. Instead, as Staiger notes, reception studies need to "recognize the dialectics of evidence and theory, and take up a critical distance on the *relations* between spectators and texts" (emphasis in original; 81). In keeping with Staiger's advice, this chapter looks at reception with a focus on gender and the genre's address to female patrons. My intention is to outline the reception climate for horror in the early 1930s with a view to highlighting the ways in which the industry's self-regulatory and promotional efforts opened up viewership to a wide spectrum of patrons and an even wider range of affective responses to the genre. The chapters that follow take that context as a starting point and combine original materials with close textual analysis. The task in those chapters will be to illustrate that many of the meanings deployed at the site of reception, which I will explore here, are also built into texts at the narrative level.

Taking Staiger's comments as my guide, I cannot possibly know *exactly* how male and female viewers responded to horror in the 1930s. What I do know is that their reactions were contested in reviews and Production Code files, hoped for and promoted in Pressbooks, and overtly manipulated in exhibition ploys. How men and women were believed to react to horror movies was given contradictory attention by reviewers and promoters.[5] Precisely what spectators did with those diverse messages remains a matter of speculation—my guess is that they responded with a matching dose of contradiction and complexity, at least when behind theater doors.

Many horror reviews from the 1930s addressed spectators in unspecified terms. Reporters used gender-neutral language such as "horror fans" and "audiences." As Mordaunt Hall remarked of *Dracula* (Universal, 1931): "It is a production that evidently had the desired effect upon many in the audience yesterday afternoon, for there was a general outburst of applause when Dr. Van Helsing produced a little cross that caused the dreaded Dracula to fling his cloak over his head and make himself scarce."[6] The *Motion Picture Herald*'s reviewer, McCarthy, made similarly unspecified claims regarding *Mark of the Vampire* (MGM) four years later: "This is a picture that should give the 'horror' fans all they want. It's full of shrieks and screams, gasps and shudders."[7] Edwin Schallert was convinced that *Frankenstein* elicited a range of affective responses from spectators when the film ran at the RKO Orpheum in 1932, but the audience remains a genderless mass for him: "This weird shiver feature seems to cause the audience not only to experience the spinal chills, but also to laugh, cry and otherwise express hysteria of the moment."[8]

While Louella O. Parsons gave viewership a more dramatic flair in her review of *King Kong* (RKO, 1933), she was equally vague when it came to gender: "Breathless with suspense, nervous with suppressed emotion and thrilled with continued horrors, the audience greeted 'KING KONG' at the Chinese Theatre last night, as something entirely new in the way of motion picture entertainment."[9] This lack of gender specification in a good portion of reviews is instructive, for it suggests that while assumed differences in male and female spectatorship are crucial to more recent scholarship on horror cinema, they were of less concern to critics when classic horror first appeared. What mattered most consistently to reporters was whether or not films were good, and whether they were suitable for children.

Despite the focus on other criteria, gender was referenced in a number of reviews. Critics usually offered one of three perspectives:[10] (1) they remark upon the terrors endured by both men and women in the audience; (2) they are surprised or convinced that women respond well to horror movies; and (3) they suggest that male and female viewers appreciate different aspects of films. Leo Meehan's 1931 review of *Frankenstein* in the *Motion Picture Herald* is a good example of the first critical perspective on gender: "Women come out trembling, men exhausted. I don't know what it might do to children, but I wouldn't want my kids to see it."[11] One reviewer for Warner Bros.'s *The Mystery of the Wax Museum* (1933) painted an almost identical portrait two years later: "Adults of both sexes will find more than enough in the way of startling excitement to interest them, but because of its gruesomeness, *Wax Museum* is a little too strong for juvenile patronage."[12]

In one of the few instances in which a reporter was revealed to be a woman, she assumed she could speak for all members of her sex when she made the following remarks about *Doctor X*: "All we can tell you—and we'll grant that our sisters will agree, and let the boyfriends do the real figuring in this case—is that 'Doctor X' moves swiftly from start to finish [and] it's an amusingly creepy way of spending an afternoon or evening."[13] As late as 1935, when the first horror cycle neared its end, reviewers continued to emphasize horror's draw to men, women and children: "In 'The Bride of Frankenstein,' Boris Karloff comes again to terrify the children, frighten the women and play a jiggling tune upon masculine spines."[14]

Like the other critics cited, *Time* magazine's reporter responded to *White Zombie* in 1932 by affirming that men, like women, are scared of monsters, but went a step further by critiquing the star's performance: "Bela Lugosi looks like a comic imbecile, [and] can make his jawbones rigid and show the whites of his eyes. These abilities qualify him to make strong men cower and women swoon."[15] The anonymous reviewer's critical tone suggested disdain not only for the movie and its star, but also for patrons who respond with fear in spite of Lugosi's botched performance. In fact, *White Zombie* is an excellent example of a horror movie that fared poorly among critics but well with the public. As Michael Price and George Turner note: "*White Zombie* opened on Broadway at the Rivoli Theatre. No movie ever received a more thorough critical scourge, although the public loved it and it brought in a great deal of money."[16] *White Zombie* is a reminder that 1930s reviews are limited gauges of spectatorship. Since classic horror films were released during an era when audience studies were scarce,[17] historical research can describe the environment for spectatorship but not the minutiae of viewer reactions.

The second approach to gender evidenced by reporters—surprise or conviction that horror movies delighted female patrons—was articulated in a *Variety* review for *Dracula* in 1931. As Rush noted: "Here was a picture whose screen fortunes must have caused much uncertainty as to the femme fan reaction. As it turns out all the signs are that the woman angle is favorable and that sets the picture for better than average money at the box office."[18] Universal had a hand in eliciting female interest in the film. The studio released *Dracula* with an explicitly romantic campaign targeted at women. The movie opened in New York City on February 14, 1931—Valentine's Day— accompanied by suggestive cutlines: "The Story of the Strangest Passion Ever Known;"[19] "The Strangest Love Story of All;"[20] and "The Strangest Love a Man Has Ever Known"[21] (figure 3.1).

The assumption that women might have a romantic stake in vampire movies may not have been surprising at the time, given that fiends often sweep heroines off their feet. But the same *Variety* reporter thought female patrons hooked on *Frankenstein* as well: "Appeal is candidly to the morbid side and the screen effect is up to promised specifications. Feminine fans seem to get some kind of emotional kick out of this sublimation of the bedtime ghost story done with all the literariness of the camera." Although Rush did not elaborate upon why he or she thought women were drawn to James Whale's movie, a more general viewer profile was provided: "The audience for this type of film is probably the detective story readers and the mystery yarn radio listeners."[22]

Who were those detective readers and mystery listeners? Rush did not say. Yet clues appeared in two industry magazines geared toward exhibitors: the *Motion Picture Herald* (MPH) and its predecessor, the *Exhibitors Herald-World* (EHW). In a 1933 issue of the MPH, the following headline appeared: "Girls Want Mystery; Boys War Pictures." The brief article announced the results of an Edinburgh, Scotland, study of children's spectatorial preferences. The gender lines were drawn between mystery and war movies but, noted the report, neither group liked romance films.[23] The column went on to suggest that girls will, eventually, become women with a continued investment in mysteries.

That they might also grow up to crave romance was an assumption made by the motion picture industry at the time.

That assumption was articulated in a 1930 article in the EHW entitled, "B. O. Explodes Idea That Women Dislike War and Crook Pictures. Feminine Attendance at Four Productions Classed as Lacking in Love or Romantic Interest Averages 61 Per cent of Total at Matinees and 59 Per Cent at Night." Although the films cited were war and gangster pictures, the unconventional results predicted female horror attendance—*Dracula* debuted and was a box-office success only five months later. "Smashing a traditional theory of the

Figure 3.1. Dracula's allure (Bela Lugosi) for women was depicted in publicity stills from the film, as this image of Mina (Helen Chandler) and the count suggests. *Copyright © by Universal City Studios, Inc. Courtesy of MCA Publishing Rights, a Division of MCA, Inc.*

Figure 3.2. This poster promises generic rewards for male and female spectators. Helen Grosvenor (Zita Johann), the heroine of *The Mummy*, lies vulnerable to the advances of monstrous men, while the cutline promotes an ominous love story: "A LOVE THAT DEFIED TIME DRIVES A BEAUTIFUL GIRL TO HER DOOM!" *Copyright © by Universal City Studios, Inc. Courtesy of MCA Publishing Rights, a Division of MCA, Inc.*

box office," the article continued, "investigation has brought to light some pertinent facts to disprove the idea that women, who decide the fate of motion pictures, object as a rule to war pictures, crook dramas, and films in which the love or romantic interest is conspicuous by its absence."[24] While the percentage of men attending matinees increased in the early part of the 1930s, due to rising unemployment rates, women remained a significant viewing force. Thus, the study's announcement of female interest in gangster and war films was also a promising sign of horrific things to come.

Although the EHW article encouraged exhibitors to quell their anxieties about female attendance at rough-and-tumble movies, classic horror marketing rarely took women for granted. Films often included romance at the narrative level, which was promoted as a selling point to women viewers. In McCarthy's review of *The Mummy* (Universal, 1932) in the MPH, for example, he or she articulated the gender divide assumed in spectator tastes: "It has that type of romance, which, although far-fetched and entirely visionary, is nevertheless fascinating to feminine patrons, while the mystic unrealism should provide the men folk something new."[25] Men and women may enjoy horror movies, McCarthy claimed, but their pleasures are found in divergent aspects of films. Furthermore, McCarthy thought that the source of fascination for women was decidedly unimpressive, "far-fetched" romance in the reporter's own words (figure 3.2).

Not surprisingly, given the goal of as wide a viewership as possible, classic horror movies were made and marketed with a general audience in mind. As an MPH reviewer noted of *King Kong* in 1933, the film "has everything—romance, drama, spectacle, unrealism, thrill terror and 'love interest.'"[26] The same combination of disparate themes was proclaimed in a 1931 MPH advertisement for *Dr. Jekyll and Mr. Hyde*. As the cutline notes: "PARAMOUNT BRINGS YOU THE THRILLER OF ALL THRILLERS!—PLUS A GREAT LOVE STORY." Later in the same advertisement, diverse promotional possibilities were emphasized: "Swell cast; great director and a fascinating story. Mystery and horror! Heart-warming romance and intense-drama! Everything! Its appeal is unlimited."[27] Just in case that appeal was divided along gender lines, *Variety* ran what David J. Skal calls a "split-personality review" (144). A sidebar commentary entitled "The Woman's Angle" recasts some of the film's supposed failures in the horror department as draws for female spectators. As *Variety*'s reporter remarked: "Classic shocker loses much of its stark horror and consequent unpleasantness for women, by growing logical with psychoanalytical motivation and daringly presented sex appeal. Latest version made enticing instead of repellent to the girls."[28]

Along the same lines, one exhibitor of Paramount's film literally split his lobby display in two and separated the horror from the romance theme. As the MPH reported:

> In connection with one of the recent so-called "Horror" pictures, "Dr. Jekyll and Mr. Hyde," contrasting lobby displays were most effectively used by George Laby, manager of the Washington Street Olympia Theatre, Boston, Mass.; so effectively, in fact, that the displays were thought to be a contributing factor obtaining the highest weekly gross over the period of the year. The accompanying photo speaks for itself. At the left, now the famous "Doctor" in characteristic poses of himself and other self, treated from the "horror" angle. At the right are featured characters representing the romantic side of the picture.[29] (see figure 3.3)

The romantic side consisted of a poster of actresses Miriam Hopkins and Rose Hobart flanking heartthrob Fredric March, who stars in the eponymous role. The dual-focus display parallels the film's dual theme and highlights exhibitor assumptions about male and female spectatorial preferences. Thus, although some reviewers claimed that women and horror were a fine match, others believed that female patrons had to be courted with romance themes and promotional stunts.

II

Classic horror's promotional gimmicks took various forms, including updating techniques from the silent era. The ambulance parked outside the theater door, for example, was a popular ploy in the 1920s and was refurbished by exhibitors in the next decade. As the MPH reports, the following sign was displayed in front of the Princess

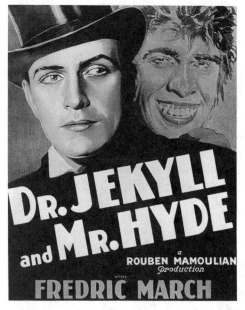

Figure 3.3. The horror side of George Laby's lobby display in Boston, Massachusetts included an image like this one, in which Mr. Hyde (Fredric March) threatens his handsome second self, Dr. Jekyll (also played by Fredric March). *Copyright © by Universal City Studios, Inc. Courtesy of MCA Publishing Rights, a Division of MCA, Inc.*

Theatre in Aurora, Mississippi, for performances of *Bride of Frankenstein* (Universal) in 1935: "No parking here, space reserved for ambulance."[30] Holden Swinger, manager of the Palace Theatre in Akron, Ohio, went a step further—he "stationed an ambulance at his curb during his 'Bride of Frankenstein' date with lobby easel and sign on ambulance calling attention to the free emergency service for those who 'couldn't take it.'"[31] Both stunts, used earlier in the decade for *Frankenstein* (Universal, 1931), are variations on a ploy listed by John F. Barry and Epes W. Sargent in their 1927 guide to exhibitors, *Building Theatre Patronage: Management and Merchandising*.

Barry and Sargent had clear ideas about the appeals of the ambulance to motion picture theater managers and, by extension, to spectators:

> A standard comedy stunt is the ambulance parked in front of the theatre to carry out those who may be overcome with laughter. The ambulance may be paraded through the streets with signs to the effect that the occupant is being rushed to the hospital because he nearly died laughing at the named comedy. If you can get a man who can laugh naturally and infectiously, it will not hurt to have him stagger from the house, and be helped into the ambulance, laughing all the way.[32]

While the ideal comedy stunt participant, according to Barry and Sargent, is a man whose laughter is infectious, horror exhibitors preferred women for exploitation purposes in the 1930s.

For example, in order to draw as many patrons to *Mark of the Vampire* (MGM, 1935) as possible, a first aid stretcher was placed in the lobby of the Loew's Colonial Theatre in Reading, Pennsylvania. The in-house stunt was accompanied by advertisements in the town's daily newspapers addressed to "women who are not afraid." The notices recounted the film's storyline and challenged female viewers to attend a screening. As the copy for the advertisement suggests, the contest winner was expected to respond *against* her conventional gender role; she was supposed to be brave.[33] A year later, the Wicomico Theatre in Salisbury, Maryland, devised a tie-in prize for *The Invisible Ray*, which targeted women again. A free permanent was offered by the town's leading beauty salon to any woman willing to sit alone in the theater and watch the film at midnight. According to the MPH, there were twenty applicants for the stunt and "crowds gathered at the theatre to watch the gal enter."[34] Both exhibitor efforts used women as prototypical viewers, drew upon stereotypes that assumed that female patrons will be frightened by watching horror and invited women to defy those stereotypes as a means of garnering prizes and proving their prowess as spectators.

In an analysis of the relationship between women and early exhibition tactics, Diane Waldman mentions that the manager of New York's Rialto Theatre took pride in promoting horror movies to a predominantly male clientele. Waldman uses the manager's claim as a springboard to analyze horror's sadistic address to women in the early 1940s:

> If other theatres showing horror films were anything like the Rialto, one piece of exploitation aimed at women takes on ominous tones: a theatre exhibiting Universal's *Frankenstein Meets the Wolf Man* (1943) offered a prize to any woman who would sit through the midnight show alone. It is not clear whether the danger was supposed to derive from the terrors of the screen or from the other patrons of the theatre. This stunt, then, made explicit the connection between horror films and the terrorizing of women, capitalizing on one of women's most common experiences: fear of harassment when alone, especially at night, in a public place heavily frequented by men.[35]

While Waldman is right to take note of the midnight terrors endured by women in American society, she reduces the Rialto stunt to vulgar sexism and assumes that it fully encapsulates horror's relationship to women. Waldman is not far off in claiming that the choice of a female patron resulted from conventional assumptions about women in a patriarchal culture, but she is wrong to assert that the choice only connoted attack and harassment.

Women were classic horror's central stunt participants because they were thought to personify the genre's favored affect: fear. The upshot was that if women could survive the viewing of a horror film and, moreover, if they could respond bravely, then other patrons, meaning *men*, can do the same. While Waldman's claim has some validity, it was not exhibitors' primary motivation. Given that the woman chosen was expected to view *Frankenstein Meets the Wolf Man* alone in the theater, harassment by men was not part of the contest's requirements, but solitary bravery was. Female responses to horror were used by exhibitors to prove that the films should and could be seen by all patrons and to highlight the performative elements of terror. For if women were asked over and over again to *act* out or refuse to act out their fears in front of crowds or to garner prizes, their gender roles—though conventional and promoted—were also highly theatricalized.

Take the efforts of the Loew's Majestic Theatre in Bridgeport, Connecticut, for instance. During screenings of *Mark of the Vampire* in 1935, "[a] woman was planted in the audience at each show to scream and faint, after which she was carried out to an ambulance parked in front of the theatre and whisked away."[36] While the female scream is a popular on-screen trope, it was also promoted heavily as a horror gimmick, a performance intended to incite viewer response. So powerful was the female scream for audiences that Marquis Busby claimed it sparked his reaction to *Dracula* at the beginning of the decade: "I wasn't really scared until some lady in the audience let out a piercing scream. Maybe it was just a pin, but it was disconcerting to the rest of the audience."[37] Maybe it *was* just a pin, maybe she was a plant, maybe the viewer was terrified, or maybe she pretended to be. Whichever explanation holds true, the sound of a woman's scream promoted fear, guaranteed the genre's effectiveness, and linked female gender behavior to an overwrought performance.[38]

While some theaters addressed female patrons with tame ploys—for example, the Capitol in Dallas premiered Universal's *The Black Cat* (1934) with a contest for the most beautiful cat[39]—others tried to create as large a ruckus as possible. Owners of the Palace Theatre in Chicago, for example, placed advertisements in newspapers noting, "EMOTION TEST HITS ON '[BRIDE OF] FRANKENSTEIN.'" The exhibitors remodeled a lie-detector exam to register the affective roller coaster experienced by viewers. The prototypical spectators chosen for the stunt were two female subjects, aged five[40] and twenty-five respectively, who were hooked up to the contraption as they screened the film. A first-aid booth was placed in the lobby to dramatize the health hazards of horror viewing. The promotional efforts were rounded out by a tie-up with the Loop department store, which utilized "a professional mannikin [sic] modeling evening gowns, surrounded by color enlargements from the picture."[41] As was true of other stunts, female responses to horror were promoted vociferously and used to gauge the genre's ability to frighten, amuse, and satisfy patrons.

Although department store tie-ins were initiated by local theater managers, they were also suggested in Pressbooks. The promotional materials distributed for *The Mystery of the Wax Museum,* for instance, include a full-page game plan for linking the film to a local department store. Exhibitors were advised to approach a store as follows: "Here is a tie-up that is a natural for any store that uses the finer grade of lifelike wax models for gown displays. Offer to furnish the store with such equipment, the services of an experienced gown model, and one that in general dimensions, sizes up to the wax models to be used."[42] The idea was for the store to announce a window fashion show, at which time the live model would pose with the wax figurines, stand frozen for a few moments, and surprise the audience by smiling and bowing. The logic ran as follows: exhibit beautiful gowns at local department stores to pique women's interest in the latest horror film, and they will arrive at the next showing with their dates and friends in tow (figure 3.4).

Although the exhibition ploys listed thus far appeal to women as prototypical horror viewers and consumers of feminine wares, other promotional tactics were developed. One popular technique was to link women with monstrosity, as well as suggest their desire for a fiend. The RKO Theatre in Los Angeles, for example, sent masked women into the streets to hand out "Beware" notices announcing the premiere of *The Invisible Man* (Universal, 1934).[43] While the announcements targeted male as well as female patrons, women were used to promote the picture as fiendish doubles—like the film's monster, their identities remain hidden. The MPH added yet another dimension in its advice to exhibitors for the same film: "There are a million more [exploitation angles] you can concoct, not the least of which are those that can be applied to women to stir their curiosity. How would they like to be embraced, kissed, by an invisible lover?"[44] Here, the MPH urged managers to address women in terms of their desire *for* the invisible man, and not their resemblance to him.

The publicity ploys for *Island of Lost Souls* (Paramount, 1933) also targeted female patrons in dual terms. Prior to the release of the movie, Paramount conducted a nationwide search for the Panther Woman of America. Basing the competition on the female monster in Erle C. Kenton's screen adaptation of H. G. Wells's novel *The Island of Dr. Moreau* (1895), the search gained public attention and boosted pre-release interest in the film. Paramount chose a winning entrant for each state and decided on a national victor amid fanfare in Chicago. The winner received a prize, the Panther Woman of America title, and the promise that Laughton would turn her into a beast.[45] The contest was mentioned in newspapers across the country and *Photoplay* hinted at it in a review: "A thriller of thrillers. Among the monstrosities created is *Lota*, the much publicized 'Panther Woman'" (emphasis in original).[46] The movie's Pressbook is filled with references to Kathleen Burke's prize-winning portrayal of the Panther Woman. Theater managers were advised to plant stories regarding her contest travails in local newspapers two days before the film's release. Proposed headlines include: "A STAR BEFORE SHE STARTS! 'PANTHER WOMAN' ACHIEVES NEW OVERNIGHT FILM SUCCESS" and "WINS 60,000 TO ONE SHOT! OFFICE GIRL CAPTURES 'PANTHER WOMAN' ROLE."[47]

Other publicity materials for *Island of Lost Souls* tempered the horror theme through an appeal to stardom. In the February 1933 issue

Figure 3.4. While department stores were supposed to attract women to *The Mystery of the Wax Museum* with figures modeling evening gowns, posters promised spectators a sexually suggestive tale of female creatures that "THROBBED WITH HUMAN PASSION!" *Photo courtesy of Ronald V. Borst/Hollywood Movie Posters. Copyright © 1933 Turner Entertainment Co. All rights reserved.*

of *Photoplay*, a three-page story was devoted to Charles Laughton who played the mad doctor of Kenton's film. The profile, which included glossies of Laughton in and out of costumes, and a still of him posing with his thespian-wife Elsa Lanchester in a moment of conjugal bliss, presented him to *Photoplay*'s readership as a character actor of great versatility and a husband of exceeding warmth. This piece appeared in the same month that *Island of Lost Souls* was reviewed and advertised in the magazine. Laughton may have played a horrid man in the film, fans were told in the ads, but he was a gentleman in real life, according to the star profile.[48]

A full-page advertisement for *Island of Lost Souls* appeared near the beginning of the same *Photoplay* issue. Depicting a drawing of a partially clad woman surrounded by wild animals, the cutline intoned: "HE TOOK THEM FROM HIS MAD MENAGERIE . . . NIGHTS WERE HORRIBLE WITH THE SCREAMS OF TORTURED BEASTS . . . FROM HIS HOUSE OF

Figure 3.5. Lota (Kathleen Burke), the Panther Woman of *Island of Lost Souls*, holds hands with the hero, Edward Parker (Richard Arlen), as the evil Dr. Moreau (Charles Laughton) confronts the viewer with his steady stare. Photo courtesy of Ronald V. Borst/Hollywood Movie Posters. *Copyright © by Universal City Studios, Inc. Courtesy of MCA Publishing Rights, a Division of MCA, Inc.*

PAIN THEY CAME RE-MADE. . . . HIS MASTERPIECE—THE PANTHER WOMAN THROBBING TO THE HOT FLUSH OF LOVE."[49] The publicity simultaneously positions the mad doctor as a sadist, a passion-inspiring figure, and a man capable of transforming women in terrifying and desirable ways. *Photoplay*'s readers were invited to view Lota, the monstrous Panther Woman, as both tortured and positively transformed by Laughton, her equally monstrous creator (figure 3.5).

The doubling of heroines and fiends persisted in publicity for other films as well. A striking advertisement for *Svengali* (Warner Bros., 1931)[50] appeared in *Photoplay* in July of 1931 and positioned John Barrymore, who played the title role, as a simultaneous object of fear and desire for Marian Marsh's Trilby, as well as a double for her: "HE IS GENIUS—MADMAN—LOVER! HIS HYPNOTIC SPELL REACHES OUT OF DARKNESS CONTROLLING LOVE—HATE—LIFE ITSELF. SHE IS THE BEAUTY WHO HAD ALL PARIS AT HER FEET—WHO WINS MEN WITH A SMILE—WHO HATES SVENGALI THE SINISTER LOVE-MAKER—UNTIL HIS MAGIC SPELL FORCES EVEN HER TO BEAT TO HIS MANUFACTURED LOVE!" (emphasis in original).[51] In a mimicry of Svengali's hypnotic abilities, Trilby, the advertisement proclaims, is not only subject to the fiend's control but exhibits her own brand of hypnosis—she has Paris at her feet and wins men with a smile.

Like *Photoplay*'s presentation of *Island of Lost Souls* two years later, this advertisement banks on multiple modes of address to, primarily, female readers. The cutline aligns fiend with heroine, suggests they desire each other *and* introduces stardom into the mix. Cut across the center of the layout, in capital letters, are the following words: "JOHN BARRYMORE AS 'SVENGALI' THE HYPNOTIST." The typeface is largest for the actor's last name—it literally slices the advertisement in half and draws the most visual attention.

III

Fan magazines mediated the relationships between viewers and stars in a paradoxical manner during the 1930s. *Photoplay*, in particular, presented its predominantly female readership with a complex portrait of stardom. Writing of the interactions between women and star magazines during the 1920s, Gaylyn Studlar notes: "Instead of automatically reinforcing female powerlessness and marginalization before a patriarchal system, [fan magazines] explored, albeit in ideologically contradictory terms, the historically specific locus of women in American cinema, culture and society."[52] The contradictory ideologies, which Studlar mentions, found form in a multiple address to women readers in the 1930s as well. As they were represented in print and publicity stills, stars promised fans both an adherence to traditional mores and the transgression of familiar values.

From 1930 to 1934, for instance, *Photoplay*'s letters to the editor highlighted a heated debate between proponents of Greta Garbo and those of Marlene Dietrich. Each side consisted of missives from female fans who made vehement claims regarding the superiority, power, and attractiveness of the actresses. "Garbo carries us away from our modern, humdrum existence to a dream world," wrote Thelma Holland of Ann Arbor, Michigan, in one such printed debate. Holland's adoration was balanced by a letter from Betty Ferguson of Brooklyn, New York, who sang Dietrich's praises: "Dietrich is superior to Garbo in everything. She has twice the looks, twice the acting ability and an utterly charming talking and singing voice that Garbo can never aspire to."[53] In a fascinating display of the contradictory negotiations put into play between viewers and stars, the debate elicited the passions of female fans who unleashed their feelings for female performers, stars who each connoted traditional notions of beauty, as well as independence, androgyny, and danger to men.

According to Studlar, critics are mistaken to assume that the investment of female readers in fan discourses represents their loss of identity and their overinvestment in fantasies of Hollywood glamour. As she claims:

> Instead, what is evoked by both the tone and content of fan magazines is more on the order of an identification with stardom as a kind of "masquerade," a play with identity. Bringing elements of make believe and pretense into play—on both sides of the screen. Such a masquerade would have elicited the understanding of many women who themselves were engaged in an attempt to resituate themselves in relation to changing concepts of female social and sexual identity. ("PP" 15)

Studlar's use of disguise as a means of describing viewers' relationships to stars and images is important. Like the concept of spectatorship-as-drag I have detailed in chapter 2, Studlar's version of masquerade makes viewing a playful negotiation, an engagement of spectators in a game of fantasy. Studlar asserts that viewers have interpretive power in their relationships with actors—performers and fans masquerade for each other.

But how does the spectator-star masquerade take form in horror? One means of conceptualizing this rapport is to accept viewers' abilities to interpret films—and the publicity that surrounds them—in a complex manner. Quite possibly, spectators recognize the interplay between the fiction of roles and the, different but related, fiction of extratextual discourses. In fact, magazines and Pressbooks promoted the conflation of contradictory on- and offscreen personae, which complicated the stability of both character portrayals and star images in the 1930s.

The potential impact of this combination of elements in reference to classic horror is that actors may have portrayed sinister or helpless characters on-screen while being promoted as kind or capable stars offscreen. This representational paradox engages spectators as active agents in the construction and comprehension of the inherent contradictions and complexities of cinematic discourses. Viewers likely refused to interpret on-screen portrayals in a vacuum in the 1930s and probably opted, instead, to infuse films, characters, and stars with diverse meanings—Maestro Svengali's monstrosity, then, existed alongside John Barrymore's heartthrob reputation.

In 1931, for example, *Photoplay* ran a series of articles on Marian Marsh, *Svengali*'s heroine, which illustrates the multiple identities created for horror stars. "And Who Is This Girl?" is a story that includes photos of Marsh and links her to John Barrymore: "Surely the young lady [in the photo] on the left is Mrs. John Barrymore, Dolores Costello that was. And the girl on the right must certainly be either Constance or Joan Bennett. But the fact is that both girls are Marian Marsh, the child still in her 'teens who has been chosen to play *Trilby* to John Barrymore's *Svengali* in the Warner Brothers's talking version of that famous Du Maurier story" (emphasis in original).[54] In this article, Marsh's on-screen assignment is collapsed with an offscreen relationship to Barrymore (she looks like his wife), while her resemblance to glamorous female stars is emphasized.

The following month *Photoplay* ran another article on Marsh that trades more thoroughly in fantasies of stardom. In "You Should See My Kid Sister," Marsh's motion picture debut is attributed to a sibling who coaxed her to a place where, "like Cinderella, in the fairy tale, she met Prince Charming. Only in this story, Prince Charming is John

Barrymore—but nothing could have been more princely or more charming to Marian than Barrymore's acceptance of her for the role of Trilby."[55] Marsh's impending starring role is considered romantic and her casting deemed a matter of Barrymore's personal choice. The article smacks of a rags-to-riches tale of transformation in its associations with Cinderella and Sleeping Beauty. Romance connotations are reinforced by the conflation of Marsh's extrafilmic roles (ingénue and Barrymore's adoring waif) with her narrative position (Svengali's unwilling yet compliant object of desire). Given the range of messages circulated, Warner Bros.'s actual production of *Svengali* was but one discourse among many. Marsh's on-screen incarnation of a heroine subjected to the horrifying advances of Barrymore's devious maestro appeared simultaneously with articles proclaiming that she resembles Barrymore's wife, was discovered by him, and was well matched with the actor in her on-screen portrayal.

Throughout the decade *Photoplay* and other fan magazines ran stories on horror's heroines as they posed in the latest fashions and tendered advice on makeup, grooming, and romance. Fay Wray was especially popular, given her starring roles in a range of films, including classic horror and jungle-adventure movies such as *Doctor X* (Warner Bros., 1931), *King Kong* (RKO, 1933), *The Most Dangerous Game* (RKO, 1932), *The Mystery of the Wax Museum* (Warner Bros., 1933), and *Vampire Bat* (Majestic, 1933). In February 1931, the year Michael Curtiz's *Doctor X* debuted in Technicolor, Wray was profiled in a number of publications. *Picture Play* detailed her efforts to control her star image: "Resolutely Fay Wray set about to overcome the handicap of being overpublicized as a swansdown heroine at the beginning of her career [in 1927]. So well has she succeeded by dint of hard work that now she's placed by critics among the select few."[56] The same month that *Picture Play* commented on her popularity with critics, *Screenland* asked readers to determine her stature: "There seems to be quite an argument over Fay Wray. Is she still a pleasant ingénue, or a real dramatic artist? Fay thinks she has grown up—do you agree with her?"[57] By the spring of 1931, Wray was offering tips to *Photoplay*'s readers on how to steam their hair to "bring out the wave."[58] Whether ingénue or not, her publicity focused on a good girl image, the same image she projected as the heroine of Curtiz's film.[59]

Nearly two years later, *Photoplay* ran a publicity still for *King Kong*, which focused again on Wray: "Introducing you to just one of Fay Wray's bad moments in that new hair-raiser, 'King Kong.'"[60]

Although the image depicts Wray dangling precariously from Kong's paw, the casual tone of the description, combined with the mentions of her in other publications, are striking counterpoints to the horror elements. For example, her ingénue demeanor was replaced by strength and an immunity to terror in a piece that claimed her athletic abilities in 1933.[61] And in a Lux soap advertisement that appeared in the *Los Angeles Examiner* upon the film's release, *King Kong*'s star promised "A THOUSAND THRILLS AND HERS THE THRILL OF SUPREME BEAUTY."[62] Wray's simian troubles on top of the Empire State Building are nothing compared to her thrilling loveliness, according to the advertisement. The actress may look tormented on-screen, the *Photoplay* still suggested, but her stardom and advertising appearances assured readers she was alive, beautiful, and athletic off-screen.

Heroes and monsters were also subject to scrutiny and adoration in fan magazines. Boris Karloff, who plays the fiend in movies like *Frankenstein* and *The Mummy*, was presented to *Photoplay*'s fans as a skilled actor. In an article entitled, "Meet the Monster!" readers were introduced to the man behind the masks. Ruth Rankin's descriptions of Karloff's rise to fame from "incredible hardship and frustration" are almost as dramatic as his film roles. Karloff's on- and offscreen personae are conflated by Rankin and marked by high drama, suffering, ambition, and dissimulation. Rankin, for instance, highlights the tortures endured by Karloff during the hours of makeup application required of so many of his roles. Here is an actor who has to suffer in order to become a monster that makes others suffer, Rankin tells her readers.[63] In the month following Rankin's piece, *Photoplay* published a personable glossy of Karloff with an ominous caption: "And now his bosses have issued orders that hereafter Boris Karloff is to be photographed only in character. So this is the last straight portrait you will see of *The Monster*."[64] Photoplay thus shifted from humanizing Karloff, as in Rankin's exposé, to confirming that his monstrous roles were paramount.

Other horror actors received acclaim in *Photoplay* as well. In the case of Fredric March, who plays the dual eponymous roles in Paramount's *Dr. Jekyll and Mr. Hyde* and who went on to win an Oscar for his monstrous thespian efforts, his hero and star status were reinforced in the magazine, while his links to monstrosity were downplayed. In one review, for example, March was praised in an intimate fashion: "Fred handles the difficult dual role superbly."[65] In other references to the film, he was presented as either a dashing star or hard-working actor whose efforts pay off.[66]

Photoplay's focus on Miriam Hopkins, the actress who plays the woman killed by the fiendish Mr. Hyde in the movie, similarly avoided the horror theme. A January 1932 production still depicted Hopkins's thespian travails. She is shown bare-shouldered under the covers of a bed. The shot is from an early scene in which the kind-hearted Dr. Jekyll visits her boudoir, and the following commentary frames the still: "Miriam Hopkins suffers. Imagine having to lie in that soft bed all day while the director gives instructions. She makes the sacrifice so your lives will be brighter."[67] While in the film Hopkins endures the sustained abuse of a monstrous Fredric March in her role as the working-class character named Ivy, the sarcastic caption beneath *Photoplay*'s still announced that her cinematic sacrifices are primarily glamorous not painful.

Photoplay's publicity ploys complicated horror's reception by contrasting narrative events, in this case Hopkins's on-screen torment, with innocuous star profiles. The net result is an environment for spectatorship that provided female patrons with a range of prospective responses to the genre: women were told they are terrified of horror movies but crave romance with fiends. They were also informed they resemble monsters but do not need to take the genre too seriously because its stars are only play-acting. This combination of contradictory discourses disabled viewer efforts to streamline the genre's gender address. If male and female spectators saw classic horror as a purveyor of traditional values and roles, which I am sure some did, they did so *against the grain* of publicity discourses and against the narratives of some of the films as well.

IV

It was probably easy for 1930s viewers to find more in horror movies than a classic tale of monster attacks heroine. This is true especially given the genre's employment of offscreen space as a stylistic device. Thus, although classic horror implies monstrous attacks, most films reserve acts of violence for a location just outside the margins of the frame. This attribute was fostered by the Studio Relations Office (SRO) of the Motion Picture Producers and Distributors of America (MPPDA), the office charged with enforcing the 1930 Production

Code. For example, in a letter to Carl Laemmle Jr. at Universal, the SRO's Jason S. Joy advised that scripted scenes in *Frankenstein*, which showed the body of a hanged man and "other gruesome incidents which make up a part of the script," should not be depicted directly.[68] Laemmle Jr. heeded many of Joy's recommendations for *Frankenstein* and built them into subsequent films produced by his studio. Innuendo became a generic staple in the early 1930s.

This self-censorship tactic had an impact on the genre's representations not just of violence but of romance as well. For the erotic aura that infuses so many of the interactions among horror's characters, especially the meetings between monsters and heroines, also finds form in offscreen innuendo. In fact, *implying* versus representing elements of the storyline serves a dual function in classic horror. First, it satisfied censors, who were rather shortsighted in their equation of sight with knowledge, and, second, it heightened the risqué connotations of monstrous attacks. Here, violence and romance are generically conflated and both are hidden from direct view. While this device was intended to diffuse the supposedly socially destructive components of actually *seeing* violence, its impact on viewers was probably more complex. For this device invited spectators to assume that what occurred offscreen was as significant as what happened onscreen and that offscreen events were not solely acts of violence (the monster attacking the heroine) but were displays of romantic/sexual desire as well (the monster seducing the heroine). I will return to this point shortly.

These censorship tactics were, however, rather mild, at least in the early 1930s. It is as if horror came onto the scene too late in the reformist efforts, which were very pronounced during the 1920s, to be a subject of much debate. As David J. Skal remarks in *The Monster Show*: "The obsessively detailed Production Code itself had been drawn up in 1930, before *Dracula* had flapped its way out of Universal City. The document had nothing to say about supernatural monsters, even though horror did have a vague and unsavory connection to the libido, even if you couldn't quite figure out what kind of hanky-panky was being hinted at" (161).

In an MPPDA file memo dated a month before *Dracula*'s release, an employee named James Fisher wrote a report that confirms Skal's claims in retrospect: "All the characters except Dracula and Von [sic] Helsing are English. There should be no cause for any objections on this point since they are all honorable and upright. Dracula is *not really a human being* so he cannot conceivably cause any trouble" (emphasis added).[69] At the time of *Dracula*'s debut, the MPPDA was concerned with portraying foreigners and foreign countries positively, hence Fisher's reference to characters being honorably English. Any other concerns he might have had about the film were quelled by the fact that the count is not human and, therefore, not subject to the same censorship concerns as are other characters. Given the lack of specification for horror films in the Production Code, which served as Fisher's guide, he assumed that *Dracula* would be treated as a harmless fantasy by censors and viewers alike—meaning, that the film's illicit connotations would either be overlooked or would bear little relevance to people's everyday lives, behaviors, and attitudes.

Although historians concur that the 1930s is a decade marked by social protests against the movies, they disagree as to the effectiveness of industry self-regulation. Whereas 1934 is often cited as the moment at which the industry fully enforced the Production Code, via the formation of Joseph Breen's Production Code Administration (PCA) at the MPPDA, Lea Jacobs makes a compelling argument that censorship existed in a different form in the early thirties.[70] In her analysis of the fallen woman cycle, in her book *Wages of Sin*, Jacobs remarks that the efforts of the SRO were aimed at ensuring that films meet the requirements of state and municipal censor boards. Thus, in order to strike a compromise between studio sensibilities and the boards' reformist impulses, the SRO devised three tactics of indirect representation: (1) the deletion of explicit and offensive words from scripts, such as *whore, rape* and *prostitute*; (2) the use of narrative ellipses to imply but not represent certain events (e.g., a couple having sex); and (3) the punishment of bad characters at the conclusion (Jacobs 35). In Jacobs's estimation these tactics were successful enough to satisfy most censor boards but not extensive enough to prevent intimations of proscribed behavior in the fallen woman cycle.

Joy's memo to Laemmle Jr. regarding *Frankenstein* suggests that the SRO employed indirect representation as a self-regulatory tactic for horror as well. Jacobs's third point, the punishment of evil characters, also finds expression in the genre, for films usually conclude with the supposed demise of the monster. Most domestic censor boards responded well to the SRO's approach to classic horror, at least until the release of the Payne Fund Studies in 1933, which were used by reformers to prove horror's adverse effect on children.[71] The impact of the SRO's indirect approach on viewers, however, is another matter.

If Jacobs is right and patrons were getting used to assuming that a narrative ellipsis following a scene of a man and woman entering a bedroom, for example, meant an out-of-sight sexual encounter, they were probably inclined to read sexual meanings into similar ellipses in horror. Thus, although a cut away from Dracula leaning over Mina's supine body in her bedroom does much to relegate his attack to offscreen space, it also heightens the sexual connotations of their encounter for spectators. Out of sight is not, then, out of mind, as censors would have it (figure 3.6).

While the PCA, which took over the SRO's duties in 1934, required more in the way of censorship, connotations of multiple sexualities, female aggression, and homosexuality endured, as the case of *Dracula's Daughter* (Universal, 1936), outlined in chapter 1, confirms. In fact, some post-1934 censorship may have contributed to those connotations, as I believe to be true of *Bride of Frankenstein*. In

Figure 3.6. Despite the cut-away that follows the count's (Bela Lugosi) menacing approach toward Mina (Helen Chandler) in this scene from *Dracula*, editing choices not only suggested offscreen violence but also implied an out-of-sight sexual encounter. *Copyright © by Universal City Studios, Inc. Courtesy of MCA Publishing Rights, a Division of MCA, Inc.*

Figure 3.7. The Monster (Boris Karloff) and his "friend," Dr. Pretorius (Ernest Thesiger), share a candlelit meal atop a casket in this scene from *Bride of Frankenstein*. Photo courtesy of Ronald V. Borst/Hollywood Movie Posters. *Copyright © by Universal City Studios, Inc. Courtesy of* MCA *Publishing Rights, a Division of* MCA, *Inc.*

response to an early draft of the script, then called *The Return of Frankenstein*, Joseph Breen made the following recommendation to Harry Zehner at Universal: "Scene F-26: The monster's use of the word 'mate' should be dropped in this scene. All material which suggests that he desires a sexual companion is objectionable. We suggest that you substitute the word 'companion' in the dialogue, or some synonym for it."[72] Zehner implemented Breen's suggestion and opted for the word "friend" instead of companion (figure 3.7).

Although this word substitution was designed to temper connotations of sexual desire on the part of the monster, the final effect is somewhat more complex than Breen intended. For the substitution of terms in James Whale's film equalizes the monster's relationships with all characters, male and female alike. In the effort to desexualize the bond between the monster (Boris Karloff) and the bride (Elsa

Lanchester), an effort doomed to fail because of the connotations of matrimony in the movie's title and the persistent doubling of the doctor with his creature, the PCA in effect *sexualized* the bonds among men in the film. If the monster's relationship with the bride is the same one it has with Dr. Pretorius (Ernest Thesiger), a man whom the fiend refers to as a "friend" at one point in the story, and if the monster's rapport with the bride is sexual, then homoerotic connotations are produced, not deleted, by this particular censorship effort.

These Production Code examples suggest that, like reviews and marketing materials, the industry's regulation of classic horror cinema was far from straightforward. As is true of the fallen woman cycle, which Jacobs addresses in detail, sexually illicit meanings were reinforced by the SRO's use of indirect representation and created in some instances by the PCA's insistence on deletions and substitutions. In both cases, viewers encountered censorship and marketing campaigns that offered contradictory meanings.

The diverse connotations promoted to viewers of classic horror films will be my starting point in chapter 4, where I will argue that those meanings find textual footholds in the hypnosis subgenre. What was promoted offscreen is what viewers often faced on-screen. Narrative construction, like reception, was far from simple. But what of those spectators in the movie theater who watched horror films in the 1930s? Like obedient male viewers, they may have protected their dates or bitten their lips, held their girlfriends close or responded bravely. Like exemplary female patrons, they may have screamed or swooned, cowered or fainted. Or they may have taken the contradictions at face value and let loose, growled if they were women, fainted if men, and put the cultural expectations of proper gender behaviors to shame in the very act of spectatorship.

4

Looks Could Kill: The Powers of the Gaze
in Hypnosis Films

"Why do you stare at me?"
Why do you think I stare at you,
I stare at you because I am a monster
and you are a monster and I want to see
what it is I will become!

—Anne Rice, *Cry to Heaven*

I

A month before Tod Browning's *Dracula* (Universal) debuted in February 1931, *Motion Picture Classic* ran an article entitled, "The Feminine Love of Horror." Gladys Hall's two-page piece was composed almost entirely of direct quotations from the stage and soon-to-be film star who developed the eponymous vampire role. As Bela Lugosi pronounced: "But it is *women* who love horror. Gloat over it. Feed on it. Are nourished by it. Shudder and cling and cry out—*and come back for more*" (emphasis in original).[1] Lugosi's prose is punctured by ghoulish and orgasmic metaphors—metaphors that cast female fans as both monsters and victims, not to mention vocal sexual beings as well. Patrons "fed on" and were "nourished by" his vampiric performance, while they also shuddered, clung, and cried out for more.

Hall's column was both a promotional stunt to elicit female attendance at Universal's new movie and a morbid commentary on women's investment in the genre. According to the more or less apocryphal stories that followed Lugosi from stage to screen, his cinematic impact on female fans created as large a ruckus as did his theater performances. The actor was said to have received countless love letters from viewers enamored of his on-screen incarnation of a blood-sucking fiend, missives from women who hoped for a comparably thrilling real-life encounter with him (figure 4.1).

According to Lugosi, women have a deeply embedded stake in Bram Stoker's tale. *Dracula* gives them an entrée into illicit sexuality and fulfills ravenous desires, which the actor details with confidence:

> When I was playing Dracula on the stage, my audiences were women. *Women.* There were men, too. Escorts the women *had brought with them.* For reasons only their dark subconscious knew. In order to establish a subtle sex intimacy. Contact . . . Men did not come of their own volition. *Women did.* Came—and knew an ecstasy dragged from the depths of unspeakable things. Came—*and then came back again.* And *again.* . . . Women wrote me letters. Ah, what letters women wrote me! Women from seventeen to thirty. Letters of a horrible hunger. *Asking me if I cared only for maidens' blood.* . . . And through these letters, couched in terms of shudderings, transparent fear, there ran the hideous note of—*hope.* (emphasis in original; Hall 33)

Lugosi describes women's desires for horror in not-too-veiled sexual terms. Appealing to phrases that allude to the real or imagined specificity of women's sexual urges, Lugosi thinks that female patrons are drawn to his performances more than once. Likening theater attendance to multiple orgasms, or to a feminine form of repetition compulsion, Lugosi believes that women came to his shows again and again.

But what hope is hidden behind these women's displays of fear and their sexually suggestive shudderings? According to Lugosi, women search for monstrous love and a means of escape from their everyday lives. They also hope for the brutal demise of mortal men. His female fans, Lugosi intones, have "a ghoulish compulsion to see men torn and bloody and in agony" (86). For Lugosi, then, female shudders are but the surface manifestations of deeper needs and urges. Beneath the veneer of fear, women display sexual hunger and cry out for radical change in their lives. Change that, according to Lugosi, includes intimate contact with monsters, or the men who play them on-stage and on-screen, and the sadistic punishment of mortal men. Female fear and sexual pleasure are woven together, fused in the actor's rendering of the powerful, illicit, and dramatic links between vampirism and female desire.

Certainly Lugosi's pronouncements have to be taken with a grain of salt, or garlic as the case may be. Promotional discourses are as much fantasies about spectatorship as commentaries on it. Yet Lugosi's words also ring true, at least insofar as they describe the vampire story as a tale of female transformation, a narrative of well-behaved women who fall under the spell of hypnotic creatures, respond with a good dose of aggression toward mortal men, and exhibit a remarkable degree of sexual allure. The effects of hypnosis upon heroines are usually profound in classic horror. They float through rooms with a vapid stare, an unfocused gaze that signifies their transformation into victims—and doubles—of the fiend. Under the guise of affective paralysis, they do the creature's bidding. They comply with the fiend's demands, behave monstrously, are sexually appealing, and often attack the heroes they supposedly love.

As this description suggests, hypnosis films explore at the narrative level what publicity stunts promote in the extratextual domain— women are drawn to horror for a variety of reasons and are invited to act out a range of behaviors, some conventional and others not, in their rapports with monsters. From a traditional perspective, the heroine's vacant stare is a physical sign of her plunge into a nether world of monstrous control. It signifies her victimization at the hands, or in this case the eyes, of a powerful creature. Yet, like the female scream, the vapid stare is a cover of sorts. Monstrous desire and sadistic behavior reside beneath a passive veneer. Most hypnosis films, by which I mean vampire, mummy, and zombie movies, are inverted fairy tales. Girl gets boy at the conclusion, but her best times, the moments that give her free rein to throw all caution to the wind, are spent with the monster in the narrative middle.

I want to explore that middle more fully in this chapter. For although hypnosis films appear to play out female masochism and passivity at the manifest level, they celebrate female sadism and mobility beneath that surface tale. Hypnosis movies of the early 1930s provide a fictional home to the meanings and motives that Lugosi attributed to his female fans, as well as a textual ground for the diverse modes of address that confronted women in horror's reception context. According to hypnosis films, women love horror. It fulfills their desire for freedom from conventional ties and punishes men in the process. The hypnosis subgenre suggests that, given half a chance, women always come back for more.

Figure 4.1. Bela Lugosi takes his place as a Hollywood screen idol in this glamorous publicity still from the early 1930s. *Source unknown.*

II

In its classic and contemporary forms, horror cinema is a genre of looking. The visual realm and the act of seeing are paramount. While contemporary films often represent movies-within-movies,[2] in which theater audiences watch fictional audiences watch horror, hypnosis films prioritize looking in more conventional ways. The looks shared between characters, especially the monster and heroine, are this subgenre's favorite mode of communication. The hypnosis film is filled with eyes—close-ups of the monster's mesmerizing gaze and reverse shots of the heroine's wide-eyed response. Seeing is constructed as both powerful and terrifying. When looks are exchanged, vision is equated with possession and acts of seeing and being seen play out flip sides of a monstrous power dynamic (figure 4.2).

As a subgenre obsessed with vision, hypnosis films have their own economy of looks. Monsters mesmerize heroines, heroines respond with a vapid stare, and heroes cannot see much of anything at all. As I mentioned in chapter 1, horror's heroes often fail miserably in their

Figure 4.2. The primacy of vision and the hypnosis of women were portrayed in posters from other subgenres as well, as in this example from the mad-doctor movie *Mad Love* (a.k.a. *The Hands of Orlac*). Photo courtesy of Ronald V. Borst/ Hollywood Movie Posters.   *Copyright © 1935 Turner Entertainment Co. All rights reserved.*

efforts to save the day. They make their way through narratives, salvaging whatever meager self-respect they can muster, given their inability to vanquish the fiend. The hypnosis film's male lead is a prime example of the genre's disrespect for heroics. Not only is he unable to control the outcome of narrative events, he sometimes falls prey to the monster in offscreen space and endures the heroine's attack to boot. As if his obstacles were not challenging enough, the hero is displaced visually as well. In the most blatant of cases, he literally cannot see the fiend that confronts him.

Dracula, the tale of a vampire that travels from Transylvania to London to turn women into creatures of the night, furnishes a prototypical example. The hero's failure to command the visual realm is most dramatically depicted in a scene in Dr. Seward's (Herbert Bunston) parlor late in the film. At a crucial moment in this sequence, John Harker (David Manners), the hero, grasps a cigarette holder encased with a mirror. As Dracula engages in conversation with the heroine, Mina (Helen Chandler), and her father (Seward), the fiend is unaware that Harker's mirror reveals the count's true identity. Although Dracula is shown conversing with Mina and Seward in a number of tableau shots, only the heroine and her father are reflected in the cigarette case mirror. Although the count's voice can be heard, he is nowhere to be *seen*. Dr. Van Helsing (Edward Van Sloan), the older man charged with interpreting the clues to the mysterious goings-on and the man who kills the monster at the conclusion, notices Dracula's absence from the mirror and thus confirms his suspicions that the aristocrat is a vampire. John Harker, however, is left in the dark. While he holds a clue to Dracula's true identity in the palm of his hand, he literally cannot see what is in front of him. He never looks closely at the reflection and never notices Dracula's monstrous disappearing act.

Unlike *Dracula*, Lambert Hillyer's 1936 sequel, *Dracula's Daughter*, seems to provide a valiant hero. In the end, however, Dr. Garth's (Otto Kruger) ability to control events is nearly as limited as John Harker's. From one perspective, *Dracula's Daughter* is a feature-length exploration of Garth's journey toward Oedipal adulthood. He moves from a childish position of helplessness and ignorance at the film's beginning—he relies on his secretary, Janet (Marguerite Churchill), to pick him up from vacation, help him dress, and warn him about Countess Zaleska (Gloria Holden)—to an adult, heterosexual position by its conclusion. The film's closing image shows Garth supporting Janet in his arms as she awakens from an hypnotic stupor. While she propped him up, so to speak, earlier in the movie, he takes care of her at the film's close.

Yet a significant segment of *Dracula's Daughter* focuses on the psychiatrist's failure to see the countess for what she really is. Although he earns his living as an analyst, Garth's powers of interpretation are worthless when it comes to vampires. Whereas Janet is suspicious of Zaleska from the start, in part because she competes for Garth's affections, the good doctor mistakes the countess for just another neurotic woman. Garth's inability to guess Zaleska's true identity throughout most of the film not only throws his powers of analysis into question, it also precipitates his feeble heroics at the conclusion. He is hardly a dashing figure as he tries to save his secretary from the countess's clutches. While the vampire is killed at the conclusion, Garth has little to do with her demise. Instead, he is reunited with the heroine *in spite* of his efforts to save Janet and not because of them.

The conclusion is played out thus: an over-the-shoulder shot shows Zaleska move slowly toward her hypnotized captive. There is a cut to Garth attempting to gain entry into her castle, and a cut back to Zaleska who almost bites/kisses Janet. Finally, Garth breaks in and tries to reason with the countess. Zaleska promises to release the heroine on the condition that Garth receive her bite/kiss in Janet's place. Just as Garth is about to sacrifice himself for Janet, Zaleska's assistant Sandor (Irving Pichel), who is jealous of Zaleska's affection for Garth, shoots a fatal arrow into his mistress's chest. Because of Sandor's efforts, not his own, Garth gets the girl at the end. Yet Garth comes awfully close to *becoming* Janet—to taking up the narrative role usually reserved for horror's heroines. Thus, although Garth tries to fight Zaleska, his actions and powers are nothing compared to her supernatural strength and mesmerizing gaze. While he looks Zaleska in the eye near the conclusion, doing so is his act of submission and not challenge to the fiend.

As the case of *Dracula's Daughter* suggests, heroines are the most spectacular victims in hypnosis films. Janet's yielding body is the focus of attention in the final scene, and her vacant stare, even when she is revived from her stupor by the hero, is much more visually compelling than the promised attack on Garth. The conclusion thus reveals an important subgeneric component. Men, too, fall prey to fiends when given half a chance, but always in less spectacular terms than heroines. Hypnosis movies often *imply* male victimization in off-screen encounters with creatures or threaten to make men suffer in the very act of saving the heroine, as is true of Garth. However, as with horror cinema in general, women remain the most spectacular sufferers (figure 4.3).

To repeat a point made by Carol J. Clover about the occult film: "For a space to be created in which men can weep without being labeled feminine, women must be relocated to a space where they will be made to wail uncontrollably" (105). Hypnosis films offer a twist on this approach. Instead of heroines displaying terror in extremis, as when they scream, male victimization is disguised behind the heroine's vacant stare. The *absence* of affect on the part of heroines, their vapid paralysis, allows men to endure unspeakable terrors in this subgenre and still emerge with their masculinity somewhat intact.

In fact, the heroine's vapid stare may have as much to do with the hero's ineptitude as with the allure of monsters. For as long as heroines are frozen in affective paralysis they cannot, ostensibly, witness their boyfriends' failures. Garth may come close to succumbing to Zaleska at the conclusion of *Dracula's Daughter*, then, but Janet does not, for all intents and purposes, witness his near demise. Thus, while hypnosis serves as the heroine's vehicle for doubling fiends and attacking heroes, it also ensures that heroines, too, are not fully in charge of the visual realm. While the hero often fails to recognize and destroy the monster in hypnosis movies, the heroine usually misses witnessing the hero's emasculation and punishment.

Tod Browning's *Mark of the Vampire* (MGM, 1935), like *Dracula's Daughter*, relishes the heroine's victimization as a cover for male suffering and ineptitude. Here, the most pronounced vampire attack is endured by Irena (Elizabeth Allan), the heroine whose father dies mysteriously at the film's start. The two puncture wounds on her father's neck and his blood-drained body are enough to warn Irena that vampires are nearby. Part of the sequence in which Irena herself is attacked by a vampire occurs in full view of the audience. Irena is beckoned from inside her room by the silent, yet insistent, gaze of a female vampire named Luna (Carol Borland). As soon as Luna sets her sights on Irena, the heroine responds with a vacant stare. Accompanied by her vampire-escort, Count Mora (Bela Lugosi), Luna approaches Irena slowly and silently from the garden. The heroine responds with parallel movements and leaves her room to glide across the terrace to meet the monster. Shots of Irena, Luna, and Mora are intercut to increase the momentum of their impending meeting. Eventually, Mora stops his approach and watches Irena

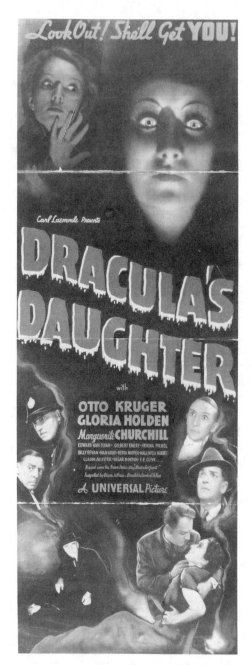

Figure 4.3. In this one-sheet from *Dracula's Daughter*, the spectator is cautioned to watch for the female fiend—"LOOK OUT! SHE'LL GET YOU!"—and women are portrayed as spectacular sufferers.   *Copyright © by Universal City Studios, Inc. Courtesy of MCA Publishing Rights, a Division of MCA, Inc.*

and Luna's encounter from afar. Near the scene's conclusion, Irena sits in a chair and swoons at the precise moment that Luna leans over the heroine and hides her vampiric bite/kiss with her gown (see figure 2.5).

In many ways, this sequence is a precursor to Countess Zaleska's attack on women in *Dracula's Daughter* a year later. As I pointed out in chapter 1, the Production Code Administration (PCA) saw fit to warn that film's producers against heightening the lesbian connotations of the attack. Tod Browning's movie, however, garnered no such advice from Joseph Breen's office. The only deletions recommended by the PCA were sequences in which the Lord's name was used in vain; in addition, in a letter to Louis B. Mayer, Breen wanted to "keep the corpse [of Irena's father] out of sight as much as possible."[3] Nowhere were Luna's advances toward Irena remarked upon as perverse or worthy of censorship.[4]

Reviewers were similarly silent on the topic, although they had much to say about Borland's vampire role. "A legendary tale serves as a medium to bring forth all types of shocking materials," noted *Film Daily*'s reporter, "one of which is a girl who sometimes moves about as a bat, who when seen in close-ups has such glaring eyes as to give one the creeps."[5] The reviewer was so impressed with Borland's portrayal of Luna, and with her mesmerizing gaze, that she or he made no mention of Lugosi at all. Char's review in *Variety* focused on Borland as well: "[Borland] almost takes the picture away from Lugosi on the chiller end, her performance being exceptional."[6] *Time* magazine offered more in the way of narrative description, but little in terms of connotation: "Irena . . . is attacked by a glassy-eyed lady in graveyard clothes who first puts Irena in a trance, then bites her on the neck."[7] Although the sexual connotations of vampires were recognized by critics and censors in the 1930s, *Time*'s reporter offered a deadpan approach and assumed that Luna's attack solely signified a vampiric bite and not sexual desire (figure 4.4).

Despite this failure to remark upon the homoerotic elements of Irena and Luna's union, reviewers were savvy enough to assert the centrality of the heroine's attack to the film. For this sequence is the only vampire scene that is given extensive visual representation. Thus, although Irena's boyfriend, Fedor (Henry Wadsworth), is supposedly attacked by a vampire, his victimization occurs in offscreen space, outside of the spectator's view. As *Time*'s reviewer phrased it: "Irena's gallant young sweetheart is waylaid one evening by a mysterious what-not. When he wakes up there are spots on his neck also."[8] In fact, Fedor is attacked twice in the film. The first time occurs before Irena falls under Luna's spell. Fedor stumbles into the house one day and recounts that he fell asleep outdoors and awoke with two marks on his neck. The second attack is implied when Count Mora is shown going into Fedor's bedroom. In both instances vampire encounters are reported by a character, or implied by editing, but are never shown directly to the audience.

Unlike Fedor, Irena succumbs to a vampire in full view of the theater (and diegetic) audience. Her meeting with Luna confirms that women, vacant stares and all, offer the most spectacular performances of victim roles in hypnosis films. That said, however, *Mark of the Vampire* also indicates that behind every hypnotized heroine lies a hero in greater distress. Late in the film the audience is informed that Luna and Count Mora are not vampires at all, but actors hired to play the part in order to capture the film's real murderer who turns out to be Irena's guardian, Baron Otto (Jean Hersholt). When the ruse is revealed, Irena admits that she played a role all along. Her vacant look at Luna, her fainting spell upon the fiend's embrace were but a show, indeed, a spectacular performance.

But what of Fedor? He is as surprised by Irena's revelation as is Baron Otto at the film's conclusion. He knew nothing of the vampire performance during the course of the narrative. How, then, was he attacked twice by nonexistent vampires? Why did he have two marks on his throat? Although this aspect of the film was not remarked upon by critics at the time, probably because the genre was thought to be filled with loopholes of this sort, Fedor's unexplained attacks are a crucial subgeneric trope: they suggest that while female fear is explicitly performed by the heroine, the hero's victimization—such as Mora's late-night visit to his chamber—is a narrative loose end that confirms the genre's investment in male suffering behind the appearance of female abuse. In *Mark of the Vampire*, Irena merely looks as if she is under attack by a beautiful female fiend—she emerges from the narrative unscathed, having acted her victim role with flair. Poor Fedor, on the other hand, is marked for life.

As I have already noted, the hero's power to look in hypnosis films, his ability to see what is happening, is often ineffectual. This subgenre undermines the male gaze—the hero's control of the visual realm, which Laura Mulvey once thought characterized Hollywood

Figure 4.4. Carol Borland, who plays Luna the vampire in *Mark of the Vampire*, is photographed as an eerie and alluring fiend in this publicity still.   *Copyright ©* *1935 Turner Entertainment Co. All rights reserved.*

narrative cinema.[9] It is incorrect, then, to assume that the hypnosis film's hero gazes sadistically, while the heroine takes up a traditionally masochistic position. As an extension of this concept, it is equally unwise to assume that the male spectator identifies with the sadistic gaze of the hero, for, as I have indicated thus far, such a gaze does not exist.

In "White Privilege and Looking Relations," Jane Gaines introduces a concept that is helpful in this context: "Framing the question of male privilege and viewing pleasure as the 'right to look' may help us to rethink film theory along more materialist lines, considering, for instance, how some groups have historically had the license to 'look' openly while other groups have 'looked' illicitly."[10] Gaines's notion of the "right to look" reframes the male privilege of cinema's visual dynamics in less totalizing terms and suggests that acts of looking can take various forms. Some may be straightforward and commanding, as is the case with monsters, while others are more illicit or vapid, as is true of heroines. Thus, instead of assuming that the hero always looks and the heroine is solely looked at, the following questions need to be asked of hypnosis movies: Who looks at whom, in what way, and for how long? Is the look returned? What power does the character looking have within the diegesis? And what power does the character being looked at have? Not only do these questions pry film theory away from a paradigm that totalizes gender dynamics at the levels of narrative construction and spectatorship, they also allow for a more expansive and expressive model of diegetic viewing.

III

According to Rick Altman in "Dickens, Griffith, and Film Theory Today," the field of film studies considers the nineteenth-century realist novel a far more significant influence on cinema than staged plays. In an effort to legitimize cinema as a cultural artifact, the literary model was granted supremacy. The result has been an emphasis on "omniscient narration, linear presentation, character-centered causality, and psychological motivation"[11] as the dominant modes of cinema. Altman argues that this emphasis overlooks the fact that many Hollywood films are adaptations not only of literary texts but of plays as well. Moreover, stage versions often foregrounded elements of novels deemed unworthy by critics, such as melodramatic material, which includes lengthy spectacles and the display of extreme emotional states. The latter material has been termed "excessive" by the field—that is, the leftovers of the dominant approach.

Altman argues against this polarization of the dominant and excessive, and calls for a double system of cinematic meanings instead:

> Unmotivated events, rhythmic montage, highlighted parallelism, overlong spectacles—these are the excesses in the classical narrative system that alert us to the existence of a competing logic, a second voice. Hollywood's excesses, like those of the novel, systematically point toward the embedded melodramatic mode that subtends classical narrative. . . . However strong the dominant voice, excess bears witness to another language, another logic. Unless we recognize the possibility that excess—defined as such because of its refusal to adhere to any system—may itself be organized as a system, then we hear only the official language and forever miss the text's dialect, and dialectic. (347)

Classic horror is especially well-suited to Altman's view of cinema, given the genre's fondness for spectacles of ghoulish fiends and images of heroines in emotional distress.[12] Horror was recognized as inherently melodramatic by critics during the 1930s[13] and reviewers assumed it defied logical narrative organization by introducing elements that seemed extraneous to story continuity.[14]

The genre was also thought to be filled with characters who were visually compelling. Both heroines engaged in histrionic or catatonic displays, and monsters in elaborate makeup were fascinating to look at. In fact, heroines often react expressively in response to the *sight* of monsters.[15] Thus, the camera photographed creatures with regularity and style, as publicity stills attest, and lingered on their made-up features and elaborate costumes. As the *New York Times* reviewer remarked of *Frankenstein* (Universal, 1931): "Imagine the monster, with black eyes, heavy eyelids, a square head, huge feet that are covered with matting, long arms protruding from the sleeves of a coat, walking like an automaton."[16] The *New Yorker* review by J.C.M. also took note of Boris Karloff's appearance and offered much in the way of praise: "The makeup department has a triumph to its credit in the monster and there lies the thrills of the picture."[17]

Makeup departments worked to ensure that monsters were eye-catching creations aimed at clinching viewer interest. *The Mummy*, for example, received accolades for Karloff's fiendish appearance: "As 'The Mummy' Karloff achieves something new and very unusual in the art of makeup."[18] *Time*'s reporter declared *The Mummy* a makeup marathon: "Boris Karloff keeps his press agent busy estimating the amount of time he expends in putting on make-up. For *The Mummy*, Karloff's preparations took eight hours. He dampened his face, covered it with strips of cotton, applied collodion and spirit gum, pinned his ears back, covered his head with clay, painted himself with 22 kinds of grease-paint, then wound himself up like a top in bandages which had been rotted in acid and roasted."[19] Not only were actors' makeup ordeals described in detail by reviewers, as the Karloff example suggests, but most reporters thought monsters were spectacles of vast proportions, creatures that drew a critical eye (figure 4.5).

In writing of Rudolph Valentino's rise to stardom, Miriam Hansen describes him as an on-screen hero who became a spectacle. Like the women who are the objects of his gaze, Valentino is a sight to be seen. She writes: "Valentino's appeal depends to a large degree on the manner in which he combines masculine control of the look with the fem-

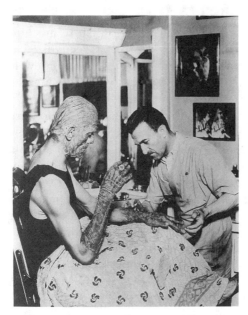

Figure 4.5. Boris Karloff endures arduous makeup application on the set of *The Mummy* in order to transform himself into a fiendish spectacle of vast proportions. *Copyright © by Universal City Studios, Inc. Courtesy of MCA Publishing Rights, a Division of MCA, Inc.*

inine quality of 'to-be-looked-at-ness' . . . When he falls in love—usually at first sight—the close-up of his face surpasses that of the female character in its value as spectacle."[20] According to Hansen, part of Valentino's fascination is his ability to conjoin the powers of looking with the allure of being looked at. This same duality marks hypnotic fiends, as Bela Lugosi's opening remarks make clear. For in order to mesmerize women, creatures must be both objects of desire *and* desiring subjects. On the one hand, fiends must act out their monstrous cravings in order to propel narratives toward near-apocalyptic endings. They have to set their sights on women and pursue them with vigor. On the other hand, monsters must be objects of the viewer's and heroine's gaze. Through the excesses of makeup, heavy-handed accents, and bulky or unusual costumes, they have to look and act the part of a creature destined to be looked at.

The staging of classic horror's most famous films as melodramatic plays prior to their cinematic debuts reinforces their status as spectacles. Some movies, in fact, were written for the screen by the playwrights who conceived theatrical versions, as is true of John L. Balderston's work on *Dracula*. This theatrical heritage, in which makeup artists first constructed grotesque monsters for the stage, ensured that the films appealed to melodramatic conventions and elaborate makeup techniques and wardrobes.

One of the theater conventions that endured in early classic horror films (and cinema in general) is the staginess of camera work. The numerous tableau shots in *Dracula*, for example, led Frank McConnell to remark: "The film is basically a succession of stage scenes, from a proscenium-arch point of view."[21] It is noteworthy that some of the only moments in the film in which the fourth-wall perspective gives way to close-ups is when the count fixes his mesmerizing gaze on the heroine, and when Mina returns his insistent look. Classic horror, then, is a genre indebted to both stage and novel, a genre that focalizes Altman's arguments about cinema as a whole.

Support for Altman's perspective appeared in an unlikely form in a 1930 report in the *Exhibitors Herald-World*: "More Pantomime, Less Dialog [sic] to Form Screen Techniques, says Laemmle. Universal Production Chief Sees Need for Greater Use of Silent Film's Methods." Carl Laemmle, the German émigré who founded Universal in 1914, and spearheaded its horror output with his son in the 1930s, added: "It is my opinion that in the future we should develop as much of the drama as possible in pantomime (as we used to do in silent film days) and use the dialog [sic] and sound to give emphasis to the highlights of the production."[22] According to Laemmle, silent cinema's highly gestural form of acting is suited perfectly to sound film.

Not surprisingly, hypnosis films, which depend on close-ups of hypnotic and *silent* stares, are an ideal home to Laemmle's advice on sound cinema. The visual realm and the importance of nuances in character expression and response are heightened in the subgenre. Given that Universal's *Dracula* debuted six months after Laemmle's comments were published in the *Exhibitors Herald-World*, and given the film's stagy quality, Laemmle's opinion on acting can be read as either a directive at his studio or a description of techniques already applied to the new horror cycle. Either way, Browning's movie is full of emotional performances and melodramatic spectacles that do more than drive the story toward a conclusion. They also orient viewer attention to the relationship between the mesmerizing fiend and its victims and to the organizing powers of visual excess in the subgenre.

The hypnosis film is literally built upon two seemingly divergent meaning systems—narrative movement via conventional means, such as character psychology, and excess in the form of heightened emotional states and riveting images of creatures. The subgenre is grounded on the narrative trajectory of boy meets girl, boy loses girl to monster, and boy gets girl back from monster. But it is also built on excessive displays, such as lingering shots of the monster's physique or mesmerizing gaze, reverse shots of the heroine's vapid stare, and narrative glitches, like the attacks on Fedor in *Mark of the Vampire*. While film theory conventionally views these two cinematic strains as mutually exclusive and of differing importance, they are interdependent and equally significant in hypnosis films.

In fact, the dual meaning systems may help explain spectatorial variance in the subgenre. Some viewers, for example, may privilege spectacle over narrative in hypnosis films, a point suggested by Lugosi in his claim that women love horror because it offers escape from their everyday lives. The female fans who thought Lugosi might remove them from their day-to-day grind and take them into a fantasy world of romance, read more than sadism into the vampire's attacks on women. They likely understood the messages proffered by the system of excess, which invited them to gaze at monsters for a long period of time and assume that untold desires and pleasures were communicated through the heroine's vacant response.

Part of the hypnosis film's narrative trajectory is to pause and emphasize the exchange of looks between victim and fiend. Yet looking into a monster's eyes in close-up or lingering on the heroine's vapid stare are not only moments of narrative import but also signifiers that monster and heroine are bound together as spectacles in a game of mutual desire. Here, Linda Williams's arguments about the monster-woman bond are instructive. Williams contends that while the looks exchanged between fiends and heroines express victimization on the part of women, they also speak of their shared status with the fiend as outsiders to patriarchy. Williams elaborates: "In the classic horror film, the woman's look at the monster offers at least a potentially subversive recognition of the power and potency of a non-phallic sexuality" (90). Williams's focus on the visual realm, and her assertion that looking and sadism are not always a perfect match, reinforces the subgenre's doubling of woman with fiend.

This doubling was recognized by critics in the early 1930s. In his description of Mina's role in *Dracula*, for example, Edward Churchill had the following to say about the actress who portrayed her: "Helen

Chandler, as the creature of the vampire, who finally is saved by David Manners, contributes to the generally weird effect."[23] While in a trance, Mina is a monster whose eerie performance embellishes the film's horrifying atmosphere. Actually, Mina's likeness to the count was used to market the film. In a section of the Pressbook, entitled "Here's How to Sell DRACULA," one printed poster includes a drawing, in the upper left hand corner, of Lugosi staring down at Mina and John, who occupy the lower right portion of the advertisement. The count's arms are raised in an hypnotic gesture, while the following cutline comes between Dracula and the other figures depicted: "UNDER THE SPELL OF A MAN..WHO WAS DEAD..WHO LIVED AT NIGHT ONLY..OF A HELLISH FIEND..WHO DEMANDED THE BLOOD OF THOSE SHE LOVED."[24] Here, the twist of phrasing lends a homoerotic mystique to the vampire's relationship with the heroine. Dracula is not, it seems, interested in Mina; rather, he is enamored of the blood of those whom she loves. The bottom image, then, confirms that Dracula yearns for the blood of the hero, for Mina is shown staring intently at John Harker. The image also reinforces the doubling of heroine and fiend—John clutches his heart in a dramatic gesture, while Mina stands behind him, gazes at him with both an hypnotic and hypnotized stare, and, in a threatening move, places her hand close to his neck. Mina, it seems, is both a woman who swoons in Dracula's embrace, as well as one who is likened to the count—they are both creatures of the night.

Like *Dracula*'s Mina, *Mark of the Vampire*'s heroine was also described as a woman with a dark side. *Time*'s reporter presented her condition in rather comic terms: "When it appears almost certain that Irena, overcome by ghoulish tendencies, is about to gnaw her fiancé's jugular vein, the police inspector on the case makes a remark which can be considered classic in its style: 'There are things going on around here that I don't like.'"[25] The hypnotism of *White Zombie*'s heroine garnered similarly light-hearted remarks in the *New York Times* in 1932: "Necromancers waved their sinister hands from the screen of the Rivoli yesterday and tried to hypnotize blondes into killing their boy friends."[26] Madeline (Madge Bellamy), the heroine in *White Zombie*, is charged with more than threatening her boyfriend. Like Mina in *Dracula* she was doubled with the hypnotic fiend, according to the trades. "Murder [Legendre], too, has come under the spell of the girl and plots to make her his own," was how Abel put it in *Variety*.[27] While Legendre (Bela Lugosi) plots to possess the heroine, Madeline casts a spell over him—she, too, is a hypnotist of sorts.

Figure 4.6. Doubling the heroine with the fiend, this Pressbook advertisement illustrates the victimization of the hypnosis film's hero, renders Mina (Helen Chandler) monstrous, and implies a homoerotic component to Dracula's (Bela Lugosi) vampiric desires. *Copyright © by Universal City Studios, Inc. Courtesy of* MCA *Publishing Rights, a Division of* MCA*, Inc.*

IV

The persona of the hypnotized heroine dates back to nineteenth-century literature. Writing of the reception in the 1890s of George du Maurier's novel *Trilby*, upon which the film *Svengali* (1932) was based,[28] Bram Dijkstra paints a rather conventional portrait: "What made Trilby attractive to readers of her story was that she was the epitome of the passive, yielding woman whose only identity came from what the men around her made of her."[29] According to Dijkstra, connotations of female passivity persisted in fin-de-siècle sources, such as the fairy tale of Sleeping Beauty whose state of suspended animation connoted both virginity and near death (61–2). The hypnosis film's heroine possesses similar attributes to those described by Dijkstra. In being hypnotized, in staring out of eyes that look glazed over and vacant, she, too, appears to incarnate death-in-life.

While he paints a familiar portrait of the hypnotized heroine, Dijkstra's is also an incomplete canvas. Instead of the frozen passivity attributed to Victorian women, the hypnotized heroine, whether of du Maurier's *Trilby* or Tod Browning's film version of *Dracula* is a transformative figure, a woman who looks as if on the brink of death but who surges with a hidden life inside. As Nina Auerbach remarks of the literary and real women of the Victorian era: "If we look at her simply as a literal woman, her recurrent fits of vampirism, somnambulism, mesmerism, or hysterical paralysis illuminate powers that were somewhat fancifully and somewhat fearfully imagined in women throughout the [nineteenth] century; the passage of our own century has not entirely dispelled them."[30] In *Woman and the Demon*, Auerbach maintains that in texts such as du Maurier's *Trilby* and Sigmund Freud's *Studies on Hysteria* (1895), hypnotized and hysterical women are granted "self-transforming power [which surges] . . . beneath apparent victimization" (34) (figure 4.6).

In a sense, the hypnosis of literary and film heroines, their "apparent victimization," is the price they pay in order to break the bounds of convention. If heroines, and their counterparts in the audience, insist on desiring fiends, aggressing against boyfriends, and behaving independently, as Lugosi believes they were apt to do, their desires and powers are masked by a victim role. Lest their nontraditional behaviors get too out of hand, however, most hypnotized heroines return to conventional mores by the narrative conclusion. Those who do not pay a heavy price for their independence; they wander aimlessly in a nether world of narrative obscurity and lost plot lines, as is the case with Lucy (Frances Dade) in Tod Browning's adaptation of *Dracula*.[31]

While heroines are forced to relinquish their fiendish potency eventually, their experiences while hypnotized are probably worth the price. For in addition to trying to murder heroes, their transformations usually offer physical benefits. For example, just prior to his near-attack by Mina, John, *Dracula*'s hero, gazes at his fiancée and exclaims: "You look wonderful." Irena, too, is positively transformed by *acting* like an hypnotized heroine in *Mark of the Vampire*. Her late-night meeting with Luna leaves her energetic and playful. A verve for life replaces the lethargy that she displayed earlier in the film.

Even those films that provide little textual evidence of a positive transformation on the part of the heroine were marketed with illicit female desire in mind. While *White Zombie*, for one, is a rather gruesome tale of a ruthless man named Legendre who turns his victims into zombies that do his bidding, the film was not promoted solely as a thriller (although the Pressbook includes a wonderful poster in which *White Zombie* is likened to *Scarface*). In fact, one advertisement includes the following cutline, in fine print, just beneath the film's title: "HERE'S A GLAMOROUS LOVE-TALE TOLD ON THE BORDERLAND OF LIFE AND DEATH, STRANGER AND MORE FASCINATING THAN ANYTHING YOU EVER DREAMED! WITH BELA (DRACULA) LUGOSI." The poster's parenthetical reference to the actor's earlier role suggests that Victor and Edward Halperin, the film's producers, were hoping to cash in on Lugosi's reputation as a lady-killer, so to speak.[32] By the same token, their use of the phrase *love-tale*, given the modes of address employed at the time for luring female patrons to horror films (see chapter 3), indicates their interest in speaking to and of female desire (figure 4.7).

The same interests were expressed in another poster for the film: "HERE'S THE BURNING GLAMOROUS LOVE-TALE TOLD ON THE BORDERLAND OF LIFE AND DEATH . . . THE STORY OF A FIEND WHO PLACED A WOMAN HE DESIRED UNDER THE STRANGE SPELL OF 'WHITE ZOMBIE' RENDERING HER SOUL-LESS, LIFELESS YET PERMITTING HER TO WALK AND BREATHE AND DO HIS EVERY BIDDING! SEE THIS LIVE, WEIRD, STRANGEST OF ALL LOVE STORIES!"[33] Like *Dracula* a year earlier, *White Zombie* is described as "the strangest of all love stories," a tale of compelling, yet bizarre, desire. While the love story is emphasized in this advertisement for *White Zombie*, the references to a soulless and lifeless woman, combined with a drawing of Legendre holding a yielding Madeline in his arms, do much to invoke Dijkstra's vision of the hypnotized female—she looks like a passive woman, a figure who embodies death-in-life. Yet, as I mentioned earlier, at least one reviewer made reference to the heroine's aggressive tendencies, to her efforts to stab her own husband, suggesting that both the publicity and reception of *White Zombie* allowed for and mobilized contradictory meanings.

While the prizes won by heroines under hypnosis involve trade-offs—love at the cost of life, in the case of *White Zombie*—those trade-offs often pale in comparison to the gains. *The Mummy* offers an instructive example along these lines. In Karl Freund's movie, the heroine not only experiences horrible terrors, especially in the final moments of the film in which she comes close to perishing in a vat of boiling fluid, but hypnosis also ensures that she looks great, feels won-

Figure 4.7. In this one-sheet for *White Zombie*, Madeline (Madge Bellamy) embodies a passive, yielding heroine who succumbs to the will of her monstrous and hypnotic lover (Bela Lugosi); she is a woman who signifies death-in-life. Photo courtesy of Ronald V. Borst/Hollywood Movie Posters. *Copyright © 1932 Amusement Securities/United Artists.*

derful, journeys through her past life in Egypt, and bonds with a fiend that was once the man of her dreams.

Here, the status of the monster as an object of fear *and* desire is rendered explicit—in present-day Egypt, the mummy is a mesmerizing yet frightening creature; in his past incarnation he was a handsome and welcome suitor. When the monster, which has adopted the persona of a man named Ardath Bey (Boris Karloff), arrives at the home of Sir Joseph Whemple (Arthur Byron), the archaeologist who discovered his tomb, he walks into the living room and happens upon the heroine, Helen (Zita Johann), who is fast asleep on the couch. As Bey stares at her, Helen awakens and rises to meet him. When Sir Joseph, Helen's suitor Frank (David Manners), and Dr. Mueller (Edward Van Sloan) enter from another room, they find Helen and Bey staring at each other, as Helen announces: "I've never felt so alive before." Like a revived Sleeping Beauty, Helen's prior melancholy and exhaustion evaporate as she stares into Bey's eyes (figure 4.8).

The Mummy is the tale of a cloth-bound creature that finds his Egyptian princess reincarnated as a modern-day woman named Helen Grosvenor. Bey pursues Helen in her present incarnation in order to revive their magnificent love of days gone by and to free himself of an ancient curse. His pursuit takes the form of hypnosis. The most important set of hypnosis scenes begins when Helen is shown lying on a divan and speaking to Frank on the telephone. When Frank asks of her plans for the afternoon, she tells him she is going to remain in her hotel room. The action shifts to an extreme close-up of Bey, whose eyes glow as he stares into the camera. A shot of Helen walking through the Cairo market is then superimposed over his face. His image fades as Helen arrives at his doorstep. Here, Bey's visual powers are rendered explicit, as is his role as rival for Helen's affections. For Helen's plan to remain in her hotel room, which she articulates to her suitor on the phone, is disrupted by Bey's mesmerizing eyes.

In the next scene Bey continues to hypnotize Helen, tells her of her previous incarnation, and conjures images of them together in the distant past, which are "projected" in a circular pool in his living room. The scenes conjured by Bey are Hollywood's rendition of Egyptian culture—spectacles of monumental architecture and intricate stage design. Elaborate costumes and sets form the environment against which Bey and Helen's ancient love story is played out. When Bey finishes recounting and illustrating their age-old romance in voice-over, the images shift back to Bey's living room, where Helen

Figure 4.8. Helen (Zita Johann) first meets the mummy (Boris Karloff) in Sir Joseph's (Arthur Byron) living room, where she stares into the fiend's eyes and declares: "I've never felt so alive before." *Copyright © by Universal City Studios, Inc. Courtesy of* MCA *Publishing Rights, a Division of* MCA, *Inc.*

awakens from her trance and tells him that she remembers dreaming of ancient Egypt.

Helen's links to Egypt not only are in the past but race through her blood in the present as well. Her mother is Egyptian, the viewer is told, while her father is British. In a sense, her connection to Bey is a maternal link, her means of exploring her Middle Eastern heritage through and with him. When Bey gazes at Helen, calls her to him, and unfolds her ancient life in the form of images in his magical pool, he connects with her not only on the basis of desire but on ethnic identity as well. *The Mummy*'s visual dynamics, then, are also ethnic dynamics to the extent that Bey represents both Egyptian immortality for Helen as well as difference from the British norm.

That norm is personified by the film's hero, Helen's mundane suitor, Frank. Frank is played by David Manners, the same actor who had been less than heroic in *Dracula* the previous year. In his role in *The Mummy*, Manners's ineptitude recalls his problems with heroics while portraying John Harker. While Frank represents normalcy and the West in *The Mummy*, Bey is a far more fascinating figure, and Frank's efforts to court Helen are less than impressive. Frank nearly loses Helen to Bey at the end of the movie, and she has never felt better than when she looks into her mummy's eyes. The visual and romantic lures of the Middle East run deep for Helen.

Those lures were so deep, in fact, that exhibitors were encouraged to market Zita Johann as an actress shrouded in mystery—like Karloff's Mummy, a being whose existence defies all laws of science, so, too, was Johann cast as a woman with an inexplicable past. One publicity story in particular, "Zita Johann Another Enigma to Hollywood," collapses the actress with her on-screen role to a startling degree: "Zita Johann is Hollywood's latest *mystery*. The *olive-skinned* Hungarian actress with the *exotic brown eyes* who is featured in Universal's fantastic 'The Mummy' . . . is one of the *most secluded* members of the film colony, and is rarely seen at parties and functions in Hollywood" (emphasis added).[34] Johann, like her character Helen and her monstrous suitor Ardath Bey, is described as exotic and a loner, a woman with a dark side.

In an interesting twist of editing choices, the ethnic connotations of the film were heightened by director Karl Freund prior to its release. During production Freund shot a number of sequences that show Helen in various past lives, most of which are as white Western women. The excised scenes include one in which Johann plays a first-century Christian martyr about to be fed to lions, another in which she is an eighth-century Barbarian queen who commits suicide, and a third in which she is a Medieval Lady of the Court who watches the Crusaders set off on their journey. Freund also shot Johann as a French aristocrat and a thirteenth-century noblewoman. Johann claimed in a 1989 interview that Freund's decision to cut the scenes was the final blow in his sadistic treatment of her. According to the actress, the director treated her miserably throughout the shoot, and when she complained to Carl Laemmle about Freund's savagery, Freund's response was to cut some of her best scenes.[35] Whatever the reason for Freund's decision to edit out these sequences, their absence reinforces the Egyptian focus and equates Bey's monstrosity—and Helen's attraction to him—with their shared heritage and their difference from the British norm. Helen's return to that Western identity at the film's conclusion, her partnering with Frank after Bey's demise, is a feeble effort to reinforce Western supremacy in a film that celebrates, albeit in monstrous ways, ethnic difference (figure 4.9).

A provocative two-page layout for *The Mummy* appeared in the *Motion Picture Herald* a week before the film was released commercially. In that advertisement, which was geared toward exhibitors, Karloff's mummified head occupies the page on the left, while a full-figure shot of Johann seductively embraces the word *Mummy* on the right. Two electrifying bolts travel between Karloff's and Johann's eyes, while the following headline heralds the movie's hypnosis theme: "THE LIVING EYES BLAZED LIKE BALLS OF FIRE AND FASTENED THEIR HUNGRY GAZE ON THE GORGEOUS CREATURE."[36] Since the direction of the lightning bolts is not illustrated, the poster's phrasing can be read in two ways. Not only is Johann a fiendish recipient of Karloff's stare but her eyes are hungry for Karloff as well, the creature that serves as her object of desire. Johann's romantic interest in the

Figure 4.9. Helen's (Zita Johann) Egyptian heritage courses through her veins and ensures her attraction to Ardath Bey (Boris Karloff), as in this still from *The Mummy*. Photo courtesy of Ronald V. Borst/Hollywood Movie Posters. *Copyright © by Universal City Studios, Inc. Courtesy of* MCA *Publishing Rights, a Division of* MCA, *Inc.*

monster is represented literally in the advertisement as her arms enfold its name. The monster and heroine, this image proclaims, are linked together by hypnotic stares and shared monstrous identities.

A similar doubling of monster and woman appeared in at least two one-sheets from the film's Pressbook. In one poster, in particular, Karloff and Johann are represented as hypnotic creatures that stare at the prospective viewer with horrifying intensity. An image of Karloff's cloth-bound head and a slightly smaller shot of Johann's face occupy the center of the advertisement. While the monster's gaze is implied (his eyes are shaded), the heroine's stare is rendered in full view. Her eyes are enlarged, her brow slightly ruffled, and her gaze fixed on the viewer who dares to stare back. Here, Johann's expression is anything but vapid—she is not the passive heroine of the hypnosis film. Instead, she is a powerful monster in her own right.[37]

V

One of the questions I asked near the beginning of this chapter was how do characters look at each other in hypnosis films? I am interested in specifying the differences, for example, between hypnotic monsters, which often gaze at their victims with ruffled brows and concentrated stares, and heroines, who usually respond with an absence of facial movement and affect. In an attempt to define the gazes of contemporary horror, Carol J. Clover describes two forms: (1) an assaultive gaze that attacks or reaches out to a victim, which she terms "predatory" (173); and (2) "the horrified gaze of the victim," which she calls "reactive" (175). Clover notes that the two gazes are not always separate in contemporary films, as the case of *Peeping Tom* (1960) makes clear. In Michael Powell's work, the protagonist is both an assaultive gazer who pierces women with a camera that houses a deadly blade and a reactive gazer who turns his device on himself at the conclusion (Clover 176).

Assaultive and reactive gazes appear in hypnosis films as well. Although slightly different in form than *Peeping Tom*, the subgenre explores the collapse of diverse looks in a single character. Near the beginning of *The Mummy*, for example, Ardath Bey murders Sir Joseph, the archaeologist who discovered his tomb, because he came too close to learning the mummy's true identity. In a series of crosscut shots, Bey reaches out visually to Sir Joseph by staring at the camera. In response to Bey's insistent gaze, Joseph clutches his chest in pain. While the creature counters with ever-intensive looks, Bey also begins to display physical discomfort. With each exchange between Bey, the predator, and Sir Joseph, the victim, the mummy exhibits dual responses: aggression and suffering. And when Joseph finally falls to the floor in distress, Bey collapses in a parallel move. It is as if Sir Joseph's torture turns back upon the creature. Although Bey succeeds in his murderous efforts, the sequence illustrates the conflation of assaultive and reactive components in the figure of the fiend. While Bey is on the attack, he is also a victim of his own efforts. Here, the suffering of monsters, when they lock eyes with victims in hypnosis movies, doubles them with their prey. Bey's relationship to Sir Joseph is a gender exception, however, for the most overt examples of assaultive/reactive responses occur between creatures and female leads.

Archie Mayo's *Svengali* explores the assaultive/reactive rapport between monster and heroine quite well. *Svengali* is the story of a singing teacher's (John Barrymore) obsession with a young girl and his hypnotic transformation of her into a stage star. The film is filled with close-ups of the fiend's ghoulish eyes and the heroine's wide-eyed response. In fact, Svengali's assaultive gazing was articulated in a poster displayed at the Old Colony Theatre in Massachusetts, which declared: "The most amazing character ever portrayed—as only Barrymore can—Playing the mad pianist with the terrible eyes of the hypnotist—who looked at women and transformed them—or destroyed them—as he willed."[38]

Svengali's hypnotism of Trilby (Marian Marsh) begins when he sees her suffer from a headache. In a series of intercut shots, which depict his focused gaze and her vacant stare, Svengali wrests her headache from her and internalizes it. Like Bey, Svengali feels another character's pain. Unlike the mummy, however, Svengali's agony results from his efforts to relieve, not cause, injury. In a second sequence, in which Trilby again endures a headache, Svengali calls to her at night through a series of close-ups of his eyes. This sequence, in which Svengali's eyes are cross-cut with Trilby as she endures her pain across town, was much remarked upon by reviewers in 1931. *Time*'s reporter was duly impressed: "He can hypnotize her at any distance, and one of the best shots in the picture suggests how his influence bores through the night, over the roof-tops from his window, and into her mind."[39] Mordaunt Hall of the *New York Times* found the scene even more remarkable: "In one sequence, where Svengali casts his spell over Trilby from his abode to her's, there is unusual artistry. This is undoubtedly one of the most striking and interesting camera feats ever accomplished in a film."[40]

Svengali's gaze is so powerful that one reviewer thought it had an impact on female patrons inside the theater as well. As J.C.M. commented in the *New Yorker*: "The stunt of the picture is the way in which the hypnotic powers of old Svengali have been suggested—camera tricks responsible, I hear, for a number of susceptible ladies' being carried out in violent hysterics."[41] As I suggested of other gimmicks, in chapter 3, the episode described by J.C.M. may have been a planned stunt and not the spontaneous reaction of female viewers. Nevertheless, the narrative suggests that Svengali's or Barrymore's influence might not only hypnotize but terrorize women as well. When Trilby arrives in the maestro's studio after being summoned in the night, he offers to relieve the headache that plagues her. She responds, however, with fear and resistance: "No, no, take your eyes off me. Let me go, let me go." Not surprisingly, given his keen interest in the heroine, Svengali refuses to let her out of his sight and internalizes her pain once again (figure 4.10).

The first time Svengali succeeds with his hypnotic trick, he tells Trilby: "Your headache is here in my heart." Over and over again the film confirms this claim. That is, Svengali's tortured expression suggests that her headache is *literally* in his heart and, by the conclusion, his heartfelt torment is too great to bear. Before her final performance, Svengali tells Trilby: "Tonight I want you to watch me very closely, do not take your eyes off mine for an instant." Trilby complies and as she completes her song, Svengali collapses and dies. Although this sequence, like Svengali's prior feats of hypnosis, indicates that the assaultive and reactive gazes are conflated in the figure of the maestro, it is also possible to locate them in Trilby as well. Svengali's pain may have been *caused* as much by Trilby's returned look as by his focused gaze. After all, he tells her to keep her eyes on him at all times, which she does remarkably well—meaning, her eyes are also hypnotic, capable of bringing Svengali under her powers and, finally, precipitating his demise.

The contemporary telekinesis film, according to Clover, may be "the one subset of horror which regularly features females as assaultive gazers" (223). Contemporary films are often quite obvious

Figure 4.10. Maestro Svengali (John Barrymore) gazes deep into Trilby's (Marian Marsh) eyes and wrests her headache from her with the aid of his hypnotic powers. Photo courtesy of Ronald V. Borst/Hollywood Movie Posters. *Copyright © 1931 Turner Entertainment Co. All rights reserved.*

in depicting women who gaze aggressively and destructively, as in David Cronenberg's *Scanners* (1980). Classic hypnosis movies, however, are much more indirect in aligning heroines with visual aggression. Instead of presenting Trilby as an independent gazer, for example, *Svengali,* and the publicity materials that surrounded the film, alternates between highlighting her victimization and emphasizing her willful investment in the fiend. The film's Pressbook intersperses posters depicting Barrymore as a controlling gazer with stories that promote Trilby as a heroine who looks back. In fact, viewers were urged to return Svengali's gaze as a marketing ploy. One Pressbook column opens with the following headline: "Look! Trilby looked into these eyes. See What Happened to Her! Look Inside."

Yet another piece declares: "23,000 Women! have been fascinated by 'Svengali'! Spellbound by its soul-searching drama of woman's strangest passion. Entranced by its bitter-sweet romance of a love that has no happiness! Dare you deny yourself the supreme thrill they have enjoyed? Dare you miss the chance to learn the dark mysteries of synthetic love!"[42] Although framed by Svengali's mesmerizing powers, this story implies that women have a choice about whether to look at the maestro. It also suggests that looking might bring benefits for the heroine and viewers alike, such as strange passion and manufactured love.

The melding of assaultive and reactive gazes is a significant element in other hypnosis films as well, especially in monsters' death scenes. Here, the role of heroines as foils for the suffering endured by other characters takes center stage. Neither Count Dracula in Browning's 1931 version nor Countess Zaleska in Hillyer's *Dracula's Daughter*, for example, display conventional reactive gazes when staked. Instead, their hypnotized victims do so on their behalf. In *Dracula*'s staking scene, Van Helsing dispatches the fiend in offscreen space. During the vampire's demise, however, Mina's body becomes a surrogate medium for the count's death throes. The camera frames Mina clutching her chest—the conventional seat of romantic desire, as well as the place where Dracula is pierced—while the count's gasps are heard on the soundtrack. This sequence both confirms Mina's doubling with the fiend and makes literal the genre's conflation of painful *performances* with women. No doubt, Mina's responses to Dracula's staking are complex. Her pain may signify the loss of a romantic partner, as well as the rite of passage she must endure to return to normalcy. Yet, her reaction can also be read as a displacement. Although Dracula is the one being dispatched just beyond the margins of the frame, Mina *acts out* his pain for him.

The conclusion of *Dracula's Daughter* is a variation on *Dracula*'s closing scene. At the end of Hillyer's sequel, Countess Zaleska threatens the psychiatrist-hero Garth, while Janet lies dormant on the couch. The countess begins to hypnotize the hero, but is stopped mid-gaze when Sandor shoots an arrow that pierces her in the chest. Like *Dracula*, the monster's agony is shared with and then channeled through the heroine. The sequence takes place as follows: a close-up of Zaleska being staked and in pain is quickly replaced with an insert shot of Janet writhing in agony. What is striking is that Janet is not awake while the fiend is staked, yet she experiences Zaleska's torment nonetheless. Just as Mina endures Dracula's pain, so too is Zaleska's suffering represented upon Janet's body.

On the one hand, the pain experienced by these heroines signifies their release from the clutches of mesmerizing creatures. On the other hand, their reactive displays imply the devastating impact of the monsters' demise: the women suffer the loss of the fiends. More significant, perhaps, is the suggestion that they may well keep the creatures' legacies alive. For one way to interpret the displacement of affect that occurs in these films is to claim that, in the act of dying, supernatural monsters pass their torches on to heroines. This is convincing especially in vampire tales, narratives of the undead that defy the normative conventions of mortality. After all, Van Helsing may have killed the count at the end of *Dracula*, but Lugosi was paid handsomely to sit on the set for the sequel. In the end, Hillyer and screenwriter Garrett Fort decided not to have the actor appear in the film. But Lugosi was prepared to remind the audience that the undead refuse to die.

Perhaps, these films' conclusions suggest, the endurance of hypnotic fiends is personified by the heroines who survive them. This is that much more convincing in *Dracula*, in which Lucy, a woman who is transformed into a vampire early in the film, is never staked. As a result, her survival might well confirm that the genre is filled with narrative loopholes, but it also suggests that threats of monstrosity endure in women who survive narrative closure.

The hypnosis film offers viewers a double-edged promise: the heroine will be fiendish as she travels through the narrative middle, but she will take her place at the hero's side at the conclusion. The heroine can be a scary creature for a while, but the hope is that the fiend's demise in the closing moments will save her for patriarchal culture. Thus, while I agree with Linda Williams that the heroine's look at the monster confirms their doubling, I also believe that the different ways in which they look at each other—the fiend with a focused and assaultive gaze, which exerts power over the heroine, and the heroine with a vacant and paralyzed stare, which often signifies her pliability in the hands, or eyes, of the monster—guarantee that they face different fates at the finale. The only problem is that there is no handbook on hypnosis, no assurance that its effects are temporary. Instead, there is every likelihood that happily ever after is a pipe dream for the couple. The threats of the undead, not to mention sequels, ensure that the monster will mesmerize others in the future, that the hero is destined to get blindsided all over again, that the heroine will yearn to look more fiends in the eye, and that spectators will continue to set their sights on creatures and their prey.

5

The Interpretation of Screams: Female Fear, Homosocial Desire, and Mad-Doctor Movies

Whatever happened to Fay Wray?
That delicate, satin-draped frame.
As it clung to her thigh
How I started to cry
'Cause I wanted to be dressed just the same.

—Dr. Frank N. Furter, *The Rocky Horror Picture Show* (1975)

I

It has often struck me as curious that in the gender-bending universe of *The Rocky Horror Picture Show* Fay Wray is the heroine invoked by the lipstick-wearing Frank N. Furter (Tim Curry) during one of his musical numbers. Despite her sartorial status in the stanza quoted above and her role as a signifier of Furter's gender mobility (he wants to dress like her), Wray's fate in the world of classic horror seems less relevant to *The Rocky Horror Picture Show* than do the exploits of other heroines. After all, Jim Sharman's movie not only invokes comedies and musicals, it parodies the vampire film, the haunted-house movie, and James Whale's *Frankenstein* pictures as well. Although situated squarely in horror's field of meanings, *The Rocky Horror Picture Show* does little to invoke *King Kong* (RKO, 1933), the movie with which Wray is most regularly aligned. What purpose, then, might Wray serve in a parody that disrupts gender roles and depicts malleable sexualities?

The answer to this question lies less in the generic associations attached to Wray—her alignment with jungle-horror—than in the performative connotations she inspires. For in addition to her fame as the heroine who struggles to free herself from the huge paw of her simian captor, Wray is credited with immortalizing the on-screen display of female fear. As Mordaunt Hall remarked of her character in *King Kong* upon the movie's release: "It often seems as though Ann Redman [sic], who goes through more terror than any of the other characters in the film, would faint, but she always appears to be able to scream."[1] No matter what horrors confront Ann in *King Kong*, Hall notes in the *New York Times*, Wray manages to let out blood-curdling yells. In fact, the scream may be Wray's trademark, as Calvin T. Beck makes clear: "Fay Wray, the reigning empress of all Scream Queens, refined the deepest aspects of beast versus beauty into an art form that remained virtually unchallenged through one decade and well into the next"[2] (figure 5.1).

Wray's screaming legacy is modernized in *The Rocky Horror Picture Show*. While one of her vocal descendants is Janet (Susan Sarandon), the frightened heroine who happens upon the bizarre household in which Dr. Furter and his cohorts reside, the film's more dramatic

Figure 5.1. Fay Wray—the Scream Queen of Hollywood horror cinema—poses for a glamor shot in this publicity still from *King Kong*. Photo courtesy of the Academy of Motion Picture Arts and Sciences. *Copyright © 1933 RKO Pictures, Inc. Used by permission of Turner Entertainment Co. All rights reserved.*

scream *queen* is Frank N. Furter himself. Depicting a world in which the rules of heterosexual patriarchy are overturned, in which Furter is the queen of his castle, *The Rocky Horror Picture Show* portrays a gender-bending screamer, a mad doctor who wears makeup and feminine clothes and sleeps with men and women alike.

The Rocky Horror Picture Show's most direct links to classic horror are its invocation of Fay Wray and its modern recycling of the mad-doctor scenario. The film is a musical send-up of prior narratives, as well as a comic representation of the terrors embedded in classic mad-doctor movies. For Dr. Furter dares to invent life, a beautiful blonde hunk to be exact, with the same test tubes and other gadgets used by 1930s physicians to perform their feats of creation. Like Furter, the classic mad doctor is obsessed with men's bodies, with dissecting, manipulating, and joining them together. His deistic aspirations to construct or reconstruct men (and, in a few instances, women) are both the narrative motors and the horror components of these movies. Mad-doctor films are about male scientists' terrifying efforts to create living men from dead matter. They are *mad* doctors, then, because of their deistic aspirations and, furthermore, because they are physicians who are less intent upon healing the sick than they are obsessed with animating the dead.

The Rocky Horror Picture Show is the classic mad-doctor movie with its internal machinery laid bare. The film *openly* celebrates Furter's homoerotic impulses, desires that lead him to build a man. Classic movies, on the other hand, depict man-to-man dynamics as monstrous; they also punish physicians for venturing into god's territory, becoming too attached to other males, and putting women at risk of extinction. Mad-doctor movies, therefore, are not only male creation fantasies—consider their appropriation of mothering roles[3]—they are also about anxieties concerning the male body and male bonding. Contrary to tradition, mad-doctor narratives dissolve age-old reproductive functions. They shift the terms of human interaction from heterosexual intercourse to scientific and homoerotic discourse.[4] Even those films centered on female monsters, such as *Island of Lost Souls* (Paramount, 1933) and *Bride of Frankenstein* (Universal, 1935), are built on relationships between men. The latter examples disguise the horrors of homoeroticism and male-to-male social rapports behind a female-coded body, behind a monstrous woman. That body, however, is not so much a corrective to male bonding as a vehicle for its expression.

So where is the scream queen in all this? She is the mad-doctor movie's cover, the generic convention that, yet again, places women at the center of horror. Like the heroine's hypnotic stare, which I have outlined in chapter 4, the screaming and frightened woman, whether she is Fay Wray in *Doctor X* (Warner Bros., 1932) and *Vampire Bat* (Majestic, 1933), or her counterpart in other films, takes center stage in the subgenre. She guarantees that the terrors experienced by men, homoeroticism and suffering being the most pronounced, are nothing compared to what is endured by women. Thus, while *The Rocky Horror Picture Show* gives male transgressions of conventional gender roles free rein and lets Furter preen through the film as a scream queen of spectacular proportions, classic movies disguise the physician's social transgressions behind the heroine. Her body, like the bodies of female creatures given life in the subgenre, is a medium of expression not only for her own fears and aspirations but for male anxieties, desires, and terrors as well.

The heroine's body also serves as a more traditional vehicle for terror and pain than male bodies—while men suffer in mad-doctor movies, women (patriarchal society's most popular victims) do so more frequently and in more spectacular terms. Yet the performances of terror offered by heroines may be a disguise of yet another sort: a cover for women's own pleasures in male suffering. In a society that relishes representations of female victimization over and above male victimization (except, perhaps, in depictions of war), the heroine's bouts of screaming can be read as her means of disguising her *enjoyment* of male suffering behind a conventional behavior. Here, I want to repeat a quotation from Bela Lugosi, which I included in my discussion of the hypnosis film in chapter 4. In his ruminations on the relationship between women and horror, Lugosi asserts that women love the genre and, moreover, that they have a "ghoulish compulsion to see men torn and bloody and in agony."[5] While the hypnosis film offers heroines and female spectators few opportunities to witness male suffering in a graphic fashion, mad-doctor movies offer such opportunities with regularity. If they can be pried away from their screams for a brief moment, heroines (and female spectators) bear witness to male anxiety, pain, and terror in mad-doctor narratives. And, moreover, women may very well enjoy what they see—tormented and terrified men—in spite of or with the aid of their own displays of terror.

The performative and homoerotic qualities I have just outlined are depicted in Technicolor in Michael Curtiz's *Doctor X*. The film is about a maniacal physician who strangles, slices, and eats his victims. The police discover that the scalpel used by the murderer is only available to the professors who teach at Dr. Xavier's (Lionel Atwill) Academy of Surgical Research. In order to protect the reputation of his school, Xavier convinces the authorities to give him forty-eight hours to interrogate his colleagues and find the fiend. Lee Taylor (Lee Tracy), a crack newspaper reporter, follows the story from start to finish by sneaking into the city morgue as well as Dr. Xavier's home laboratory.

Xavier invites his colleagues to his house on Long Island for a controlled experiment. He informs the professors that his thermal tubes and other contraptions are part of his efforts to study the emotive composition of blood. Xavier proposes to locate the murderer by hooking the doctors to his machinery and registering their reactions. The premise is that strong mental repression can be studied in heart palpitations, which should, in turn, lead Xavier to the killer. Xavier decides to recreate one of the murder scenes on a small stage in his lab. Whoever becomes most agitated by the spectacle, he theorizes, is the murderer. Professor Wells (Preston Foster), one of his colleagues, is charged with administering the test. Because he only has one arm, Wells is assumed to be incapable of strangling anyone and thus innocent of the murders.

The first recreated murder scene is performed by Xavier's butler and maid. The maid Mamie's (Lila Bennett) performance highlights the masquerading function of female fear in *Doctor X*; her rendition of terror literally masks offstage events. Posing as a washerwoman who was brutally attacked by the fiend, Mamie's screams echo on the soundtrack as the butler feigns an attack. Suddenly, the room is plunged into darkness and insert shots are shown of hands unclasping the diodes attached to the professors' wrists. When the lights come up, Professor Rowetz (Arthur Edmund Carewe), one of Xavier's colleagues, lies dead on the floor. Xavier then searches for Wells, whom he finds disoriented and injured. As he tells Xavier, he was thrown through a glass door by an unknown assailant. Finally, the reporter, Taylor, is discovered locked in a closet, where he missed witnessing the murder because he fainted. As these diverse offstage events suggest, men are the *real* victims in the experiment. Mamie looks and acts like a frightened female, but she survives her performance without a scratch. The offstage and offscreen suffering of Rowetz, Wells, and Tracy is, however, much more extensive and far less theatrical.

The film's second performance scene occurs the next day. Xavier tries to prevent the earlier fiasco by chaining the professors, including himself, to diodes and bolting their chairs to the floor. When Mamie refuses to act in the scene, Joanne (Fay Wray), Xavier's daughter, agrees to play the part of a young woman murdered in her hospital bed. After each professor, except Wells, is latched to his seat, and after Wells returns to his backstage post, the fiend's identity is revealed. Staring out a window at the full moon, Wells becomes agitated. He dons a fake arm that he places in an electrical current. Miraculously, the limb comes to life. He then sits in front of a vat of synthetic flesh and covers his face and arms with the fake skin.

Wells then attacks Xavier's butler in the wings and takes his place as the fiend on-stage. As soon as he appears, Joanne is immobilized by fear, or at least she performs that response for her captive audience. When the professors finally deduce that the monster is real, they struggle to free themselves from their chains. Firmly locked in place, however, they are forced to watch Wells approach Joanne. Stage lights shine on the heroine who lies immobile, as the creature moves in for the attack. Taylor finally arrives and dispatches Wells (thus making up for his fainting spell earlier in the film)[6] and ensures that at least one horror hero saves the day.

The second staged sequence, like the first, highlights the performative connotations that surround women and, in this instance, the monster as well. Whereas the professors are shrouded in shadow in their roles as offstage spectators, Joanne's on-stage fright is depicted in full view. Like Mamie, she performs for men in two ways in this scene. She both *acts* the part of a terrified woman for those who watch her in the on- and offscreen audiences and *enacts* the pain and paralysis endured by males in offscreen space and in the dark of the laboratory.[7] In other words, while Joanne is approached by the fiend in spectacular and theatrical terms, men are as profoundly victimized as she is in this sequence. Wells injures the butler in the wings, for example, and although Joanne appears frozen on-stage, the professors are literally chained to their seats. This sequence offers a fictional parable for male spectatorship in classic horror. While male spectatorship has a sadistic reputation (which the professors put into effect by vicariously enjoying the *sight* of the heroine's attack), it is profoundly masochistic as well (they are as helpless as she) (figure 5.2).

The performative connotations of this scene also double Joanne with the fiend. They both assume on-stage roles, playing the parts of

Figure 5.2. Locked firmly to his chair, Dr. Xavier (Lionel Atwill) is forced to watch the monster (Preston Foster) attack his daughter, Joanne (Fay Wray), on a makeshift stage in his laboratory. Photo courtesy of Ronald V. Borst/Hollywood Movie Posters. *Copyright © 1932 Turner Entertainment Co. All rights reserved.*

victim and attacker respectively. Like Joanne, and Mamie before her, Wells might also be credited with playing the part of a victim with style. If he is the film's monster, how, then, was he thrown through a glass door earlier in the narrative? All clues suggest that he was his own attacker and, therefore, his own victim as well. In the closing moments of the film, the doubling of monster and heroine is reinforced. As Taylor telephones his story into the newspaper, he notices a shadow on the wall. Outstretched and foreboding arms enter the room and move toward him. In response to the approaching creature, he quivers in fear. Eventually, the shadow is revealed to be Joanne, and Taylor laughs nervously at his error in judgment. "You've got my heart going a mile a minute," he notes, playing on a double-entendre of fear and desire. This same doubling of heroine and fiend was suggested by an odd twist of phrasing for a poster that appeared in the *Motion Picture Herald* just before the movie's release: "Weird

Doctors and a Helpless Girl—And among them a savage whose victims disappeared in the night!"[8] Although she is described as passive, the advertisement also implicates the heroine in monstrous savagery—the murderer is to be found in a group composed of male professors and a woman.

Like female performances of fear, male passivity and an aura of homoeroticism are recurrent motifs in *Doctor X*. The most striking clues to homosexual relations occur the night of Rowetz's murder. Turning restlessly in her bed, Joanne awakens suddenly. When the knock on her father's door receives no response, she goes downstairs. There is a cut to a darkened room in which Rowetz's prone body lies on a stretcher. The sheet that covers him is then lifted by someone who leans mysteriously over the corpse. Joanne enters the doorway and screams at the sight of the intruder. The figure, revealed to be her father, jumps back from the body with a start. Joanne and Xavier then approach the exit, but before they depart the heroine spots yet another man lifting the sheet. When confronted, Dr. Haines (John Wray) notes that he wanted to make "a more thorough investigation of the body." Joanne then returns to her room as Haines whispers to Xavier: "Since we retired, this body has been . . . it's been—." "I know, but I don't want her to know," is Xavier's response. Neither doctor articulates what has been done to the man's body—the truth of the matter remains unspeakable.

This brief scene reiterates a number of elements introduced in the performance sequences. For Joanne's response acts out terrors that occur elsewhere, in this case on Rowetz's body. There is every indication that she is not at risk in the scene but screams nonetheless. In fact, the one character who cannot scream, and is forced to remain silent, is Doctor Rowetz himself, the corpse subjected to the late-night intrusions of men. Joanne's reaction, then, expresses horror *for* Rowetz—her yells both focus and shift attention away from the terrors enacted in the dark by male professors on a man's supine body.

The unspeakable nature of what Joanne witnesses that night is reiterated the following day at the beach when she tells Taylor: "I saw my father bending over Rowetz's body. I saw . . . oh, it's a terrible thought." Joanne is no more explicit about the previous evening than the professors. The viewer is left to wonder whether she witnessed her father committing a monstrous act—a scene of cannibalistic delight—or a perverse primal scene with a dead man. Whatever happened is too horrible for her to articulate, too evil to say out loud. The only information given is that the event took place at night, on a bed, and between men.

Doctor X offered viewers an unusual and potentially contradictory love story from the perspective of marketing. A two-page Pressbook Herald that was distributed for the film is a wonderful sample of the multiple meanings used in marketing strategies. On the right side of the page an oversized shot of Doctor X's head stares down at the yielding body of Joanne. Although connected by sight lines, father and daughter are separated by the letter "X," which literally separates the doctor's head from his unseen body and announces that Joanne is off-limits to him. Here, the image suggests that father desires daughter, that his desire is taboo ("X" may mark a spot on Joanne's chest, but it also protects her from her father), and that his desire may be channeled elsewhere, meaning toward men.

The advertisement reinforces the suggestion that men may be Doctor X's social and erotic destiny, since four of his colleagues glare at him from the upper left side of the notice. The remainder of the advertisement not only depicts the hero and heroine staring at Doctor X with expressions of fear on their faces, but the paragraph that accompanies the image speaks of unusual desires. Here is an excerpt: "An adventure in the realms of mystic romance with *lovers fascinatingly different from any you've ever known*" (emphasis added).[9] Spectators are invited to read the film, or at least its promotional machinery, in a complex manner. They are offered multiple connotations, such as father-daughter incest, homoerotic desire, and heterosexual romance (figure 5.3).

II

The scene that distresses Joanne so thoroughly in *Doctor X* is about homosocial encounters among men. I am using the term *homosocial* in two ways: first, as the combination of the social and erotic charges that bind rivalrous men together in narratives and, second, as a description of the manner in which patriarchy excludes women. The first meaning is articulated by Eve Kosofsky Sedgwick: "Homosocial is a word . . . [that usually] describes social bonds between persons of the same sex; it is a neologism, obviously formed by analogy with 'homosexual,' and just as obviously meant to be distinguished from 'homosexual.' To draw the 'homosocial' back into the orbit of 'desire,' then, is to hypothesize the potential unbrokenness of a continuum between homosocial and homosexual."[10] Homosocial desire—social bonds underscored by an erotic thrust—is a significant narrative attribute in the majority of 1930s mad-doctor movies. In one sense, then, this is a subgenre that celebrates male homosexuality by ensuring that a repressed component of dominant culture returns with a vengeance.

Yet to assume that these films are merely progressive beacons of a marginalized male homosexual voice is to misread the dual function of homosociality. For these movies also figure homosociality as the culmination of misogynistic impulses, the ultimate in patriarchal power, and a sign of the oppression and elision of women. From this perspective, homosocial desire has to be understood along the lines of Luce Irigaray's term *hom(m)osexual.* "Hom(m)osexuality," according to Irigaray, is the "law that orders out society . . . [as] the exclusive

Figure 5.3. Multiple meanings are portrayed in the Pressbook Herald distributed for *Doctor X.* Father-daughter incest, homoerotic desire, and heterosexual romance are either depicted or hinted at in this advertisement. Photo courtesy of Ronald V. Borst/Hollywood Movie Posters. *Copyright © 1932 Turner Entertainment Co. All rights reserved.*

valorization of men's needs/desire, of exchanges among men."[11] Homosocial desire is, therefore, as embedded in the exchange and exclusion of women as in the celebration of male homosexuality. When I use the term *homosocial* in the discussion that follows, my intent is to invoke both meanings.

A number of classic horror movies, including hypnosis films, depict homosocial relations. Few critics, however, remark upon them, as illustrated by Andrew Tudor's oversights regarding *White Zombie* (United Artists, 1932). In this film, the fiend Legendre (Bela Lugosi) is paid by a plantation owner named Beaumont (Robert Frazer) to turn the heroine, Madeline (Madge Bellamy), into a zombie in order to lure her away from her husband. Legendre, however, decides that he wants Madeline to himself and transforms his benefactor into a zombie as well. As Tudor recounts:

> Legendre has his own purposes (the plantation owner also becomes his victim), though apart from his satisfaction at exercising power for its own sake they are never entirely clear. That there is an underlying sexual element to his domination, however, can hardly be doubted. In turning Madeline into a zombie he makes her entirely compliant to his will, although nowhere does the film fully draw out the implications of this absolute power.[12]

Through a subtle rhetorical displacement Tudor sidesteps the sexual connotations of Legendre's exercise of power over Beaumont by shifting to the fiend's relationship with Madeline. Yet the scene in which the near-paralyzed Beaumont confronts Legendre makes clear that the victimization of the plantation owner parallels the monster's sexual pursuit of the heroine. The exercise of power and sexual desire are likened in the film, thus equating Legendre's relationships with Beaumont and Madeline (figure 5.4).

Tudor's reading of *White Zombie,* and his rhetorical slide from homosexual to heterosexual desire suggest the ease with which homosociality can be ignored and overlooked. In his study of Karl Freund's *Mad Love,* Richard Koszarski performs a similar oversight. Here, the focus is on a physician's desire for the heroine: "Yvonne, seen by Gogol (and first seen by us) as a classically helpless female figure yielding to the brand of a red hot poker, must be weaned away from her artist husband by means of scientific prowess. Gogol is not the screen's first scientist to attempt to win love in this manner, but the conflict between the scientist and the artist over the woman's body is here uniquely clear."[13]

While Koszarski's reading is plausible, it is also partial and inaccurate. Koszarski is incorrect to note that the audience meets the heroine when she is being tortured. The truth is that the viewer first sees Yvonne (Frances Drake) in her dressing room *before* she assumes her role as a victim on-stage. Second, Koszarski assumes that the relationship between Gogol (Peter Lorre) and the hero, Stephen (Colin Clive), is solely rivalrous. While that component of their rapport certainly exists, Gogol also operates on Stephen after the hero is in a train crash, thus serving as his caretaker as well as his rival. When Gogol sutures the hands of another man to Stephen's wrists, the surgeon's gesture recalls the point I made earlier about the subgenre's affection for combining men's body parts. Koszarski may be right, then, to call Yvonne the movie's most spectacular victim (meaning,

Figure 5.4. Legendre (Bela Lugosi) commands Madeline (Madge Bellamy) to do his bidding, while Beaumont (Robert Frazer)—his other victim—looks on helplessly in this still from *White Zombie*. *Copyright © 1932 Amusement Securities/United Artists.*

artificial and theatrical), but he is quite wrong to note that she is solely a helpless figure and the only object of desire. From this perspective, the film's "mad love" may have as much to do with the homosocial bonds formed among men—especially between Gogol and Stephen—as with the physician's obsessive desire for the heroine, a point I will return to later.

In her book *Epistemology of the Closet*, Sedgwick suggests that maddoctor narratives are especially prone to homosocial desire. She analyzes the erotic male dynamics of a number of literary texts and argues that the Gothic genre foregrounds "intense male homosocial desire as at once the most compulsory and the most prohibited of social bonds."[14] Most striking about Sedgwick's claim is that many of the novels she addresses, such as *Frankenstein* (1818), *The Strange Case of Dr. Jekyll and Mr. Hyde* (1886), and *The Island of Dr. Moreau* (1895),[15] were made into mad-doctor movies in the early 1930s.

According to Sedgwick, the Gothic depiction of homosocial relations was both socially sanctioned and shunned. It was considered a necessary narrative element, as well as a monstrous possibility that threatened to subvert the status quo. Homosocial desire was represented as ambiguous, as flipsides of the paradoxical definitions of homosexuality that appeared in cultural discourses circa 1900. On the one hand, Sedgwick maintains, homosexuality was likened to the "trope of inversion," in which male desires for other men were explained as female and feminine. On the other hand, the "trope of separatism" claimed homosexuality and, by implication, homosociality as the natural end point of masculinity and men's superiority over women (*Epistemology* 87). In the first instance, homosexuality is deemed undesirable, in the second, unavoidable. The combination of these two attitudes is expressed in homosocial narratives—male bonding is both horrifying and guaranteed, entailing the simultaneous introjection and expulsion of femininity.

In the film versions of these narratives, homosocial desire is embodied by the subgenre's lead characters: crazed physicians. Like their Gothic predecessors, effeminate and macho connotations are combined, in this case *within* the mad doctor. For example, in *The Crime of Dr. Crespi* (Republic, 1935), the eponymous character is played by Erich von Stroheim with a skillful combination of the sinister traits and effete aura for which the actor was famous. Thus, Crespi wears a very delicate, feminine bracelet on his wrist throughout the film, while he also beats up one doctor and tortures another (figure 5.5).

In her study of *Foolish Wives* (Universal, 1922), Janet Staiger addresses the diverse meanings that surrounded the movie and its star-director, von Stroheim. According to Staiger, von Stroheim's film role is contradictory: "As a consequence of the combination of Karamzin [von Stroheim] as masculine and feminine but also 'foreign' and desirable, 'foreignness' assumes connotations beyond designations related to national origin. Apparently, viewers of the period were interpreting films such that American women desired 'non-Americans,' a confrontation not only to sexual ruling norms but, then, to political ones as well."[16] One of the results of Karamzin's paradoxical image is that "a submerged homosexuality lies barely beneath the textual surface" of the film and of von Stroheim's character (Staiger 136). Thus, according to Staiger, although Karamzin pursues women enthusiastically in the narrative, he is also a figure around whom homoerotic connotations circulate.

Similar connotations were mobilized for von Stroheim's 1935 appearance in *The Crime of Dr. Crespi*. Banking on his star status, and in an effort to foster the controversy that surrounded *Foolish Wives* thirteen years earlier, the film's producers promoted Republic's B-movie with the same cutline used in 1922: "THE MAN YOU LOVE TO HATE."[17] The phrase was especially useful from a marketing perspective and is repeated throughout the Pressbook. As a selling ploy, the phrase could be broken down into diverse and intriguing component parts: the man you love, the man you hate, the man you love to hate, and the man you hate to love. All meanings are collapsed in the phrase as a means of addressing as wide a viewership as possible. Thus, depending on the particular poster in which it appears, the headline offers different modes of address to audiences and emphasizes divergent messages.[18]

For example, in one Pressbook advertisement von Stroheim gazes out from the upper left hand corner, while the film's romantic couple is trapped in the lower right. "THE MAN YOU LOVE TO HATE ERIC [SIC] VON STROHEIM" is printed across the center of the image and separates the mad doctor from his victims. In this case, von Stroheim is depicted as a threat to the heterosexual couple—the hero and heroine clasp each other against his intrusion. A second Pressbook poster utilizes the catchy phrase as well but configures characters differently. Here, the heroine, Mrs. Ross (Harriet Russell) looks across the poster from the upper left at Crespi, who stares at the viewer from the lower right. Whereas the first image emphasizes von Stroheim's danger to the couple, the second underscores the heroine's desire for the fiend. Still a third type of advertisement is promoted in the Pressbook. In this instance, "The Man You Love to Hate" is shown leaning over the prone body of the hero, Dr. Ross (John Bohn). The two men's eyes are locked together and, like Count Dracula in 1931, Crespi looks as if he is about to bite or kiss his patient.

The range of meanings represented in these posters appears in the film itself. The narrative's manifest storyline consists of Crespi trying to steal Mrs. Ross away from her husband by performing (and, supposedly, botching) a life-saving operation on him and administering a drug that makes Ross appear dead. Crespi's plan is to murder Ross by burying him alive. Crespi dares to destroy the conventional couple and substitutes himself as Mrs. Ross's monstrous partner. Yet the meanings of the second poster, in which the heroine desires the mad doctor, also circulate in the film. Mrs. Ross appeals to Crespi for help based on an old friendship that smacks of an affair, and as the narrative progresses she relies on him more fully. Thus, like some women spectators who found von Stroheim sexually appealing in 1922, Mrs. Ross is drawn to the actor in his 1935 incarnation. Like other monsters, then, Crespi is an object of both fear and fascination.[19]

Finally, although Crespi's crimes are supposedly motivated by an attraction to the heroine, von Stroheim's obsessive interest in her husband speaks of homosocial desire. For example, Crespi keeps newspaper clippings of Dr. Ross's professional and personal accomplishments hidden in his desk and gazes at them passionately throughout the film. Even as Ross lies vulnerable on his operating table while Crespi raves of murder, the surface sadism is tempered by an erotic charge. In a sense, Crespi's desire to injure Dr. Ross parallels his urge to embrace Ross's wife—both are marked by extreme affect, by the fine line between love and hate.

Unfortunately, there are few detailed analyses of the sexual and social proclivities of 1930s mad doctors. James B. Twitchell is one of the only scholars to make a compelling argument for such a reading. As he comments on Dr. Frankenstein (Colin Clive) in James Whale's 1931 film: "[Frankenstein] had been cast—I suspect quite unconsciously, until recently, at least—as bisexual" (*Dreadful Pleasures* 179). Twitchell's mention of the scientist's bisexuality is perceptive. Yet he assumes that the casting was unconscious for classic films, a point I will return to shortly, and uses Frankenstein's bisexuality solely to address unnatural reproduction: motherhood without women. Twitchell is explicit about the sexual urges the experiment engages:

the creation scene bears traces of "sexual arousal," he remarks, but Henry[20] remains "frighteningly onanistic" (DP 180). Thus, although Henry challenges heterosexuality by usurping Elizabeth's (Mae Clarke) role and giving birth to a full-grown male, his bisexuality remains a masturbatory affair in Twitchell's schema.[21]

Here, I want to spend a few moments reviewing Twitchell's claim that the bisexual casting of mad doctors was unconscious until recently. While I can only speculate on the matter, James Whale was probably aware of the sexual connotations in his casting choices, given that he was an openly gay director in Hollywood, and given that all his horror films, including the haunted-house saga *Old Dark House* (Universal, 1932), include at least one actor who is overtly effeminate

Figure 5.5. Dr. Crespi (Erich von Stroheim) plays the effete yet sadistic mad doctor in this publicity still from *The Crime of Dr. Crespi.*   *Copyright © 1935 Republic/ Liberty Pictures.*

and stereotypically gay. Whale's movies do much to suggest that conventional masculinity is more a pipe dream than a reality for men. In the case of *Old Dark House*, for example, the family that lives in the mysterious abode bears a humorous and telling surname that reflects Whale's play with gender: "Femm."[22]

My guess is that Whale cast and directed actors capable of portraying sexual ambiguities with ease.[23] He imported Colin Clive from London to play the eponymous role in his adaptation of Mary Shelley's novel. Rumor has it that Clive was bisexual,[24] which in Hollywood terms usually means gay. Whatever Clive's sexual orientation, his acting style was definitely effete, what Owen Gleiberman recently dubbed "seethingly neurotic,"[25] and what Leonard Wolf calls a "whiny performance."[26] Clive brings the same effeminate connotations to his starring role as the hero in Karl Freund's *Mad Love* at mid-decade. Thus, whether or not he was gay, his performance style connotes amorphous male sexuality.

The same is true of Ernest Thesiger who both stars in *Old Dark House* as a son of the aptly named Femm family and plays Dr. Pretorius, the scientist who convinces Henry to continue his creative efforts in *Bride of Frankenstein* (Universal, 1935). Although Thesiger was married to a woman for many years, he is the queerest of Whale's casting choices. Henry Sheehan, for example, referred to Pretorius as a "sexually ambiguous doctor" in his 1991 comments on the revival of the film. Vito Russo assert that Thesiger was a "man who played the effete sissy . . . with much verve and wit."[27] And according to James Curtis in his biography on Whale, during the shooting of *Bride of Frankenstein*, Thesiger "would busy himself in a corner of the stage with needlepoint."[28] Like Clive, Thesiger's thespian renditions in Whale's films seem anything but straight. Whether that is a result of narrative mandates, Whale's direction, Thesiger's performance choices, and/or a match between on-screen character and offscreen sexual orientation can no longer be determined. That Thesiger plays an effeminate mad doctor with panache is all that matters now.

III

Homosocial desire is a striking component of Whale's *Frankenstein* films. While the second movie in the series, *Bride of Frankenstein*, is a more powerful and obvious vehicle for the doctor's homosocial

behavior, clues also circulate through the first film, as publicity lay-
outs emphasized. In the last weeks of 1931 a series of posters were
printed in the *Motion Picture Herald* that hint at proscribed male sexuality. The first appeared on December 12th:

FRANKENSTEIN

THE LADY OR THE MONSTER

HE MADE IT WITH HIS OWN HANDS . . .

AND ON HIS WEDDING NIGHT

IT CAME . . . NO PICTURE EVER

MADE CAN TOUCH IT FOR THRILLS.[29]

The fragmented grammar of this cutline is a lesson in publicity
efforts to combine various connotations in a single advertisement,
including homosocial meanings. The mad doctor, it seems, has to
choose between a woman and a monster. The cutline's cryptic structure also suggests that Henry *is* a lady or a monster and, moreover,
that women and monsters are alike. It is unclear who came to him on
his wedding night: "The Lady Or The Monster." Although presented
in somewhat opaque terms, the advertisement also includes orgasmic allusions from the perspective of the 1990s—"on his wedding
night it *came*." To whom and with whom the monster came remains
a matter of speculation.

Other posters repeat these ambiguities and invoke the mother-
theme highlighted by Twitchell. One advertisement intones: "I GAVE
HIM LIFE BUT HE WANTED LOVE! FRANKENSTEIN. THE MAN WHO MADE
A MONSTER."[30] Complemented by an image of the creature at the left
of the page, and one of Henry in a formal suit and Elizabeth in her
wedding gown at the upper right, the cutline reinforces the film's
maternal connotations and positions Henry as a bad mother and
lover—he withholds love.[31] The image of Henry and Elizabeth in
matrimonial wear adds yet another layer of meaning to the cutline's
fragment, "He Wanted Love!" The phrasing suggests that although
he is about to be married, Henry wants love, a love that Elizabeth may
be unable to provide. From a more conventional perspective, the
phrasing can also be read in reverse: while the monster is needy,
Henry's romantic desires are already spoken for—they belong to
Elizabeth.

Clues to the monster's homosocial disposition are reinforced by a
poster printed in the final issue of the *Motion Picture Herald* for 1931:

Figure 5.6. Henry Frankenstein (Colin Clive) stares at his monstrous creation (Boris Karloff)—the fiend that "NEVER KNEW A WOMAN'S KISS"—in this still from *Frankenstein.*   *Copyright © by Universal City Studios, Inc. Courtesy of* MCA *Publishing Rights, a Division of* MCA, *Inc.*

"MYSTERY, DARKNESS, DEATH . . . WHICH SANE MEN SHUN . . . THESE MADMEN SOUGHT WHEN THEY MADE FROM STOLEN BODIES, THE SOUL-LESS MONSTER WHO *NEVER KNEW A WOMAN'S KISS.* . . TO MAKE THE 'THING' THEY PRIED INTO TOMBS, AND THEN THEIR MISFIT, SNARLING CRE-ATION ESCAPED AND ROAMED THE WORLD DRIPPING TERROR AND DEATH" (emphasis added).[32] More explicit than prior examples, this advertisement pivots around the central phrase: "the soulless mon-ster who never knew a woman's kiss." Although the creature's missed heterosexual experience is invoked as an unnatural omen, it is also heralded as a perverse romantic lure. The creature is monstrous because it lacks a woman's touch, because it only knows a man's touch (figure 5.6).

In her analysis of Mary Shelley's *Frankenstein,* Sedgwick argues that the original novel is distinctly homosocial. She maintains that Elizabeth's marginalization in the book leaves the reader with "a residue of two potent male figures locked in an epistemologically indissoluble clench of will and desire" (*Epistemology* 187). Although more attentive to Elizabeth's relationship with the doctor than Shelley, Whale's direction of Garrett Fort and Edward Faragola's script retains the novel's residue. Henry's rapport with Elizabeth is pitted against his bond with the monster.[33]

The homosocial connotations of this bond are reinforced in a scene in which Elizabeth and her friend Victor (John Boles) go to the Frankenstein castle. Upon their arrival Baron Frankenstein (Frederick Kerr), Henry's father, asks after his son and expresses disbelief that Henry would stay in a laboratory when he has a lovely home and wife to keep him occupied. In a fit of fury he rushes out the door to search for Henry, with the following words to guide him: "There is another woman, and I'm going to find her." The Baron is absolutely correct to assume that Henry's behavior is the result of illicit desire, but his search for another woman produces a male figure instead, a creature that drains Henry of his normative social and sexual responsibilities.[34] After all, the monster prevents Henry's wedding in *Frankenstein* and kidnaps Elizabeth before she and her husband can go on their honeymoon in the sequel.

Bride of Frankenstein has been hailed as one of horror's best by critics including Michael Bedford, Carlos Clarens, and Bruce Dettman. Reviewers in 1935 also thought it a fine cinematic accomplishment, as F. S. N. noted in the *New York Times*: "Another astonishing chapter in the career of the Monster is being presented by Universal on the Roxy's screen."[35] Otis Ferguson was even more complimentary in the *New Republic*: "Advertised as a chiller, this film turns out to be something else, having a lot of jollification, nice fancy, elegant mounting—there is, in short, beauty as well as the beast."[36] *Bride of Frankenstein* is, indeed, an exceptional film, one filled with wit and a directorial artistry shared by few classic horror movies.

Bride of Frankenstein opens on the exterior of a house as a thunderstorm rages. There is a cut inside where Mary Shelley (Elsa Lanchester) is seated in a parlor with the poets Percy Shelley (Douglas Walton) and Lord Byron (Gavin Gordon); Byron is the host at whose home Mary's novel was inspired. As the men discuss their work, Percy asks: "And what of my Mary?" To which Byron responds: "She's an angel." Mary looks up from her embroidery, eager to hear the compliment. Byron then invites her to the window to better witness the storm, but she refuses: "You know how lightning alarms me." "Astonishing creature," remarks Byron, "frightened of thunder, fearful of the dark, and yet you have written a tale that sent my blood into icy creeps. . . . [That such a] lovely brow conceived of *Frankenstein*. . . . Isn't it astonishing?" "I don't know why you should think so," responds

Mary, "Such an audience needs something stronger than a pretty little love story, so why shouldn't I write of monsters?" The scene closes with Mary describing the events that follow her novel's conclusion. Her voice-over narration serves as a sound bridge into the film proper (figure 5.7).

This opening sets the tone for *Bride of Frankenstein*. It introduces the creative strength of a woman yet tempers her professional achievements in the horror genre by underscoring her fear of thunder and lightning. Mary's feminine demeanor (she embroiders, is scared, and is referred to as an "angel") is counterposed against monstrous qualities (she authors a tale of terror—albeit for an audience of men—and is called a "creature" by Byron). Mary's latter role is protracted much later in the movie when Elsa Lanchester reappears, not as the famed author but as the female monster fashioned by Henry and Pretorius. Lanchester's dual role is more than a twist of casting—though Mary may be frightened of lightning, the audience learns that her monstrous double not only depends upon it as her life's blood (Henry and Pretorius channel electricity into her body to revive her), she also possesses a lightning bolt in her tresses. Lightning, then, both courses through her veins and permanently marks the surface of her body—she is an electrifying creation.

More than any other classic horror film, *Bride of Frankenstein* announces the importance of women to tales of terror. Whale's film suggests both that women write horror narratives and that they are frightened, monstrous, and—in the figure of Elsa Lanchester—fulfill all these roles at once. The appeal of Lanchester's fiend was remarked upon in the *New Yorker* in 1935. "In the prologue, Miss Lanchester also plays Mrs. Percy B. Shelley, as the movies used to call her," notes J.C.M., "but I preferred her Madame Monster."[37] Despite the genre's affection for cowering heroines, at least one critic found the monstrous female creature more compelling than either the wistful Mary Shelley or the whimpering Elizabeth Frankenstein. More recently, Leonard Wolf put into words the film's gender dynamics and the powers possessed by Lanchester's monster: "The men are effete, but Elsa Lanchester's Mary Shelley, though she speaks with the inconsequentiality of a butterfly of the drawing room, is a woman of steel who, at the same time, gives off an aura of erotic hunger. When we see her later, in the role of the Bride, this erotic aura flares up violently" (30). Not only do Lanchester's dual roles link Mary to a fiend, they also suggest that the act of authorship is a monstrous affair when accomplished by a woman: female writers both embody and spawn monsters.[38]

Figure 5.7. Percy Shelley (Douglas Walton), Mary Shelley (Elsa Lanchester), and Lord Byron (Gavin Gordon) appear in the prologue to *Bride of Frankenstein* in this one-sheet for the reissue of James Whale's film (reissue date unknown). *Copyright © by Universal City Studios, Inc. Courtesy of* MCA *Publishing Rights, a Division of* MCA, *Inc.*

On one level, therefore, *Bride of Frankenstein* portrays monstrosity as the result of a woman's refusal to adhere to her proper social role —Mary Shelley dares to defy conventions of femininity in order to write a novel filled with images of birth, death, and destruction. On another level, however, the monstrous emerges from the very display of femininity—she pens her story as a means of satisfying men, the prologue would have the spectator believe, while she herself remains a frightened and passive creature. Femininity and monstrosity are intertwined in the figure of Mary Shelley, at least insofar as she is constructed in the opening sequence of *Bride of Frankenstein*.

The enmeshment of monstrosity and femininity and, furthermore, the role of women in precipitating monstrous goings-on are also represented elsewhere in the film. An early scene shows Henry lying in bed recovering from the fiend's attack in the original *Frankenstein*. In a dramatic display of female hysteria, his bride, Elizabeth (played by Valerie Hobson in the sequel) begins the sequence by describing a strange ghostly figure that has invaded their bedroom and ends the scene by collapsing in Henry's arms in a state of utter distress:

> Listen Henry, while you've been lying here tossing in your delirium, I couldn't sleep. And when you raved of your insane desire to create living men from the dust of the dead, a strange apparition has seemed to appear in the room. It comes, a figure like death and each time it comes more clearly, nearer, it seems to be reaching out for you, as if it would take you away from me. There it is . . . there . . . it's coming for you . . . Henry, Henry!

Elizabeth becomes increasingly hysterical with each phrase until, finally, Henry grabs hold of her and she falls into his arms.

Elizabeth's tale of ghostly apparitions and, more specifically, the place in which she tells it—their bedroom—ensures that homosocial desire is a driving force in this mad-doctor movie. Elizabeth narrates

Figure 5.8. Dr. Pretorius (Ernest Thesiger) fulfills Elizabeth's (Valerie Hobson) worst nightmare and intrudes into the Frankenstein bedroom as a monstrous rival for Henry's (Colin Clive) affections. Photo courtesy of Ronald V. Borst/ Hollywood Movie Posters. *Copyright © by Universal City Studios, Inc. Courtesy of* MCA *Publishing Rights, a Division of* MCA, *Inc.*

a scenario of heterosexuality under threat; while Henry raves of creating living men from dead matter, his wife sees and, perhaps, conjures the creation that would take him away from her. There, in the privacy of their bedroom—the site of heterosexual legitimacy and desire—Henry mutters about men in his sleep, while Elizabeth assumes that those men are rivals of the most profound and intimate sort. Her distressed reaction, then, might be more than just proof that she is a conventional (read, hysterical) woman—it also signifies her keen awareness that her husband is lost to her and, moreover, that their bedroom has been invaded by monstrous male forces.

This sequence also highlights the masquerading function of female fear in mad-doctor narratives.[39] Although Henry lies injured and restless in bed, raving of his maniacal deeds, it is Elizabeth who re-enacts his experience for him. She conjures up an image of the monster, becomes increasingly agitated, and articulates the fear that her husband will be drawn away by a male-coded creature. Like Joanne's response to the sight of her father bending over Rowetz's body in *Doctor X*, Elizabeth performs on behalf of an injured man. According to her tale, she is not in direct danger, but Henry is, and she becomes hysterical *for* him.

The timing of this sequence indicates that expressions of female fear do more than conjure apparitions, they precipitate the appearance of male rivals: directly after Elizabeth's outburst, Dr. Pretorius arrives at the castle and enters the Frankenstein bedroom. Putting Elizabeth's terrifying daydream into effect, Pretorius comes for Henry (urging him to resume his experiments) and invades the sanctity of heterosexual matrimony (luring Henry to his laboratory and away from his honeymoon bed) (figure 5.8).

Pretorius's threat is announced by the maid (Una O'Connor): "He's a very queer looking old gentleman, sir. . . . On a secret, grave matter." Minnie's description of the doctor is compelling and a good example of the comic double-entendres planted throughout the film. Not only does Pretorius intend to discuss matters of the grave (he wants Henry to revive his work with dead bodies), he is also a very queer figure (he is effeminate and has an unusual fondness for Henry and his fiend).[40] Moreover, Pretorius brings the creature back into Henry's life and rekindles Frankenstein's experimental passions (albeit under the guise of saving Elizabeth from Pretorius, who soon commands the monster to kidnap her).

In writing of Elizabeth and Pretorius's first meeting, Syndy M. Conger and Janice R. Welsch acknowledge their rivalry: "Despite their gentility, the exchange presages the opposition between them, an opposition based on Elizabeth's concern for Henry's health and her desire that he return to his traditional role within society and Praetorius's [sic] disregard of the established social order."[41] Conger and Welsch imply that Elizabeth and Pretorius's battle over Henry is sexual in nature. For if the heroine's future depends on Henry's return to his proper social role as a heterosexual husband, and if Pretorius shuns all conventional mores, it follows that Pretorius is a sexual danger insofar as he urges Henry to abandon Elizabeth and all she represents.

Pretorius's menace is quite explicit in the film: he helps promote heterosexuality as a frightening construct, a monstrous phenomenon when engendered by men. In a scene in the tomb where Pretorius arrives with grave robbers in search of female bodies, the doctor and male monster first meet. After exhuming a casket, Pretorius dines on its cover by candlelight. The creature approaches and, after brief niceties, inquires: "You make man like me?" "No, woman," replies Pretorius, "friend for you." This interaction is marked by romantic overtones—Pretorius and the creature share a candlelit meal—and introduces the physician's brand of monstrous romance: male-coded characters wine and dine over a dead woman's body (see figure 3.7).

More significant, perhaps, is that the biological sex of the soon-to-be-manufactured creature is of no interest to the monster (a "friend" is someone who will be kind to him, including Pretorius). This interaction highlights both the monster's ignorance in matters of sexual difference (he tells Pretorius, "Woman? Friend? Yes, I want friend like me")[42] and Pretorius's disinterest in the romantic aspects of the woman-man bond. For while Pretorius wants to make a woman, he is also intent on making a monster—a creature that, even if she were to mate with Frankenstein's fiend, would spawn more monsters in a parody of heterosexual coupling. Pretorius is, then, not a maternal figure most intent upon playing the part of midwife to the birth of a female monster. Rather, he is a puppeteer of heterosexual desire, a mad scientist with deistic aspirations to turn heterosexual reproduction and romance into a fiendish affair.

The film's most striking homosocial interactions occur in the creation scenes. Henry and Pretorius become increasingly excited with the completion of each stage of preparation. The first, and most suggestive, phase of their experiment centers around a heart that beats on its own in a glass beaker. Each cardiac pounding is registered on a meter that Pretorius and Henry watch with expectant looks. The images are edited at a fast pace, in sync with the increasing rapidity of the heartbeats, and are shot at extreme angles so that the cuts between Henry and Pretorius have an unnerving effect. The images alternate between two-shots—in which both doctors appear, stare at the heart positioned between them, and look at each other with mounting excitement—and one-shots in which an image of each physician is intercut with inserts of the cardiac meter.

The scene is so striking that it was one of two sequences given special attention by *Time*'s reviewer in 1935: "There is one scene in which Pretorius and Frankenstein make a heart for their she-demon out of the still warm organ of a young girl murdered by their assistant, and another in which they impregnate her with crackling life from a lightning bolt brought down on gigantic kite-cables."[43] The heart scene makes literal the romantic connotations of the doctors' relationship. The men become increasingly agitated and impassioned while staring at a human heart, the conventional seat of desire. The pounding meter appears between them, joining them in the two-shots and drawing their attention in the singles. The fast-paced cutting and heartbeats thus suggest that the doctors' rising expectations refer not only to the fiend they are creating but also to a shared sexual thrill that their experiment engenders (figure 5.9).

The doctors' illicit sexualities are developed further as the scene continues. In preparation for stimulating the creature electrically, Pretorius and Frankenstein implant the heart. They listen to the storm rage outside the castle, stand at their patient's bandaged head, and then gingerly fold back the blanket that covers the corpse. In close-ups, their hands gently clamp metal objects to each side of the patient's skull. Henry and Pretorius then release kites from the roof, place diodes around the fiend, and channel electricity into it. After a lengthy series of shots, in which images of Henry and Pretorius are intercut with flashes of lightning, the creature is untethered from the machines and Henry exclaims: "She's alive!"

Just as the pounding heart serves as the vehicle through which Pretorius and Henry are conjoined, so, too, does the female-coded monster foster male bonding and arousal. To borrow the term used by *Time*'s reporter, the doctors "impregnate" the creature with the storm. In a parody of heterosexual intercourse, they join forces within the monster's body—she is the site where long bolts of lightning meet. Thus, when the doctors grasp the wrists of their monster after she is electrocuted, their gesture substitutes for their own handholding. Pretorius and Henry touch each other through their crea-

Figure 5.9. In this advertisement for the 1953 rerelease of *Bride of Frankenstein*, a heart beats on its own in a glass beaker, while Henry (Colin Clive) and Pretorius (Ernest Thesiger) alternately gaze at each other and at the cardiac meter with mounting excitement. *Copyright © by Universal City Studios, Inc. Courtesy of MCA Publishing Rights, a Division of MCA, Inc.*

ture. Although the scene ends in destruction and only Henry and Elizabeth survive, threats to their union linger. As Conger and Welsch note: "The faces of Henry and Elizabeth as they embrace and watch the castle crumble and burn . . . suggest that theirs is far from a fairy-tale ending" (304). Henry and Elizabeth's happiness is precarious because they embrace at the moment in which Henry's "children" are dispatched, and because Henry is at his best when manufacturing monsters and staring at men, not when tending to his wife.

Bride of Frankenstein is, then, a narrative of illicit homosocial desire, a film in which conventional masculinity and heterosexuality are under attack by the unrepressible forces of human "nature" (in the form of Henry's latent but insistent homosocial desires) and medical science (which takes the shape of Henry's monsters). But as Elizabeth Young has argued of Whale's film, *Bride of Frankenstein* is also a tale of race relations, a story in which female empowerment, homosocial desire, and racism converge. On the one hand, notes Young, the film transforms "the competitive force of male rivalry into a subversive mode of male homoeroticism and . . . [undermines] its apparent demonization of women with a final, fleeting moment of female power."[44] On the other hand, however, "the [male] monster appears as a marker of racial difference, and his sexualized advances to the film's women encode racist American discourse of the 1930s on masculinity, femininity, rape, and lynching" (404).

Young weaves racist discourses of the era with evidence from the film to create a compelling parallel between the horrid behavior and apelike features of the monster—features that were painstakingly planned by Jack Pierce in his makeup designs—and contemporary stereotypes of African-American men who were considered terrifying rapists by whites. Young's arguments are reminders of classic horror's investment in the dual operations of ideological transgression and containment. The film's explorations of gender ambiguity and homosociality appear alongside and in concert with a racist undercurrent. As a result, *Bride of Frankenstein* and other mad-doctor movies such as *Island of Lost Souls* and *Dr. Jekyll and Mr. Hyde*—in which experiments attempt to humanize animals in the first instance and render humans animalistic in the second—must be addressed as multivocal discourses, narratives that portray and negotiate a range of contemporary social issues and anxieties, such as racism and homosexuality.

IV

The powers of homosociality also find expression in *Island of Lost Souls*. Like *Bride of Frankenstein*, Erle C. Kenton's film utilizes a female-coded monster to disguise the mad doctor's desires for men. Although more direct in its depiction of male victimization (the movie opens with the shipwrecked Edward Parker [Richard Arlen] fainting in the arms of sailors), *Island of Lost Souls* uses female fear as a mask for male desire. The story centers on a madman who populates a desolate island with creatures that are part-human, part-animal.

In an interesting historical coincidence, H. G. Wells both acknowledges and disavows his novel's relationship to homosexuality in the preface to his collected works. He notes that Oscar Wilde's trial for homosexuality, which took place in 1895, the same year *The Island of Dr. Moreau* was published, had an impact on the author as he penned his tale of terror: "There was a scandalous trial about that time, the graceless and pitiless downfall of a man of genius, and this story was the response of an imaginative mind to the reminder that humanity is but animal, rough-hewn to a reasonable shape and in perpetual internal conflict between instinct and injunction. The story embodies this ideal, but apart from this embodiment it has no allegorical quality."[45] As described (or implied) in Wells's preface, homosexuality is a base, animalistic urge, one that results when the natural forces that surge in humanity erupt and overpower social prohibitions intended to keep heterosexuality intact. Despite Wells's warning against reading *The Island of Dr. Moreau* in terms of Wilde's trial, his novel's storyline of monstrous male figures battling each other in the depths of the jungle suggests that homosexuality was more than a literary muse for him. Homosocial desire infuses both Wells's novel and Kenton's film adaptation with monstrous possibilities (figure 5.10).

In his menagerie of creations, Moreau's (Charles Laughton) most prized experiment is Lota (Kathleen Burke), the Panther Woman of Paramount's nationwide contest (see chapter 3).[46] An early turn of events requires that Parker join Moreau's assistant Montgomery (Arthur Hohl) on his journey to Moreau's island, where he meets Lota. Parker and Lota flirt with each other, and Parker becomes Moreau's prisoner, until Parker's fiancée, Ruth Thomas (Leila Hyams), saves the hero from the madman. Lota is killed eventually and Moreau is destroyed by his creatures.

Despite the happy heterosexual reunion between Parker and Thomas, homosocial desire circulates through most of the film and confronts Parker as soon as he arrives at the island. When Montgomery tells his boss, "I'll stay with Parker tonight on the schooner," ostensibly to get an early start to the mainland, Moreau insists on keeping the hero to himself: "No, I'll take him up to the house." When Montgomery complains, Moreau counters: "I've got something in mind." Parker and Moreau then leave for the compound and, on their trek through the jungle, Parker notes: "Strange looking natives you have here." Instead of responding to Parker's comment directly, Moreau flicks his whip lightly at Parker's chest and remarks suggestively: "You'll be wanting a cold shower, I think, before dinner."

Moreau maintains this flirtatious behavior throughout the film, rendering an exceptional performance of effete villainy. The doctor's tone and movements suggest sexual interest in the hero, as did, I would venture, the rumors of homosexuality that surrounded Charles Laughton at the time of the film's release.[47] Yet Moreau's homosexual proclivities remain indirect in the movie. His desires are expressed *through* Lota. Moreau tells Montgomery that he plans to use Parker to test Lota's sexual feelings: "The only reactions we get from her are fear and terror. How will she respond to Parker when there's no cause for fear? Will she be attracted?" While Moreau articulates a scientific interest in keeping Parker close at hand—he wants to test Lota's reactions—it is noteworthy that he chooses Lota's object of desire for her; it is Moreau who decides which man will elicit a human response from the Panther Woman. Yet what qualifications does Moreau have that would allow him to choose the right man for Lota? How can he be so sure that Lota will find Parker attractive unless he, too, finds men desirable? From this perspective, Moreau's choice of Parker for Lota is a form of displacement—Moreau exhibits what are conventionallly assumed to be a heterosexual woman's emotional impulses (he flirts with Parker and deems him sexually desirable), while Lota performs the attraction on Moreau's behalf.

The masquerading quality of Lota's reactions is apparent when she meets Parker. Instead of an immediate attraction, she expresses fear.

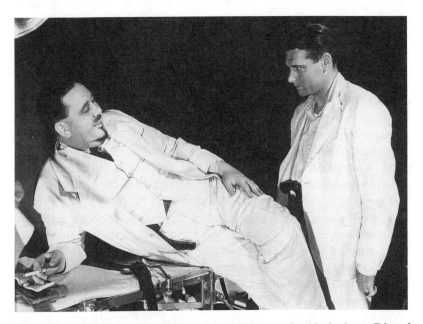

Figure 5.10. Dr. Moreau (Charles Laughton) flirts overtly with the hero, Edward Parker (Richard Arlen), in this still from *Island of Lost Souls*. Homosocial desires are combined with signifiers of hypermasculinity as guns protrude from each man's belt buckle. Photo courtesy of Ronald V. Borst/Hollywood Movie Posters. *Copyright © by Universal City Studios, Inc. Courtesy of MCA Publishing, a Division of MCA, Inc.*

Parker offers her a cigarette and she cowers in response. There is then a cut to Moreau who witnesses the scene from behind a fence, and a shot from his point of view of Lota sidling up to Parker and looking at him seductively. While a surface analysis indicates that Lota's fear easily translates into desire once she sees that Parker means her no harm, a more in-depth study of the sequence of shots reveals the masking quality of her terror. Lota's movement from fear to desire can be read as a response to the middle shot in the scene—the image of Moreau. The mere sight of Moreau, and the insertion of his point of view in the order of shots, precipitates Lota's desire for Parker. Her attraction depends, then, on Moreau's voyeuristic presence and intervention. In this way, homosocial desire gets expressed, but only when funneled through a frightened and desiring female figure.

V

Although homosocial dynamics infuse many mad-doctor movies, *Murders in the Rue Morgue* (Universal, 1932), *Vampire Bat* (Majestic, 1933), and *Dr. Jekyll and Mr. Hyde* (Paramount, 1931) are more conventional than the films addressed thus far.[48] In his analysis of *Murders in the Rue Morgue*, in which an insane physician mixes tortured women's blood with that of a gorilla, Robin Wood critiques Robert Florey's film: "The film is quite obsessive about its heterosexual relationships. . . . Even the usual gay stereotype, Pierre's plump and effeminate friend, [Paul,] fits very well into the pattern. He is provided with a girlfriend to recuperate him into the heterosexual coupling of normality. His relationship with Pierre (they share an apartment, he wears an apron, cooks the dinner, and fusses) is a parody of bourgeois marriage."[49] I share Wood's belief that this movie's rendition of homosexuality is tempered by heterosexual normativity. But that containment is less a function of Paul's (Bert Roach) possession of a girlfriend than the result of the hero, Pierre's (Leon Waycoff), depiction as a conventional male lead. By failing to look at the narrative trajectories of other mad-doctor movies, Wood misses the circulation of homosocial desire in the subgenre as a whole.

Murders in the Rue Morgue does not portray that desire with any consistency because this particular movie's hero is effective to a remarkable degree, not because films of this type are averse to homosocial portrayals. Pierre moves from a position of ignorance to a position of knowledge regarding Dr. Mirakle's (Bela Lugosi) experiments. His character's actions and psychology guide the story. While he does not dispatch the crazed physician at the conclusion, he succeeds in rescuing the heroine from a gorilla who carries her across rooftops. Thus, his valiant efforts ward off homosociality and save the day.

The homosocial dynamics of Frank Strayer's *Vampire Bat* are similarly contained. In this movie a village is seemingly under attack by a creature that sucks its inhabitants' blood. Suspecting vampires, the townspeople call upon Dr. Neiman (Lionel Atwill), their respected physician, and Carl (Melvyn Douglas), an officer of the law, to dispatch the fiend. Eventually, Neiman is revealed as the murderer. He uses vampirism as a ruse for draining his victims' blood so that he can perform devious experiments. Near the conclusion, Ruth (Fay Wray), Carl's fiancée, is captured when she overhears the doctor communicate his dastardly deeds telepathically to an assistant. But, like Pierre in *Murders in the Rue Morgue,* Carl arrives to save the heroine and precipitates the fiend's downfall. Both these films limit the connotations of illicit sexual desire and gender transgressions by figuring a powerful and effective hero. As a result, these movies also curb the range of affective and identificatory responses elicited from and offered to spectators.

Unlike *Vampire Bat* and *Murders in the Rue Morgue,* Rouben Mamoulian's *Dr. Jekyll and Mr. Hyde* depends upon a conventional heroine, not a hero, to limit homosocial desire. In this version of Robert Louis Stevenson's novella, Dr. Jekyll (Fredric March) is engaged to be married to Muriel Carew (Rose Hobart). He concocts a potion that causes a devious second self to emerge. His double, Mr. Hyde (Fredric March), is grotesque and sadistic, as indicated by his abuse of his mistress, Ivy (Miriam Hopkins). Although he is in control of his transformations initially, Jekyll soon loses mastery. The fiend then murders Ivy, attacks Muriel, and in the end is killed by the police.

This film straddles an invisible boundary between Florey and Strayer's movies (in which heroes reign) and other mad-doctor films that subjugate male leads. On the one hand, the picture relishes male suffering and the hero's failure to control events, such as his transformations into Hyde. On the other, it is strikingly heterosexual and sadistic in orientation.[50] In her book on fin-de-siècle culture, *Sexual Anarchy,* Elaine Showalter asserts that Stevenson's novella put his cultural milieu into words: "[It] can most persuasively be read as a fable of fin-de-siècle homosexual panic, the discovery and resistance of the homosexual self" (107). While Showalter's reading is instructive, it does not work well with Mamoulian's film. Although the book is populated by communities of men, the screen version includes two female leads and equates them with heterosexual desires (both their own and those belonging to Jekyll/Hyde).

As Mordaunt Hall remarked of the adaptation: "The producers have seen fit to include both a romantic theme and a sex influence in the course of the narrative"[51]—the romantic theme being Jekyll's relationship with Muriel and the sex influence Hyde's rapport with Ivy. Muriel and Ivy set the movie's heterosexual patterns into play. While the novella suggests homosexual panic via the protagonist's narcissism and rapports with men, Mamoulian's film reduces the number and importance of male characters and replaces them with women. Like *Bride of Frankenstein*, *Dr. Jekyll and Mr. Hyde* critiques heterosexuality as a monstrous orientation if left unchecked. But, unlike Whale's movie, Mamoulian's refuses to make homosocial desire look like a viable alternative.

As a further departure from the other mad-doctor movies addressed thus far, the heroine's fear and desire for the monster are split in *Dr. Jekyll and Mr. Hyde*. Hyde is solely a focus of derision for female characters, while his doubled self functions as an object of desire. The splitting of fear and desire renders Hyde much more monstrous than other fiends in classic horror, for his devious characteristics are not tempered by redeeming qualities. In addition, Ivy's terror, specifically her agonized screams when Hyde attacks her, suggests that female fear is taken to new heights in the film. Whereas most mad-doctor narratives depict heroines who endure little in the way of sustained attacks, or are subject to theatricalized violence, Ivy's pain is more lengthy, gruesome, and believable than in the other pictures I have discussed. Here, it is not so much the conventional hero who confirms the film's heterosexual dynamics as it is the traditional and suffering heroine[52] (figure 5.11).

But this description fails to account for the contradictions that publicity brought to the movie. As I mentioned in chapter 3, Fredric March was marketed as a heartthrob, a romantic lead destined to please the ladies even when in monstrous guise. Thus, while the film's dynamics are assuredly heterosexual, Hyde's sadism and torture of Ivy (remember, Miriam Hopkins was publicized in *Photoplay* as enjoying her role) are circumscribed by advertising discourses that focus on

March as an object of desire whose victims are more than willing. Even more forcefully than *Murders in the Rue Morgue* or *Vampire Bat*, which were marketed in rather simple and sadistic terms, the marketing of *Dr. Jekyll and Mr. Hyde* figures the hero as a complex actor and monster, and indicates that his female victims are, perhaps, feigning fear and torment or, at the very least, masochistically enjoying his monstrous advances.

VI

Of all 1930s mad-doctor movies, *Mad Love* is the clearest vehicle for homosocial desire and the performance of female fear.[53] Directly after the introductory scene, in which an anonymous woman refuses to go to a horror play with her date, there is a cut to Yvonne's dressing-room where the actress comments on a note and flowers she has

Figure 5.11. Mr. Hyde (Fredric March) grasps Ivy (Miriam Hopkins) and strangles her in a gruesome scene from Rouben Mamoulian's *Dr. Jekyll and Mr. Hyde.* *Copyright © by Universal City Studios, Inc. Courtesy of* MCA *Publishing Rights, a Division of* MCA, *Inc.*

received from Dr. Gogol, the man who has rented the same balcony for the last forty-seven nights. While her maid thinks "Gogol" is a nasty-sounding foreign name, Yvonne comes to his rescue: "He really is a great surgeon, he cures deformed children and mutilated soldiers." This sequence is followed by a parallel scene in which Gogol enters the theater and stands before a wax replica of Yvonne. A drunkard staggers toward the statue and talks lewdly to it. In response, Gogol champions Yvonne's integrity, but the drunk has the last word: "She's not for either of us, she's only wax."

These two brief scenes set the tone for the narrative. First, Yvonne's role as an actress is established: she is shown in costume wearing a robe with a chainlike sash around it, and the scene takes place in her dressing room. Second, Gogol's surgical expertise is mentioned, as are his maternal kindness (he cures deformed children) and aptitude for helping mutilated men. In the second of these scenes, Gogol reveals his desire for Yvonne. Yet the impossibility of his urges gets the last word: "she's not for either of us." The most obvious layer of the narrative consists of Gogol trying to prove the man wrong. The doctor buys the statue from someone who had planned to melt it for wax, and he does, briefly, have Yvonne at the conclusion—he traps her in his bedroom and clasps her to his chest.

Gogol's desire to possess Yvonne occurs at a distance through most of the film. In fact, his urges are expressed from afar in a theater scene that appears near the start of the movie. From one perspective, Gogol might be construed as an aggressive voyeur of the torture play that Yvonne enacts on stage. Here, the theatricalization of female suffering is expressed by a close-up of her face, which registers the pain supposedly inflicted on the offscreen regions of her body. The scene includes two shots of Gogol hidden by a shadow that obscures his face, while he watches the play from his box. Gogol's role as a sadistic madman in *Mad Love* was suggested by *Time* magazine's reviewer in 1935. As the reporter noted, Gogol shudders "with sadistic thrills at public executions."[54]

Yet sadism only partially describes Gogol's response to the play. In fact, the second image of him, which appears just after the camera rests on Yvonne's tortured visage, focuses on Gogol as he slowly closes his eyes with an afflicted expression on his face. Instead of enjoying the spectacle of the woman's feigned mutilation, his reaction parallels hers. As Andre Sennwald remarked in the *New York Times*: "In the theatre des horreurs, which he attends night after night, you see him in his box watching his lady tortured upon the rack, veiling his eyes in an emotion which is both pain and sadistic joy as he listens to her screams."[55]

Gogol's ambiguous response to Yvonne's grimaces is reinforced by another shot. As the play comes to an end, there is a cut to a side view of a man in the audience. Unlike Gogol, this man claps enthusiastically at the spectacle of Yvonne's staged torture. This anonymous spectator is a stand-in of sorts for horror's traditional male viewer—he delights in witnessing female terror. Yet *Mad Love* never pays him much attention, for he remains an anonymous character, one seen briefly only near the beginning of the movie. Karl Freund's film may, then, pay the sadistic male spectator brief lip service, but the movie does not tell his tale. Instead, it traces Gogol's trials and tribulations, his conflation of masochistic and sadistic responses, his position as a man who suffers from his impossible desires and torments those who deprive him of their fulfillment. Taken as a guide for the spectator as to how to react to Freund's motion picture, the fate of the anonymous man in the audience relegates the sadistic male viewer to the margins of narrative space, while homosocial desire and oscillations between male sadism and masochism are given center stage.

Mad Love's insane doctor is feminized throughout the film; specifically, he is doubled with Yvonne. Like her, he is a caretaker: he performs miraculous surgical feats as a means of tending to the less fortunate, while she supports Stephen financially and nurtures him while he recovers from his accident and operation. In fact, the same reporter who noted Gogol's sadism argued for his feminine demeanor: "Lorre, perfectly cast, uses the technique popularized by Charles Laughton of suggesting the most unspeakable obsessions by the roll of a protuberant eyeball, an almost feminine mildness of tone, an occasional quiver of thick lips set flat in his cretinous ellipsoidal face."[56] This reviewer came closer than any other to articulating the subtext of mad-doctor movies. He seems on the verge of noting that Lorre, like Laughton, is an effeminate madman obsessed by unspeakable, homosocial desire.

But what of the film's most conventional component: Yvonne's status as a woman frightened by the mad doctor? On a manifest level, she is the film's most obvious locus of fear. She performs the victim part in a play, deals with Gogol's disturbing advances, and falls prey to the doctor's raving delirium at the conclusion. Yet, like other heroines, her role is also a masquerade—a cover intended to hide her own recognition that her husband is far from traditionally masculine and to disguise Gogol's rapport with the hero. Despite Yvonne's efforts at displacement, however, Gogol touches Stephen more frequently—and in a more sustained manner—than he caresses the heroine. While he grabs Yvonne at the play's cast party and forces a kiss upon her, he spends much more time and energy working on Stephen's body. He tries laboriously to rejoin his patient's dismembered limbs and massages Stephen's hands in an effort to revive them. Therefore, in contrast to the film's publicized heterosexual motif, Gogol's most direct physical rapport is with another man (figure 5.12).

Homosocial meanings are suggested by the medical procedure itself. While operating on the hero, Gogol realizes he cannot sew Stephen's hands back to his wrists and must use the hands of a knife-throwing murderer, the hands of another man, instead. As is true of Frankenstein's labor of love in Whale's first film, Gogol sews men's

Figure 5.12   Dr. Gogol (Peter Lorre) rests a reassuring hand on Stephen's (Colin Clive) shoulder as his distraught patient displays his new limbs in this still from *Mad Love.* Photo courtesy of Ronald V. Borst/Hollywood Movie Posters.   *Copyright © 1935 Turner Entertainment Co. All rights reserved.*

body parts together and the result is a monster of sorts. While Stephen survives the procedure, he can no longer pursue his career as a concert pianist and is overcome with the urge to throw knives. As a result, *Mad Love*'s most pronounced and lasting horror is that Stephen possesses, and must therefore hold on to, the hands of another man.

The interactions among Yvonne, Stephen, and Gogol are configured as triangular, a classic horror motif addressed by Bruce Kawin: "There will be a perverse love triangle among the boy, the girl, and the monster . . . [and] the happy ending of the surviving couple will depend on their coming to some kind of understanding with the monster."[57] Writing of *Mad Love*, Kawin notes: "Stephen and Yvonne Orlac are on a delayed honeymoon when disaster intrudes, and the implication is that they must go through a horror phase, something identified with Dr. Gogol and his 'mad love,' before they can settle into their marriage" (17). While the passage quoted leaves room for a homosocial interpretation of the triangle, Kawin clarifies: "Whatever relationship there is between 'the monster and the girl' must be resolved" (17).

However, as Sedgwick's work on eighteenth- and nineteenth-century literature suggests, many rivalrous triangles highlight homosociality as significant narrative elements. *Mad Love* positions Yvonne in dual roles: she is both the object of desire in a heterosexual rivalry between men and the mediator through whom Gogol and Stephen's homosocial desires are passed. Thus, when Gogol watches Yvonne from the audience in the theater of horrors, she plays the part of a frightened heroine for two characters: both herself and her husband—she doubles Stephen's piano concert that is simultaneously taking place on-stage in another city. While the physician's sadomasochistic gaze supposedly expresses his desire for Yvonne, he is in a sense also watching Stephen, whose concert recital is crosscut with the heroine's performance. What comes to pass eventually is that Stephen's torment, the pain he endures in the train crash on his way home, is much more severe than Yvonne's thespian travails. The heroine's display is but a more spectacular version of Stephen's torture, as well as a visual circuit through which the men are bound.

In the film's closing moments, homosocial desire is finally spoken out loud. When Yvonne hides in Gogol's bedroom and takes the place of her wax statue, Gogol confesses the murder of Stephen's step-father to her. He grabs what he assumes is a wax sculpture and

Yvonne begins to scream. The doctor believes that his desire has brought the statue to life. While she begs to be let go, Gogol responds with words of love. He then begins to hear voices, first Yvonne's voice telling him that he is a hypocrite, and then his own hissing voice intoning: "Each man kills the thing he loves." Gogol mutters the phrase while he begins to strangle Yvonne. The hero and police arrive in the nick of time. As Gogol is about to murder the heroine, Stephen throws a knife and kills the fiend. Stephen then rushes to his wife and holds her in his arms. With his eyes fixed on the offscreen space in which Gogol's body lies, he croons: "My darling."

Homosocial desire orchestrates this scene with a vengeance. Stephen murders the mad doctor with Gogol's words—"each man kills the thing he loves"—echoing on the soundtrack. The implication is that Stephen has put the doctor's speech into effect and, indeed, killed the man he loves. Given that the phrase that Gogol mutters was written originally by Oscar Wilde, whose homosexuality scandalized the British social and legal system in 1895, reading homosocial desire into *Mad Love*'s closing moments is more an act of deciphering surface cues than digging for latent meanings.[58] Thus, Stephen's offscreen gaze at Gogol's body, punctuated by the remark "my darling," merely reinforces the focus on men in this sequence. Moreover, the ending leaves new horrors close at hand. As *Time*'s anonymous reporter concluded his review in 1935: "Even the music that bursts forth for the lovers' reunion has its chilling overtones, for nothing has been done about the hands of Orlac. They are still, as he clasps his wife to his breast, the hands of the guillotined knife-thrower."[59] *Mad Love* may be over, *Time* magazine suggests, but the homosocial and other horrors unleashed in the film are destined to continue their reign of terror over the heterosexual couple.

VII

In writing of Charles Ludlam's unconventional stage adaptation of *Camille*, which starred a cast of male actors, Kate Davy notes that homosexuality appears less as a manifest textual component than a latent and insistent motif. Her remarks work well as a description of the patterns of homosocial desire in most mad-doctor movies: "[*Camille*] is not gay inasmuch as its address is not exclusively homosexual, but within the dynamics of the production the machinations of homosexuality surface, 'come out,' and are rendered visible in the pockets, gaps, and fissures of an ultimately less-than-monolithic heterosexual configuration."[60] Like *Camille*, mad-doctor films portray little in the way of explicitly homoerotic relationships but much in the form of indirect desire. Just beneath the surface of monstrous displays usually lie suffering men who either make a living by joining bodies together or are linked to other men by an erotic passion that cannot be suppressed.

In the end, then, the star of *The Rocky Horror Picture Show*, Dr. Frank N. Furter, is not only a late twentieth-century icon of gender ambiguity, he is also a fitting descendant of Dr. Frankenstein, Moreau, Gogol, and their colleagues. He is a figure who rolls a crazed physician and "screaming Mimi" into a modern scream queen. The only difference between Furter and his predecessors is that he announces forthrightly the unconventional gender play and homoerotic desires that mad-doctor narratives depict in latent form. Thus, the heroine and her cries offer a traditional gender cover and object of desire for the men who act out their unconventional urges alongside her screams. In mad-doctor movies, each man may kill the thing he loves in the end, but not before he gets a chance to suffer the delight of holding its hand, grasping homosocial bonds for all they are worth, and letting go only when forced to do so.

6

White Skin, White Masks: Race, Gender, and Monstrosity in Jungle-Horror Cinema

Genuine Monster-mouthed Ubangi Savages
World's Most Weird Living Human
from Africa's Darkest Depths

—Circus ad from the early 1930s

She was discovered, it is recounted and pictured,
when a small blond-haired [sic] boy was noticed
among the black children of the natives.
The woman, his mother, was the wife of a ship captain,
whose vessel was wrecked on the rocky coast many years before.
She was the sole survivor, the child was by the native.

—*Motion Picture Herald* review of *The Blonde Captive* (Capital Films, 1932)

I

In the spring of 1930, Congo Pictures had a box-office hit with its new release, *Ingagi* (1930). Billed as a "sensation" by publicity posters, *Ingagi* promised the sacrifice of a black woman to a gorilla and emphasized "the perverse union of woman and jungle animal."[1] While crowds streamed into theaters to see the film, Will Hays's office of the Motion Picture Producers and Distributors of America (MPPDA) discovered that *Ingagi* was a cinematic fraud.[2] Parts of the film were pieced together from old documentary footage, the MPPDA learned, and the illicit scenes of nude black women cavorting with a gorilla were studio-staged performances.[3]

Hays's revelation had little impact on the film's popularity.[4] In fact, in the fall of 1930 the *Exhibitors Herald-World* announced that *Ingagi* had passed the Ohio state censor board for a second time and was enjoying an extended run in some regions. The Ohio censors imposed a minor limitation: the inclusion of a leader stating that *Ingagi* "is not an official record of any scientific expedition."[5] The audience was never informed directly that the encounter between black woman and ape, which the publicity underscored, was entirely manufactured on a soundstage (figure 6.1).

What is of most interest to me about *Ingagi* is the degree to which it blends race with gender and monstrosity. In particular, *Ingagi* constructs the "darker" races (meaning the natives as well as gorillas) as exotic and monstrous beings—exotic because of their very darkness, and monstrous because of their cross-species union.[6] And *Ingagi* figures black women and men as apelike creatures. As Frantz Fanon phrases it: "It has been said that the Negro is the link between monkey and man—meaning, of course, white man."[7] As one catchline in *Ingagi*'s Pressbook announces: "Finding of strange creatures apparently half-ape, half-human, which may represent the fabled 'missing link.'"[8] The Pressbook promises spectators a peek at monstrous offspring, a good look at beings born of an illicit and, potentially, significant evolutionary union between black woman and gorilla.

It is, in fact, the black jungle women who serve as *Ingagi*'s most powerful links: not only are they said to produce half-breed babies, but they themselves are portrayed as not fully human—in their (fantasized) union with apes, the black women signify the racist assumptions of the era in which all blacks were considered animals, black women

Figure 6.1. A monstrous ape serves as the backdrop for the opening titles of *Ingagi*. Frame enlargement courtesy of Eric Schaefer. *Copyright © 1930 Congo Pictures.*

were believed to have bizarre sexual cravings and, in general terms, *all* women (white and black) were assumed to desire their primatological ancestors. "Wild Women in Africa" is how one Pressbook story opens: "There are wild women in Africa! Not the kind referred to in some social circles of this country, however! These women are really wild—veritable amazons who dwell in the jungle depths and may be members of a strange tribe which is said to give a woman each year to the gorillas!"[9] Pressbook stories such as this one both reinforce racial differences (the targeted white spectator is meant to assume that the wild women are black natives located in a distant geographical locale) and trouble those differences (in the final analysis, they are wild *women*, merely more extreme versions of white social-circle types).

Because of its alternations between racism against blacks and a more general brand of sexism, *Ingagi* can be read as a paradigmatic pointer of sorts, a film that represents in risqué form what most 1930s jungle cinema depicts behind the mask of white civilization. First, *Ingagi* highlights the narrative function of gorillas, and black men and women, as signifiers of dark jungle depravities. And, second, the film figures all womanhood, in the guise of "wild jungle women," as inextricably linked to darkness and to illicit behaviors and desires.[10] Unlike *Ingagi*, however, most jungle films of the era relegate black women to the margins of the text (if they appear at all) and position white heroines center stage.

In her starring role, the white woman serves as a missing link in her own right—she conjoins the white and black worlds. In a move parallel to her black female counterparts, the white heroine bridges not only species but races as well. She is depicted as both white and not-white, as a double for, and potential romantic partner to, darker humans and animals. Yet, like the horror heroine whose doubling with fiends is always counterposed by victimization at the hands of her monstrous twin, the white heroine is also irrevocably different from her dark suitors—in racial terms she has it both ways.

The generic overlap between 1930s jungle and horror cinema is not restricted to the parallel representations of each genre's heroines. More general similarities between the genres were assumed by a number of critics at the time,[11] as the case of *The Most Dangerous Game* (RKO, 1932) confirms. The only link to supernatural monstrosity in Merian C. Cooper and Ernest B. Schoedsack's jungle film is that it was shot on the same set used for *King Kong* (RKO, 1933). Yet *The Most Dangerous Game* was likened to one of classic horror's first productions in at least one review: "Its theme might be considered by some as distasteful. But in view of what 'Frankenstein' did with a terror theme, this picture, too, may find unanticipated popularity with theatre-goers."[12]

Although classic horror and jungle-adventure cinema share crucial thematic and structural similarities, they also differ in important ways. Horror films often detail, at least at the manifest level, the efforts of heroes to subdue fiends whose existence cannot be explained in rational terms—that is, horror cinema's creatures cannot be destroyed via conventional means. Most jungle-adventure movies, on the other hand, portray the efforts of (usually white) characters to domesticate blacks and jungle creatures with the aid of guns and other "civilized" tools. While both genres deal with figures considered either scientifically or socially monstrous, those scientific and social menaces are dealt with in contrasting ways.

They are also dealt with in different places. Classic horror portrays monsters that must be reckoned with on home turf—fiends either descend upon or are created in England or the United States (or they travel to those countries at some point in the proceedings), and humans are required to resist their invasions, lest their homelands crumble and disappear. Jungle movies, on the other hand, depict events that occur when whites venture away from their Western habitats and confront the beasts that populate the rest of the world. Here, it is the hero who is the physical intruder, not the monster. (In a jungle-horror film, like *King Kong*, both impulses are combined—whites travel through the jungle and a monster wreaks havoc on the West.) Thus, in highlighting the alignment between horror and jungle movies, I am less interested in asserting their complete equivalence than in pinpointing some of the ways in which they share and transform certain structural and thematic conventions, especially those pertaining to gender.

Specifically, my focus is on a selection of early 1930s jungle-horror and jungle-adventure films that portray white women as midpoints between civilization and the jungle and trace the activities of "primitive"—meaning, monstrous, backward, uncivilized, and untamed—males, as in *King Kong*. Kong's exploits on his isolated island are similar to the representations of the jungle and its inhabitants in less obviously monstrous texts. Moreover, Kong's rapport with the white heroine, Ann Darrow (Fay Wray), lays bare the tenuous relationship between race and gender in jungle films. Not only does Ann serve as

Kong's victim, the blonde female who cowers before her simian suitor, she is also aligned with his monstrosity and darkness.

Like other white jungle heroines, Ann serves a contradictory racial function. She both invokes and warns against the monstrous possibility of miscegenation. Here, race is a determining and central trope. Whereas *Ingagi*'s black maidens are presented to audiences as women who do, indeed, mate with and belong to dark jungle animals, white heroines usually only threaten to do so or are rescued at the last minute from their plunge into a nether world of dark desire. At least, the hope is that they are rescued and, in turn, rehabilitated. Like so many horror heroines, then, most white women in jungle films are both conventional icons of female fear and the vehicles through which social boundaries are transgressed. They highlight the supremacy of white males when, as victims of dark creatures, they cry out for heroism. Yet in their own doubling with dark animals and black men, white heroines remind heroes that acts of bravery—and an insistence on racial purity—do not always translate into conquest and supremacy. Boundaries between white and dark, human and animal, are crossed repeatedly in the genre, no matter what white heroes do to keep them intact.[13]

Like *King Kong*, *Ingagi* invokes the threat of a cross-species sexual union in a dark jungle setting. Whereas the lighting in grassland scenes is sunny and bright, the jungle sequences are dark and gloomy. Nude black women in search of their jungle-lover, the gorilla, are hidden by shadows, shrubs, and tree branches. Problems with the lighting and camera work were noted in 1930. While the *New York Times* simply commented on the "extraordinarily bad photography of the film," another reporter noted the shrubbery problem: "The ape women are seen completely naked, but shadowed in a clearing, with the camera's vision obstructed by thickets"[14] (figure 6.2).

While certainly not the original intent of these variations in cinematography and mise-en-scène, the differences between the grassland and jungle scenes suggest an important metaphoric function for the lighting. The grassland sequences are straightforward travelogue images, shots of African animals and vegetation that have nothing to do with the risqué plot of gorillas mating with black women. The grassland scenes, then, are well lit and take place in full view of the audience. Yet because of the staginess of the woman-ape encounters, which were shot expressly for *Ingagi* on a soundstage, and because of the importance of suggesting a taboo cross-species affair, the scenes that depict the wilds of the jungle do so by emphasizing darkness and the *limits* of vision. *Ingagi* permits the viewer to discern only vaguely the bodies of the women who travel through the jungle, while the promised sexual union between ape and black maiden remains forever out of sight.

In the context of *Ingagi*, darkness is a trope for an interspecies brand of racial Otherness and a sign of obstructed vision. Black Africans are conflated with a dark animal, the gorilla, and the white Western eye, via the maker of fake documentary films, provides a blurred view of its cinematic subject. As a signifier of racial and biological difference (i.e., difference from white humans) and as a metaphor for the inadequacy of Western modes of looking, *Ingagi*'s version of darkness recalls the classic horror film. Horror also explores the spectacular and terrifying repercussions of physical differences from the norm. Here, the deformed face of Ivan (Lionel Atwill) in *The Mystery of the Wax Museum* (Warner Bros., 1933) comes to mind, as does the physically grotesque figure of Henry's male-coded monster in *Frankenstein* (Universal, 1931).

Figure 6.2. White explorers peer into jungle shrubbery in an attempt to discern the black maidens as they mate with the gorilla. The bushes, however, obstruct their vision in this still from *Ingagi*. Frame enlargement courtesy of Eric Schaefer. *Copyright © 1930 Congo Pictures.*

But the rapport between *Ingagi* and horror is even more direct: the monstrosity of the dark races has a long heritage in white Western history. According to discourses that endured well into the twentieth century, the darker races are interstitial, bridging the distance between species with little effort. This brand of racism appeared in circus publicity throughout the 1920s and 1930s. In one striking case, a South African man dubbed "Clicko," was put on display for predominantly white audiences and described thus: "He is as near like the ape as he is like the human. . . . We cannot help but wonder if [his captor] Captain Du Barry has not brought Darwin's missing link to civilization."[15] The concept of a missing link, as *Ingagi*'s Pressbook and circus advertisements indicate, was but one means of equating black men and women with monsters.

In the white imagination and mythology, blacks straddle the boundary between human and nonhuman. Like monsters, they are terrifying in their interstitiality, their simultaneous likeness to and difference from the Anglo-Saxon norm, and their very blurring of boundaries that usually remain intact. Like the sexual threat posed by monsters in classic horror, blacks, too, are sexualized in white social discourses. Specifically, black women are deemed sexually excessive, as figured by the Hottentot Venus, and black men are assumed to covet white women.[16] This white fantasy of black male desire informs jungle films. Serving as background figures in white-focused narratives, black men are usually depicted as savages whose supposed interracial urges turn them into monsters.

The narrative position of blacks (and, sometimes, Asians) in jungle movies is both like and unlike the role of monsters in horror. Blacks, especially men, are objects of fear and desire, and icons of physical differences (as is the monster). But in contrast to horror's fiends, blacks are often relegated to secondary roles. In most instances, monstrosity resides not in a single black figure but in the blackness that is attributed to shadows and unseen terrain. Thus, connotations of monstrosity inhere in the jungle itself, which becomes a repository for white racial and sexual anxieties.

The Most Dangerous Game, for example, collapses darkness and monstrosity with the mysterious jungle environs, through which the hero and heroine (played by Joel McCrea and Fay Wray) travel in order to save themselves from an evil hunter named Count Zaroff (Leslie Banks). In the film, the white fiend (Zaroff) is rendered dark through costume—he dresses in black—rather than skin tone. Thus darkness is not equated with a black character, per se, in *The Most Dangerous Game*. Rather, a white character and the jungle itself are represented as dark and therefore evil threats to whiteness. Racism manifests itself in this film's particular approach to color-coding and not in direct portrayals of black Africans (figure 6.3).

Fay Wray plays the part of the white heroine in distress in *The Most Dangerous Game*, a figure who is, or seems to be, diametrically opposed to the fiend that torments her. Thus, although Zaroff is feminized in the film, which doubles him with Wray to some degree, the heroine's most obvious role is to serve as a vulnerable object of desire for both hero and villain. Wray's portrayal of a frightened maiden is, in fact, consonant with most jungle films, which place white heroines in the narrative and visual forefront, where they are subjected to the advances of dark creatures of the jungle. Frequently possessing blonde hair and shot through filters that enhance their light skin, heroines are representatives of white womanhood and confirmations of white manhood. According to Paul Hoch, the heroine is an archetype of white culture: "The conquest of manhood by the victory of the white godlike hero over the bestial villain in a life or death struggle for possession of what Robert Graves has called 'The White Goddess' is . . . at the heart of almost all Western myth, poetry and literature."[17]

Hoch argues that saving the white goddess is the hero's urgent calling, given the unrepressible forces of sexual evolution: "The white goddess was clearly in danger; her would-be attackers were supermasculine black beasts. Sexuality itself was inherently male and bestial: a drive always thrusting up from lower males to higher females, and originating from the beasts (or 'beast') below" (51). While the rapport between the white goddess and black beast takes form in jungle movies, it is a more complex relationship than a battle between white (good) versus black (evil) archetypes.

This is true especially given the assumptions about uncontrollable black male and pure white female sexuality that mark social histories in the United States. White fears of black male sexual aggression against white women were, not surprisingly, manufactured by whites themselves—first, to justify the physical and sexual abuse of blacks during slavery and, second, to defend lynching as punishment to fit a heinous crime.[18] According to Angela Y. Davis: "Before lynching could be consolidated as a popularly accepted institution . . . its savagery and its horrors had to be convincingly justified. These were the

Figure 6.3. Fay Wray and Joel McCrea cringe in the lower left-hand corner of this poster for *The Most Dangerous Game*, while Count Zaroff's (Leslie Banks) enlarged eyes fill the upper portion of the image. As in the hypnosis subgenre, RKO placed the fiend's menacing gaze at the center of its marketing. Photo courtesy of Ronald V. Borst/Hollywood Movie Posters. *Copyright © 1932 RKO.*

circumstances that spawned the myth of the Black rapist . . . for the rape charges turned out to be the most powerful of several attempts to justify the lynching of Black people."[19] Although research by the Southern Commission on the Study of Lynching found that of the black men who were lynched between 1889 and 1929 only a handful were even accused of rape, the myth of the black rapist grounds and perpetuates violence against African-American men (Davis 189).

The mythological flip side of the black beast, the white goddess, was also constructed with care in the 1930s. For example, the presiding judge in the Scottsboro trial of 1931, in which nine black youths were accused and convicted of raping two white girls, had the following to say about the relationship between white women and black rapists: "Where the woman charged to have been raped is, as in this case a white woman, there is a strong presumption under the law that she would not and did not yield to intercourse with the defendant, a

Negro; and this is true, whatever the station in life the prosecutrix may occupy, whether she be the most despised, ignorant and abandoned woman of the community, or the spotless virgin and daughter of a prominent home of luxury and learning."[20] According to the white judge, no white woman, regardless of class, education, or desire, would have sex willingly with a black man.

Given the ways in which the relationship between black men and white women has been constructed in United States history and mythology, it is hardly surprising that the role of white heroines in jungle films is coded in racial terms. White actresses invoke an age-old rape fantasy and recast historical realities. In the history of American race relations, especially during slavery, black women were victims of white rapes, attacks that occurred within the geographical borders of the United States. As indicated by jungle movies, however, white women fall prey to black creatures in the wilds of Africa, far from the racial dynamics of their homeland.

From this perspective, jungle films are products of displacement and projection. White male guilt is conferred upon black men and white women endure terrors experienced historically by black (and white) women. Race and gender remain central tropes, but they are configured as inversions of historical events. Despite the appeals of this reading, it streamlines the frequent ambiguity of the genre's portrayals. While jungle movies rely upon the immutability of racial difference—blacks and the jungle are threatening to and different from whites—many films also challenge that racial and spatial separation, especially via white women. That is, white characters may sometimes pass as white in jungle movies, but they often possess hearts of darkness.[21]

I turn now to the white heroine's racial mobility to address the ways in which the genre both depends upon racial difference and explodes it inadvertently from within. In addition to her functions as icon of civilization and victim of black aggression, the white heroine bridges the black and white races. Just as classic horror's female leads are midpoints between humanness and monstrosity, the jungle film's white heroine is a mediator between the worlds of the white and the black man.[22] Like the Negro's function in white discourses (bridging simians with humans), the white woman has an interstitial role. She poses a threat of interspecies and interracial union and introduces the possibility that the darkness attributed to the "out there" of the jungle also inhabits the "in here" of the white domain.

By noting that the white heroine serves a mediative racial function, I risk repeating an oversight in some white feminist writings: the conflation of racism with sexism.[23] I do not want to reproduce that error here. Rather, I am interested in studying the moments of convergence between race and gender in these films. White women and black women are not the same, nor do they occupy identical positions in Western social discourses, but they are portrayed as similar in certain jungle movies. In fact, that similarity reinforces the ambiguous position of white women in dominant Western discourses of race and gender—while they are inferior compared to white men, they are also positioned as superior when placed next to black men and women.

In an article on cinematic representations of race, Mary Ann Doane describes the similarities between white and black women in Western patriarchal discourses. According to Doane, "what the representational affinity [between white and black women] seems to indicate is a strong fear that white women are always on the verge of 'slipping back' into a blackness comparable to prostitution. The white woman would be the weak point in the system, the signifier of the always tenuous hold of civilization."[24] In many jungle films, the white heroine represents the racial and sexual mobility remarked upon by Doane—the heroine signifies that whiteness is not only under attack by black jungle creatures, it is also under threat from within. As a woman, the white heroine's racial position is, then, precarious.

Thus, any attempt to analyze the heroine in jungle movies means looking at the ways in which *white* is a racial construct. Yet, as Richard Dyer laments, a heritage of white Western supremacy has posited whiteness as the norm. As a result, asserts Dyer, it often appears in social discourses as if "white is not anything really, not an identity, not a particularising quality, because it is everything—white is no colour because it is all colours."[25] In spite of Dyer's claims, the jungle heroine threatens to blur traditional racial barriers—her interstitial role implies that whiteness is not only open to analysis, it is also a mask of sorts, an identity worn by the heroine. If true, and the heroine's racial membership is unstable at best, the repercussions for white manhood are profound. Like classic horror cinema, which often relishes the ineptitude of male leads, many jungle films portray the failure of white heroism. By representing men who often attempt vainly to save heroines from their initiation into the world of blacks and apes, these films threaten to do away with heroes and their brand of whiteness altogether. The underlying threat of these movies, then, is that white heroes are extremely vulnerable in the jungle and, even more troubling, they seem to be rather dispensable.

It is wrong, therefore, to assume that jungle films are only fantasies about black male aggression against white women, or that they are simply white male projections of illicit desire. Although the latter perspective is supported by the Tarzan films, in which the white hero is literally cast as an "ape-man," as well as by a number of critical analyses of *King Kong*,[26] in a range of jungle movies the heroine is more than just a victim of dark creatures—she is also doubled with them. Jungle fiends do not *always* or *only* stand in for white or black males. Apes and black men also signify all the white man imagines he is not but should be, as well as all he believes white women desire and resemble.

II

The sight of a white woman foraging through the depths of the jungle was a showman's dream in the early 1930s. That dream reached new heights in 1931 with the release of MGM's box-office hit, *Trader Horn*. Directed by W. S. Van Dyke, the movie fictionalizes the story of a white woman adopted by a black tribe. Based on the reminiscences of Alfred Aloysius Horn, the film portrays tales from the African hunter's popular biography written by Ethelreda Lewis in 1927.[27] The cinematic adaptation has the structure and content of a travelogue, but is punctuated at key moments by scenes that forward the white woman plot. Documentary and fiction are intertwined in *Trader Horn*, with the latter assuming increasing importance as the film progresses.

Trader Horn's promotional campaign boasted a wilderness setting with white hunters in pursuit of a jungle woman—a white woman cast as a monster of sorts.[28] As one poster from Los Angeles announces: "TONIGHT YOU MEET THE CRUELEST WOMAN IN ALL AFRICA."[29] The film's Pressbook is filled with advertisements that proclaim the vicious white woman theme: "SEE THE WHITE GODDESS OF THE JUNGLE—AS SHE RULES WITH THE WHIP OVER PAGAN TRIBES" and "SHE RULED A NATION OF SAVAGES," are two excellent examples. The "Catchlines" section of the Pressbook expands the promotional angles: e.g., "AFRICA IN HER GRIMMEST MOMENTS IN THIS ASTOUNDING DRAMA"; "THE DRAMA OF WHITE MEN BATTLING THE SAVAGE ELEMENTS OF THE

DARK CONTINENT"; "ROMANCE IN SPOTS WHERE NO WHITE MAN EVER TROD BEFORE"; and "TWO TRADERS AND A WHITE JUNGLE GODDESS IN AN ADVENTURE THAT WILL LEAVE YOU BREATHLESS"[30] (figure 6.4).

Trader Horn follows the adventures of the intrepid explorer Horn (Harry Carey), his black servant Renchero (Mutia Omoolu), and a young man making his first trip to Africa, Peru (Duncan Renaldo). The explorers and their servants travel through the jungle viewing indigenous wildlife and confronting untamed beasts. Well into the travelogue portion of the film, the group meets Edith Trend (Olive Golden), a missionary searching for her daughter Nina (Edwina Booth), who was stolen from her when a tribe attacked and killed her husband twenty years earlier. Trend asks Horn to vow that he will locate Nina if she cannot. Later, when Trend's dead body is discovered, Horn, Peru, and their entourage set out to locate the girl.

One of the most striking aspects of this film is Peru's transformation once he meets Nina. Before his encounter with the white woman of the jungle, Peru is naive, frightened, and an outright coward (he climbs up a tree when a rhinoceros attacks the group, while Horn faces the beast bravely). Moreover, his relationship with Horn is homoerotic (as Horn notes early in the film when he and Peru paddle their way down a jungle river: "Sometimes, of course, it's better if two fellas run away together"). Once Nina appears and rescues Horn and Peru from tribal sacrifice, Peru drops his effeminate persona and becomes heroic. Thus, while Peru once frightened himself when he fired his rifle at a crocodile and missed, he now endures Nina's repeated slaps after he touches her without permission. The new, improved Peru does not wince, nor does he run away. Instead, the mere sight of a young white woman, albeit an aggressive and monstrous one, brings out his macho, if masochistic, side.

From a conventional perspective, Peru's renunciation of cowardice and homosocial proclivities corresponds to Nina's loss of jungle power. Peru's heroism depends not only on rescuing a white woman (he is given the task of taking Nina through the jungle while Horn and Renchero distract the natives) but also on Nina's transformation from the cruelest woman in Africa to the prototypical white heroine in distress.[31] Although Peru seems heroic and Nina distraught by the conclusion, the ending is far from reassuring. As John S. Cohen Jr. phrased it in his 1932 review: "As a finale, there is a close-up of the Trader gazing rather nostalgically at the steamer that is car-

rying away his young friend, and his bride—his bride who, one instinctively felt, was going to be as difficult a problem for civilization as any current economic one."[32]

You can take the girl out of the jungle, reporters suggested, but you cannot take the jungle out of the girl. "The white girl who had become the ferocious goddess of the savages,"[33] is how Richard Watts Jr. described Nina in the *New York Herald Tribune*. The *New York Sun*'s reporter went a step further and noted that "she had grown into a tribal chieftainess who was more cannibalish than the festooned cannibals around her."[34] According to Mordaunt Hall in the *New York Times*, Nina was "quite as ferocious as any of the blacks,"[35] and Richard Murray thought that "Edwina Booth fairly exudes cruelty as 'the cruelest woman in Africa.'"[36] It is hard to imagine that Nina's coupling with Peru and her departure from the jungle in which she had lived her entire life could exorcise the bestial and savage qualities remarked upon by reporters. Nina may look like a traditional

Figure 6.5. Trader Horn (Harry Carey) bids Peru (Duncan Renaldo) good luck as he attempts to save the heroine in distress, Nina (Edwina Booth), from the savage natives. Renchero (Mutia Omoolu), Horn's servant—who ends up being much more heroic than Peru—looks on. Photo courtesy of the Academy of Motion Picture Arts and Sciences. *Copyright © 1931 Turner Entertainment Co. All rights reserved.*

(white) woman at the conclusion, but there is no guarantee that her darker, savage qualities are a thing of the past (figure 6.5).

The theme of the white woman in the jungle reached new heights when the *Motion Picture Herald* printed reviews and full-page advertisements announcing *The Blonde Captive*. Banking on the lure of miscegenation, Louis King's picture went a step further than *Trader Horn* and promised exhibitors a spectacle of vast proportions in the spring of 1932. "THE BLONDE CAPTIVE WHO CHOSE TO REMAIN WITH HER PRIMITIVE MATE!" heralded the publicity layout in April.[37] By May, the posters had become more risqué, the lure of sexual depravity more explicit. Depicting a drawing of a topless blonde woman staring longingly at the fierce, war-painted, and partially clad black man who drags her across the bottom of the page, the cutline promises: "AN ABSOLUTELY AMAZING AUTHENTIC ADVENTURE."[38] In fine print, the

Figure 6.6. The white woman may look distraught as her jungle lover drags her across the bottom of this advertisement for *The Blonde Captive*, but the cutline proclaims that she "CHOSE TO REMAIN WITH HER PRIMITIVE MATE!" Photo courtesy of the Academy of Motion Picture Arts and Sciences. *Copyright © 1932 Capital Films.*

same advertisement boasted huge audiences in New York, Chicago, and Washington, D.C., drawing "raves from critics and crowds." By the end of June, the heroine's complicity was announced: "A WHITE WOMAN LIVING WITH HER CAVE MAN MATE—AND REFUSING TO BE RESCUED! ABSOLUTELY AUTHENTIC TRUE"[39] (figures 6.6 and 6.7).

Even more than *Trader Horn, The Blonde Captive*'s campaign was built around the interstitial qualities I have outlined in section I of this chapter. Playing on a range of themes, such as the union of a white woman with a black male, and the heroine's simultaneous attraction to and repulsion from her monstrous primate lover, King's picture promises to fulfill the moviegoer's curiosity about miscegenation and a primitive lifestyle. It also vows to upset the narrative convention so dear to many jungle movies, including *Trader Horn*— namely, the rescue of the white woman from the dark world. In *The*

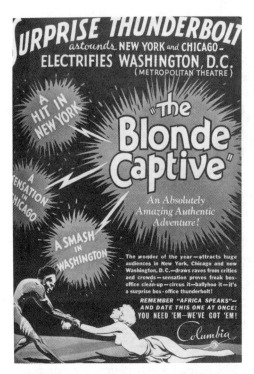

Figure 6.7. The white woman's body is both contrasted and doubled with her darker captor's physique—his body is elaborately marked, hers is blemish-free—yet both their bodies are spectacles of nudity. Photo courtesy of the Academy of Motion Picture Arts and Sciences. *Copyright © 1932 Capital Films.*

Blonde Captive, the publicity announced, the heroine refuses her real racial role and remains at the side of her jungle husband instead. Like the infamous Kong who appeared the following year, the blonde woman's captor is dark, backwards, aggressive, and alluring. His victim is both horrified and enamored by the prospect of being held by him.

The Blonde Captive and *Trader Horn* were situated squarely within the era's racial dynamics. For the 1920s and 1930s were contradictory periods in the history of white perceptions of African Americans. In some sectors, blacks were raised to the position of cultural icons: "In the 1920s a revised form of romantic racialism became something of a national fad, resulting in part, curiously enough, from patronizing white encouragement of the 'New Negro' movement and the 'Harlem Renaissance.' 'The New Negro,' as perceived by many whites, was simply a patina of the cultural primitivism and exoticism fashionable in the 1920s" (Fredrickson 327).

As George Fredrickson notes, there was a paternalistic elevation of African-American culture, especially music, by white liberals. Yet the decade also marked the resurgence of Ku Klux Klan membership, especially in Southern and midwestern cities.[40] By the beginning of the 1930s American society was engaged in a full-fledged racial battle. 1931 marked the year of the Scottsboro case, the rape trial mentioned earlier. The importance of the trial within American culture cannot be overestimated. It was publicized and debated in newspapers across the country and highlighted the nation's racial fissures.

The Blonde Captive was released into this setting. By promoting a skewed version of the Scottsboro case—the advertisements promise the story of a white woman ravaged *willingly* by a dark man—publicity rode on the racial current of the day and constructed black men as monstrous. Yet the film is not a simple reflection of the Scottsboro trial. Instead, *The Blonde Captive* takes up the racial issues of the day and twists them into a tale of white female desire designed to pique audience curiosity. The movie is, then, but one discourse among many in which racist assumptions emerged, but in a contradictory fashion. Tempered by its international scope (it is set in Australia and surrounding islands), the producers exploited racial prejudice in their address to white America. *The Blonde Captive* not only gives voice to some of the era's racial conflicts, it also transforms those conflicts into a selling ploy.

By explicitly painting the heroine's relationship to her jungle-lover as ambiguous, the publicity underscores an element only implied in other movies—namely, the white woman's similarity to her black husband. In the advertisements for the film, the chief is depicted as a victimizer (he drags the white woman along the ground), a racial Other (the darkness of his skin is visually contrasted with the lightness of hers), and a site of physical difference from whites (the skin of his body is elaborately marked in some advertisements, while the woman's body is blemish-free). As the second and third attributes indicate, the woman signifies whiteness, the racial standard against which her suitor is judged to be different. The importance of her race is confirmed within the film, in which the narrator takes note of her identity repeatedly. Here are three brief selections: "she is a white woman," "daughter of the lordly caucasian," and "there's nothing neanderthal about her."[41]

Yet the heroine is also racially unstable in the advertisements. Like the black man whose bare chest and legs are depicted in full view, so, too, is the blonde woman a spectacle of nudity. Furthermore, as the cutlines intone, she refuses to be rescued and stays with her mate in the wilderness. Thus, the white heroine is simultaneously like and unlike her monstrous jungle man. Her ambiguous racial status was suggested in reviews. The *Variety* reporter made the following comment: "She is undeniably of the Caucasian race in face and physical contour . . . though a heavy tan causes her to resemble a native as to color."[42] Mordaunt Hall, writing for the *New York Times,* was even less clear in terms of race: "[Her] skin is *relatively* white" (emphasis added).[43]

I think *The Blonde Captive* is fascinating for two main reasons; first, its advertising campaign was, as I have indicated, remarkably explicit and, second, its publicized narrative was fabricated. The film's promotional efforts literally turned *The Blonde Captive*, which is a staid and predictable travelogue set in Hawaii, Bali, Samoa, Fiji, New Zealand, and Australia, into the story of a white woman found shipwrecked among Australian Aborigines. The movie is an excellent example of what John Ellis calls a "narrative image": "the direct publicity created by the film's distributors and producers; [and] the general public knowledge of ingredients involved in the film."[44]

The film opens on a group of white men at The Explorers Club. Flipping through a book entitled *Men of the Stone Age,* one of the explorers describes a prehistoric male with ridges over his eyes. "This is what Mrs. Neanderthal had opposite her at the breakfast table every morning," the man intones, as an insert of a prehistoric male fills the frame. The men then decide to pursue the rumor that a Neanderthal still lives in contemporary Australia, and the setting shifts to Hawaii. Although the posters promise a narrative of vast proportions, that story is only briefly told. Instead, the viewer is treated to documentary footage of native peoples on various islands and presented with a smattering of animal tales, such as a turtle hunt.

The closest the film gets to a story of white female captivity follows the late and unlikely discovery of a blonde boy amidst a group of native children. After the boy is singled out, an Aboriginal man is shown wearing women's underwear. The narrator (Lowell Thomas) gingerly remarks that the inquisitive explorers followed the man only to discover a woman with light hair standing in front of his cave. Despite the narrator's claims that the woman is between the ages of thirty and thirty-five, and that she is white, the mop of gray hair on her head looks like a wig and the darkness of her skin suggests that she might be an older black woman posing as Caucasian. While the narrator notes that she has blue eyes, no close-ups confirm this claim. Though informed that she does not want to return to her white home, the spectator never hears her utter a word. The film ends with this anticlimactic scenario and the narrator's pronouncement that the white woman "seems almost as primitive and simple-minded as the Aborigines."

Despite the claims to truth suggested by the film's posters, the story met with skepticism in 1932. The *Liberty* reviewer noted that "you get a few glimpses of a middle-aged and far from prepossessing woman with bushy white hair. . . . Is all this authentic?"[45] Mordaunt Hall was so perplexed by the segment in question that he cited a quotation from a cable sent to the Liberty Theatre in New York City by the head of the film expedition (as a means of proving veracity): "I hereby certify that story of ship-wrecked white woman rescued or adopted by blacks is based on facts."[46] The precise circumstances surrounding *The Blonde Captive* will never be known. Unlike *Ingagi*, the film avoided an official inquiry, perhaps, because the theme of a white woman mating illicitly with a black man was so embedded in the white American psyche as to be completely believable (despite clues that indicate the sequence is constructed).[47]

The Blonde Captive is an excellent example of a film that trades in the rhetoric of jungle movies, invokes the risqué and monstrous lures of miscegenation, places a white woman between the black and white worlds, and revels in promised rewards that are never fulfilled (such as the *sight* of a white woman mating with a black man). It is unclear to what extent the film's narrative image, its publicized subject matter, accounted for its popularity with audiences. Undoubtedly, the image contributed in some fashion to the film's success with predominantly white viewers in 1932. But part of its success may have also been linked to the sliding of racial identities that is both portrayed (the blonde boy is identified as half-white and half-black) and implied in *The Blonde Captive* (the woman is said to be white but she does not look white).

1932 was a banner year for large- and small-budget jungle films. In addition to *The Blonde Captive*, MGM released the first of a series of Tarzan movies, which was most popular among teens, according to the trades, and Monarch Pictures debuted the fantasy-jungle film, *The Savage Girl*. Each of these movies focuses on the convergence of the white with black races via an intermediary figure—in *Trader Horn*, *The Blonde Captive*, and *The Savage Girl* a white woman is at home in the jungle, and in *Tarzan, the Ape Man* (MGM, 1932) the story centers on a white man raised by gorillas.[48]

While Tarzan achieved fame in American popular culture, the white jungle women who haunted the cinema in the 1930s have disappeared into historical archives. Although *Trader Horn* was a box-office hit and *The Savage Girl* depicted a female version of the ape-man, Edwina Booth and Rochelle Hudson's starring roles did not lodge themselves in the vernacular for decades. Despite their relative obscurity next to Johnny Weissmuller's films, however, *Trader Horn* and *The Savage Girl* are crucial texts when it comes to the relationship between race and gender in 1930s jungle movies.[49]

The Savage Girl (directed by Harry Fraser) depicts the white heroine as both an object of desire for the white hero and a character aligned with forces that threaten the masculinity and racial stability of white men.[50] Although the film does little in the way of constructing blacks as evil until its closing scenes, *The Savage Girl* pays a great deal of attention to the heroine's interstitial role. With an approach less somber than most other jungle narratives, the movie reinforces and streamlines terrors attributed to blacks and takes pains to return the white heroine to her "proper" racial and sexual domain. Like *Trader Horn*, however, the effort to restore whiteness to a state of imagined supremacy is far from convincing.

The plot of *The Savage Girl* is as follows: like the white goddess of *Trader Horn*, the heroine was born and raised in the wilds of the jungle. When white hunters enter her home, led by the hero-explorer Jim Franklyn (Walter Byron), The Girl (her character's name in the credits) is torn between two worlds—the domain of animals and the world of white people. The Girl recognizes her racial similarity to Franklyn near the beginning of the film. That recognition is figured simultaneously as a fear of whiteness (she identifies with her dark, animal compatriots against him) and as a signifier of her loss of status within the jungle (she begins to desire the hero).

The tension between the heroine's double perspective in the film, as jungle inhabitant and white woman, finds expression in point-of-view structures. When Franklyn arrives he is warned of the Jungle Goddess. Here, the jungle is linked to a female presence that is threatening (the natives will protect her at all costs) and ephemeral (she comes and goes unnoticed). Thus, the environs are identified as dark and feminine, an identity personified by The Girl. Further-more, she is one of the few characters who has an active gaze in the movie. On two separate occasions, she hides behind shrubbery and watches the white hunters from afar as they remain unaware of her presence.

Although given the power to look freely in the film, The Girl does not avoid capture. After rescuing a lion from its cage early in the movie, she is shown talking to a chimpanzee. A stream of light suf-fuses her features, and there is a cut to her point of view of a mirror and a necklace, which the hunters have placed on a tree branch to lure jungle animals. Drawn by the light, she falls into the hunter's trap. From this moment onward, The Girl becomes an object of desire for white men. It is noteworthy that her transition to a state of being looked at is achieved with the aid of a mirror, a sign of female narcissism. In a sense, when The Girl sees her own reflection, she takes up a traditional racial and sexual role: she becomes a white heroine (figure 6.8).

Figure 6.8. The Girl (Rochelle Hudson) cowers in the corner of a hut as Franklyn (Walter Byron), Vernuth (Adolph Millar), and Amos P. Stitch (Harry Myers) assess their captive creature in *The Savage Girl.* Frame enlargement cour-tesy of Eric Schaefer. *Copyright © 1932 Monarch Pictures.*

Her loss of freedom and entrapment among white men fosters behavior more in keeping with the conventions of white femininity and heterosexuality than with the wilds of the jungle. The film closes with The Girl and Franklyn embracing, thus ensuring that traditional behavior is privileged. Yet despite the conclusion, *The Savage Girl* leaves elements of the storyline at loose ends. Although The Girl and Franklyn are in love, she still does not know his language or understand his world. Given her lifelong indoctrination into the ways of the jungle—such as her ability to speak to animals and to survive in the wilderness—a few days with a white hunter seem feeble promise of a future in the West. In fact, the titles of the promotional articles and the catchlines in the film's Pressbook indicate that *The Savage Girl* was marketed on the premise that The Girl could *not* be tamed. Here are two samples: "BEAUTIFUL WHITE 'SAVAGE GIRL' MORE DANGEROUS THAN WILD BEASTS"; and "TWO WHITE MEN AND A SAVAGE BEAUTY." One advertisement went so far as to claim that the heroine is so primitive that she threatens to enslave the men who pursue her: "THE SAVAGE GIRL—WHITE!—BEAUTIFUL!—ALONE!—MEN HUNTED HER DOWN—AND BECAME . . . HER SLAVE!"[51]

Furthermore, Franklyn is a less than heroic figure in the film; he is a white man who cannot gain mastery. He is feminized by serving as an object of a woman's gaze in *The Savage Girl*, and he is not an active gazer. The only white man given free rein to set his sights on others throughout the movie is the villain, Vernuth (Adolph Millar), who is killed at the conclusion. Thus, while he facilitates The Girl's transition to white womanhood, Franklyn also functions as an object of desire. In one scene in particular, The Girl sneaks into the camp, stands outside Franklyn's tent, watches him, and, finally, sneaks in to get a closer look. Although Franklyn returns her gaze eventually, he is objectified by her for an extended period—meaning he is placed in the narrative and visual role usually occupied by heroines in Hollywood cinema. Later, when Vernuth helps black villagers attack Franklyn's expedition, the hero's helplessness is reinforced. He is tied to a stake and prepared for sacrifice. Although rescued at the last minute, Franklyn is ineffective in his efforts to protect The Girl from her attackers. In the end, a jungle animal, and not the hero, dispatches Vernuth and saves the heroine.

Like *The Savage Girl* and *Trader Horn*, a number of other jungle films of the era combine white female interstitiality with romance. *Four Frightened People* (Paramount, 1934), *Her Jungle Love* (Paramount,

1938), *The Most Dangerous Game* (RKO, 1932), and *White Hunter* (Fox, 1936), for example, associate awakening female sexuality with white women who make their way through the jungle. The combination of three elements—white femininity, jungle darkness, and white masculinity-under-threat—facilitates the heroine's transition from female sexual innocence to knowledge in these films. Her transformation is effected via her temporary, yet compelling, indoctrination into jungle environments and her close rapport with jungle creatures.

Merian C. Cooper, who codirected *The Most Dangerous Game* and *King Kong* with Ernest B. Schoedsack, had the following to say about the relationship between women and the jungle: "Woman has retained, fortunately, the fighting, dominant blood of the savage. . . . She would have perished as a distinctive individual long ago had it not been for her savage strain which has always given her the impetus of fighting for her own rights. This quality can be found in the most fragile of women. For a long time I always thought that 'the most dangerous game' naturally would be one in which a woman was involved."[52] Cooper's conflation of all women with savages, whether a publicity stunt or an honest opinion, suggests that the interstitial roles of white jungle heroines were quite consciously employed in the early 1930s, at least by the era's most famous jungle filmmaker.

A similar conflation emerges in *Four Frightened People*, in which the jungle aids Judith Jones (Claudette Colbert) in her efforts to change from a homely school teacher to an object of desire for two white men. Forced to desert their ship when cholera breaks out on board, a small band of survivors, including Jones, hikes through the jungle in search of civilization. The impact of the journey on Colbert's character is profound. Her emerging sexual attractiveness is explicitly linked to her ability to adapt to the jungle and to its mysterious and frightening ways. In fact, she becomes increasingly aggressive and independent as she moves further into the wilderness, thus putting Cooper's beliefs into practice. The environment itself, not only its black inhabitants, precipitates her transformation. Her older female companion (played by Mary Boland) is also sexually awakened in the process. She is taken prisoner by a jungle tribe and enjoys an offscreen affair with the chief. It is noteworthy that the white women's transformation in *Four Frightened People* occurs once their "half breed" guide,[53] played by Leo Carrillo, perishes. It is as if Colbert and Boland take up Carrillo's interracial role. They occupy the same position he did before he perished—they are the midpoint between the dark and white races.

III

In her fascinating book *Primate Visions,* Donna Haraway notes that before World War II, Western nations, including the United States, Germany, and France supported primate research projects intent upon discovering the scientific forces of evolution. In those projects, notes Haraway, blacks, white women, and animals are collapsed in fantasy, as well as in the working conditions of experiments.[54] The linkage of the terms *race, sex,* and *species,* which Haraway traces in primatological discourses, is a reminder that their convergence in American jungle films of the 1930s is part of an historical continuum.

In her analysis of primatological research, Haraway summarizes the efforts of taxidermist and ape hunter, Carl Akeley, which culminated in the debut of his African Hall in the New York Museum of Natural History in 1936. Throughout the teens and twenties, Akeley conducted jungle expeditions intended to find and preserve, through taxidermy, the greatest beasts of the jungle. He adhered to the Darwinian assumption that the gorilla is the human forefather, and thus spent years trying to shoot the perfect specimen (with both a camera and a gun). Despite his destruction of apes and other animals, Akeley claimed that he wanted to make hunting less attractive. His brand of killing, he maintained, was different from others because he preserved the animals for educational purposes.

According to his rather odd logic, Akeley took white women on his gorilla expeditions as a means of dissuading hunting among white men. Like Carl Denham (Robert Armstrong), the film director who employed Ann Darrow to be his lead actress in *King Kong,* Akeley invited white women to the jungle so that they could play a part. But, unlike Ann, whose rehearsed performances required that she exhibit terror when confronted with a monstrous ape, Akeley's intent was for women to become fearless hunters. According to Haraway, his thinking ran as follows: "The best thing to reduce the potency of game for heroic huntings is to demonstrate that inexperienced women could safely do the same thing" (34). Akeley relied on contradictory logic: white women are aligned with aggressive male behavior and given free rein to interact with fierce gorillas, yet their ability to aggress feminizes the sport, rendering it less attractive to white men and implying that women do not need protection from apes.

While Akeley tried to use white women as hunters in order to make expeditions less appealing, jungle-adventure and classic horror films relish the white woman's terrifying encounter with an ape. That encounter is utilized in two primary ways: (1) to align heroines with the dark creatures of the jungle (white women do not need to be saved because they are similar to, and desire, their dark aggressors); and (2) to position white women in a more conventional role (heroines are incapable of defending themselves and must be saved from their racial and primatological inferiors).

Akeley's jungle efforts are important to the consideration of *King Kong*. First, the particular ape he was most committed to preserving resembles the oversized gorilla that approaches Ann on-screen. As Haraway asserts: "There existed an image of an animal which was somehow *the* gorilla. . . . That particular tone of perfection could only be heard in the male mode" (emphasis in original; 41). In a sense, the seeds of curiosity and heterosexual romance that find form in the cross-species union of *King Kong* are part of Akeley's expeditions in the first two decades of the century. For Akeley and *King Kong*'s directors, a white woman/male ape alliance is most desirable. Second, just as *King Kong* privileges the specular realm (Carl Denham goes to the jungle to *film* Kong and directs Ann's responses to the *sight* of the gorilla before she meets him), so, too, do Akeley's efforts as a taxidermist focalize the visual realm: his apes are stuffed for an inquisitive human gaze.

But, in addition to Kong's larger dimensions, there is a significant difference between the display of Akeley's apes in the African Hall and the representation of the gorilla in *King Kong*. For the African Hall is haunted by the absence of the ape's physical movement and engagement with spectators. Although the stuffed animals at the Museum of Natural History are meant to provide the illusion that they are alive, the setting also confirms that they are not, that their threats to the white race—especially its women—are, in the final analysis, denied the museum goer.

From this perspective, the jungle-horror film, and *King Kong* in particular, negotiates sensationally the relationship between the specular surveillance of the jungle beast and the risqué encounter between a white woman and a gorilla—a creature that, unlike Akeley's stuffed animals, moves, and moves her, in more ways than one. While the convergence of women and apes in the study of primatology was limited by the requisites of science and propriety (their union could only go so far), *King Kong* lets that relationship loose in a filmic fantasy. (Yet in the censorship era of the 1930s the film was also subject to con-

Figure 6.9. A partially clad Ann Darrow (Fay Wray) acts the part of a frightened heroine to an unseen threat in this publicity still from *King Kong*. Photo courtesy of the Academy of Motion Picture Arts and Sciences. *Copyright © 1933 RKO Pictures, Inc. Used by permission of Turner Entertainment Co. All rights reserved.*

temporary social mores. By the end of the decade, the scene in which the ape removes Ann's clothes was cut from most prints.)

Like Akeley's African Hall, the cinema portrays the ape as a spectacle of vast proportions. Yet, unlike the museum's one-way setup, *King Kong* relies on the beast returning the looks offered by his on-screen spectators, especially Ann. The exchange of looks between monster and heroine unleashes female fear in *King Kong* and introduces the viewer to Ann's stock-in-trade: an ear-piercing scream. As Louella O. Parsons noted in 1933: "Miss Wray's chief duty is to scream and scream and scream, and this she does most effectively."[55] More recently, Calvin T. Beck confirms Wray's vocal powers: "One of the picture's magnetic attractions is the fact that Ann Darrow, once she's seen Kong, never seems to stop screaming."[56]

Like the heroine's displays of terror in other classic horror movies, the female scream is central to jungle-horror, and Wray's contributions should not be underestimated. Anthony Ambrogio elaborates: "Monsters just get excited when women scream, and this is where Fay Wray came in. Nobody did it better than Fay Wray."[57] While the female scream, as Ambrogio asserts, excites monsters, its function in *King Kong* is much more complex than serving solely as a signifier of female fear. As in mad-doctor movies, Wray's bouts of terror are connected directly to spectacle and performance. After all, her character, Ann Darrow, is cast as an actress who *plays the part* of a heroine terrified of a jungle fiend (figure 6.9).

In *The Philosophy of Horror*, Noël Carroll cites *King Kong* as proof that the emotions of horror's audiences parallel those of characters who confront monsters: "In the classic film *King Kong*, for example, there is a scene on the ship during the journey to Skull Island in which the fictional director, Carl Denham, stages a screen test for Ann Darrow. . . . The off-screen motivations that Denham supplies his starlet can be taken as a set of instructions for the way both Ann Darrow and the audience are to react to the first apparition of Kong" (PH 17). According to Carroll, Denham provides the audience with directions on how to be horrified. As Denham's offscreen voice instructs Ann: "Now you look higher. You're amazed. Your eyes open wider. It's horrible, Ann, but you can't look away. There's no chance for you, Ann, no escape. You're helpless, Ann, helpless. There's just one chance. If you can scream, but your throat's paralyzed. Scream, Ann, cry. Perhaps if you didn't see it you could scream. Throw your arms across your face and scream. Scream for your life." Ann is an obedient and responsive actress. She plays the part of the victim to an unseen horror with verve. And, with Denham's final direction, she lets out the film's first bloodcurdling Fay Wray scream.

There are, I think, several ways to read this scene in addition to its provision of emotional advice to viewers. The sequence is simultaneously a metaphor for the male director's function in horror cinema, a lesson in the necessity of instructing heroines on how to react to monsters, and a reminder that female terror is coded theatrically in classic films. The first function of the scene, Denham's sadistic control of Ann, is put into practice by his screen directions. He decides her thespian responses as an omniscient offscreen voice to which she responds obediently. He does, in this sense, call the shots.

Yet Denham's prescriptive role underscores the constructed aspect of Ann's fear, the artificiality of the responses she delivers. The mere need for Denham to tell Ann what her reactions are, to decide her every move in advance, suggests a skepticism about her willingness, or ability, to react as ordered *unless* he tells her to do so. The scene implies that, left to her own devices, Ann may not have responded to Kong in the same way. It follows that her reaction when she meets the creature is a protracted version of the performance rehearsed on the ship. She looks down, looks up and sees Kong, cannot scream, and, finally, screams bloody murder.

The rehearsal of Ann's terrified reactions on the ship's deck in advance of her meeting with the monster underscores the importance of female fear to *King Kong* and suggests that the heroine's traditional gender behavior is a performance of sorts. Here, I want to repeat a quotation I included in chapter 1, in an effort to draw out the highly theatricalized dimensions of Wray's screaming endeavors and emphasize the ways in which conventional gender traits—female fear in this instance—are used as overwrought and potentially self-reflexive generic tropes. In a review of *King Kong* in 1933, *Variety*'s reporter described Wray's role as "a 96-minute screaming session for her, too much for any actress and any audience." The writer then linked the film's lack of credibility to Wray's screams: "Another of the unbelievable facts is that Kong shouldn't drop her and look for a non-screamer—even if he has to settle for a brunet [sic]."[58] By suggesting that Kong could have found a nonscreamer, albeit a brunette, the reviewer indicates that Wray's vocal expertise is overwrought, unnecessary, and not credible.

In keeping with the reporter's thinking, Ann's repetition and elaboration of her rehearsed responses lend an air of masquerade to her first meeting with Kong and suggest that the relationship between the actress and the overgrown ape is not simply that between a victim and monster. This claim was reinforced by press and publicity materials. For example, a few months prior to *King Kong*'s release, Los Angeles readers were given an intimate peek at Fay Wray at home. The Sunday *Los Angeles Times* story was accompanied by a photo of Wray playing with a dog, while the following caption set the stage for her forthcoming film: "The latest in canine harmony. Fay Wray has taught her pet, *Kong*, to howl soprano."[59] Although the profile ran before the film debuted, it offers an alternate reading of Wray's rapport with Kong; like her dog, the ape may have been a playful object of affection, not just of fear.

Ann's horrified reactions to Kong were also tempered by advertisements. For example, three days after the premiere of the picture, the *Los Angeles Examiner* ran a Lux soap advertisement featuring Wray. As I noted in chapter 3, fine print encourages readers to see RKO's film, and the cutline announces: "A thousand thrills . . . and hers the thrill of *Supreme Beauty*."[60] Wray's soap promotion, in an advertisement that links her appearance in *King Kong* to female beauty tips, suggests that audiences may have viewed her cinematic performance in relation to other discourses, such as movie posters, product tie-ins, and star profiles. The net result of this environment for spectatorship may have been a willingness on the part of audiences to view and hear Ann's ear-piercing screams as less than fully credible and to accept that her performance was just an act.

Like Wray's character, Kong, too, is associated with the theater and performance in the film—thus the heroine and monster are doubled. That doubling is articulated by Carroll in "*King Kong*: Ape and Essence." As Carroll sees it, "part of the fascination of the original [film] was its openness to interpretive play . . . [And the] equation of Kong, who is introduced as the ultimate rapist, with Darrow, an archetypal victim, is not as perverse as it first appears. Both are proper objects of Depression ethos."[61] In Carroll's estimation, *King Kong* is both a conventional horror scenario, with Kong as an aggressive male figure, and a more malleable negotiation of sexual, racial, and economic relations. In fact, whereas most critics equate Kong with the expression of black or white male virility, Carroll argues that the movie is marked by a fear-of-sex theme, in which sexual desire is aligned with the destruction of masculinity.

Whereas Carroll limits *King Kong*'s doubling of the gorilla and heroine to their similar status in the Depression (she begins the film in a food line and he becomes an economic commodity), I think they share a more extensive alignment. For example, Kong, like Ann, performs for an audience. While her acting is cinematic—Denham films her with male crew members looking on—his appearance in New York is theatrical. Ann's first encounter with Kong, however, is quite similar to the monster's chained performance in the Big Apple. She is tied with arms raised between two long poles. When Kong is similarly trapped on the New York stage later in the film, he enacts what Ann cannot: he breaks free and attacks his audience (figures 6.10 and 6.11).

This reading implies that Kong and Ann are both doubles and adversaries, that had she been able to free her hands earlier in the film she would have tried to attack (or at least resist) the creature that was approaching her. This interpretation also suggests that, in being dou-

Figures 6.10 and 6.11. In the first advertisement for the 1956 reissue of *King Kong*, the monster is bound in a Christlike pose on the New York stage. Ann (Fay Wray) assumes a similar stance as she awaits Kong's approach in the second poster for the film. *Copyright © 1933 RKO Pictures, Inc. Used by permission of Turner Entertainment Co. All rights reserved.*

bled, Kong acts out what Ann might have liked to do to the audiences for whom she is a more or less captive spectacle (the audience of black male villagers who kidnap her in order to sacrifice her to Kong, and the white director and crewmen who watch her perform her fear on the ship). Ann's doubling with Kong is, therefore, a result of their similar status as spectacles, as well as their inverse positioning as victim and aggressor. From this perspective, Kong's ability to fight those who look at him through most of the movie is a surrogate action for Ann.

Ann's status as a double for that which is monstrous and threatening is reinforced by her alignment with people of color. Her affinity with nonwhites is first suggested by Charlie, the ship's Chinese cook. Charlie's job implicitly signifies conventional femininity; he is responsible for feeding men. Their doubling is reinforced by his willingness to literally assume Ann's position in the film. When he watches her screen test, standing on the (proverbial) lower rung of a ladder, he

FAY WRAY · ROBT. ARMSTRONG
BRUCE CABOT

asks: "Do you think maybe he [Denham] take my picture, huh?"
Charlie's wish to take Ann's place in front of the camera solidifies
their alignment and confirms that people of color, like white women
and racially ambiguous monsters, are the stuff of which spectacles are
made.

In an excellent analysis of the racist configurations of *King Kong*,
James Snead takes note of the connection between Ann and blacks:
"Women, similarly to blacks, appear not as people or potential partners, but as objects of others' stares, a sort of visual capital."[62] Ann's
status as visual capital is reinforced by her doubling with black women,
which occurs most obviously in a scene in which the chief, witch doctor, and villagers prepare to sacrifice her to Kong. Ann assumes precisely the same position in this ritual as that occupied by a frightened
black maiden in an earlier sequence. While I can only assume that the
black woman perished in her union with Kong, since she never reappears in the movie, Ann's fate as a white heroine is far less dismal.

Carroll takes note of the doubling function of this sequence, as
well as its racial overtones: "Darrow's sacrifice on the island bears a

number of strong formal relations to Kong's exhibition in New York. . . . If Darrow is a white speck on a dark field, then Kong is a black figure on a white ground" ("KK" 233). As the preceding examples indicate, the film establishes a congruence among people of color, a white woman, and a simian monster. Thus, while Ann, Charlie, and the black maiden are aligned with feminine passivity and victimization, they are also doubled with a dark creature that terrorizes men, women, and blacks and whites alike.

Like other horror heroines, Ann's relationship to Kong is that of a victim of a monster, a double for the monster, and a potential romantic partner to the monster. The ambiguity of her responses to Kong was well expressed by the actress in 1969. As Wray notes of her travails when clutched in the ape's mechanical paw: "When I could see that the moment of minimum safety had arrived, I would call imploringly to the director and ask to be lowered to the floor. I would have a few minutes rest, be resecured in the paw, and then the ordeal would begin all over again—a kind of pleasurable ordeal" (quoted in Beck 84).[63] Although Wray's description some thirty-six years after the fact may be nothing more than a publicity ploy, she manages to articulate the pleasure-pain, fear-desire tension of *King Kong*.

More recently, Wray reconfirmed her intimate bonds with Kong when she opened her 1989 autobiography with a candid letter to her 1933 costar:

> Dear Kong . . . I saw the cover of a Directors Guild magazine showing you in a large easy chair, wearing house slippers and watching scenes of yourself on television at the top of the Empire State Building. There were banana peels on the floor beside you and on a table nearby there was a framed photograph of me. I found that quite touching. It let me know I had been some influence in your life. I wonder whether you know how strong a force you have been in mine? For more than half a century, you have been the most dominant figure in my public life. To speak of me is to think of you. . . . I feel that you never did mean harm to me. My children knew that when they saw "our film" for the first time: "He didn't want to hurt you," they said, "he just liked you."[64]

In a mock missive to her costar of days gone by, the actress who played the simian's captive in *King Kong* writes to and of him as a fictional construct, an historic cinematic figure, and an important leading "man." Some fifty-six years after Cooper and Schoedsack's film was a box-office hit, Wray opens her life story with a message to Kong. She writes an open letter to him at an unknown address with a tone of platonic tenderness and affection. But she also writes to him as a lost lover of sorts, a monster that had a powerful influence on her life, a creature that the Directors Guild, in its musings, portrays with a glossy of Wray at his side. Like her past suitor, Wray keeps a (mental) image of Kong, and of his influence on her, close at hand.

But there is more than a lost love at work here. For Wray and Kong are bound together as doubles in her present life: "To speak of me is to think of you," she writes to him. To speak of her is to conjure an image of him, an image of both attacker and suitor, an image of monster and lover. Kong's status as more than mere fiend is articulated by the actress herself. For not only is he far from horrifying to her, her children seem equally fond of her gorilla suitor. Both she and her kids knew that he meant her no harm, Wray remarks—they knew that when it came down to it, he just liked her. And, at least from the vantage point of 1989, it seems that Wray liked him in return.

Wray's comments reinforce an assumption made by Andrew Griffin in an article on *King Kong*. According to Griffin, Kong does not personify projected male desires so much as he represents female ones. Kong embodies Ann's unconscious sexual urge, "just as big as she feared it would be if she ever gave in to it."[65] Griffin's analysis problematizes the assumption that Kong is a decidedly male figure. Moreover, the ambiguities in Ann's (and Wray's) relationship with Kong cast the heroine's bouts of screaming in a different light. In addition to serving as signifiers of fear, her vocal displays can be read quite easily as mechanisms of masquerade, her means of disguising her doubling with, and desire for, the fiend under the veneer of helplessness.

Ann's screaming masks a number of elements in *King Kong*, not least of which are the monstrosity and power of women. Her yells, which fill the second half of the movie, divert attention away from and, perhaps, are punishment for, her earlier efforts to gain independence. Throughout the first half of the film—the sections that take place in New York, on the ship, and on the island before she is kidnapped—Ann is inquisitive. She wants to see the view from the ship's deck and to watch the villagers' rituals, and she wants to know where the ship is going and what is expected of her. In the second part of the film, which is filled with her victimization, Ann is punished for her aggressiveness—her scope of experience and ability to act are narrowed.

Her screams may also serve as a disguise for independence in the realm of desire. Whereas Jack (Bruce Cabot), the hero, declares his love for her in a romantic scene on the ship's deck, Ann is ambivalent about whether or not she reciprocates his feelings.[66] Although she accepts his embrace at the end of the scene, she fails to look him in the eye and does not give him an explicit verbal or gestural response. It is noteworthy that right after this sequence—on the heels of her unconvincing reaction to Jack's display of heterosexual desire—black male villagers kidnap and sacrifice Ann to Kong. The order of events suggests that she is punished for her responses (or lack thereof) to Jack.

The exchange between Jack and Ann on the ship's deck offers an additional function for her screams and impending captivity. For in declaring his love for Ann, Jack occupies a conventionally female position. In a two-shot, he says: "I'm scared for you. I'm sort of, well, I'm scared of you, too. Ann, uh. Say, I guess I love you." Ann responds: "Why, Jack, you hate women," to which he counters: "Yeah, I know, but you're not women. Say, I don't suppose, I mean, well, you don't feel anything like that about me?" Ann says nothing in the close-up reaction shot that follows Jack's avowal. Her lip quivers and her head shakes, but she gives no definitive response.

The phrasing of Jack's declaration underscores Ann's difference from other women and establishes that his desire for her is feminized. According to Jack, being afraid *of* and afraid *for* Ann constitute love. This same combination of fear and desire marks Ann's rapport with Kong. Thus, by equating his love with fear and desire, and by telling Ann that she is not a woman, Jack doubles Ann with Kong. The monster, like her, elicits the fear and desire of a human and defies conventional designations of sexual membership. In her rapport with Jack, then, Ann is his monster and he occupies the position of a frightened heroine.

The precariousness of Jack's gender traits is represented in a conversation with Denham on the ship's deck. When Jack asks where the ship is going, Denham answers impatiently: "What's 'a matter, Jack? Are you going soft on me?" Jack then lets him know that he is not concerned for himself; rather, he is inquiring out of concern for Ann, to which Denham counters: "Oh you have gone soft on her, eh?" The sexual (and homosexual) connotations of Denham's remarks are striking. Jack is losing his phallic hardness through his desire for a woman—he is becoming feminine.

But all this changes once Ann is kidnapped. Not only does she become a traditional frightened heroine, her victimization helps Jack turn into a macho hero. Like Peru's response to Nina in *Trader Horn*, Jack needs to rescue Ann in order to be a (conventional white) man. Thus, by the second part of the film, after saving Ann on the island, Jack's gender traits are more clearly masculine. For example, when Kong is displayed on the New York stage in a gala performance, Jack complains of having to wear a "monkey suit." Like Ann earlier in the film, Jack is aligned with the overgrown gorilla.

But what of Kong's interstitial position? Like Jack and Ann, whose gender traits vacillate, so, too, is Kong an ambivalent figure, at once aggressive and gentle (Julian Fox calls his treatment of Ann "maternal"[67]). The Pressbook for the 1942 re-release of *King Kong* emphasizes the monster's dual nature in a section entitled "Tender Ape." As the accompanying story proclaims: "Kong abducts her [Ann] in the jungle, almost destroys all her companions, then treats her with an immensely awkward tenderness."[68] According to the Pressbook, Kong is both a masculine aggressor and feminine caretaker.

Kong also embodies racial and ontological slippage—he is similar to and different from blacks and humans. According to Haraway, Kong takes his place in a line of monsters spawned by the Victorian imagination (161). Like Frankenstein's creature, he is a tragic overreacher, who in Louise Krasniewicz and Michael Blitz's words, "attempts to touch across species and racial boundaries." That touch is marked by eroticism, according to Krasniewicz and Blitz: "[Kong] was allowed to touch human females as long as they were black natives, or in the racist discourses of the 1930s, as long as those women were more or less like him—merely protohuman. Touching a white woman caused new problems but also suggested new possibilities because she offered Kong the opportunity to shift the boundaries and the model for humanness."[69]

Kong's bond with Ann is, therefore, a vehicle for racial crossing. Like other white heroines, Ann is interstitial. She is the midpoint between Kong and civilization, between black and white men, and between the jungle and New York. Krasniewicz and Blitz contend that *King Kong* barely starts this process of boundary transgression before halting at Ann's refusal to touch Kong in return. Yet what of Ann's ambiguous relationship with Kong through so much of the film?

After all, the bond forged between the monster and heroine not only connotes his victimization of her, it also speaks of her fascination with and similarity to him.

IV

In his study of *King Kong*, James Snead argues that "the film's political aspects are hidden by the emotive nature of the sexual plot's covert build-up and ambiguous release" (54). That is, the movie's racial and racist obsessions are masked by Jack's romantic pursuit of Ann and by the scandal of Kong's (sexual) desire for a white woman. Snead is absolutely right to take note of the displacements effected in the film. Yet in doing so, and in arguing for the success of those displacements, he misses the importance of contradiction as an organizing force in this and other jungle movies. Although steeped in racism, films like *King Kong* are built on faulty and often paradoxical premises intended to confirm white supremacy but destined to destabilize it as well. Here, it is important to note that the film's most striking object of identification in the closing moments, at least in popular accounts of the movie, is the overgrown ape that lies bleeding on the pavement far below the pinnacle of the Empire State Building, the same gigantic figure that threatened to do away with normative relations between white men and women.

As a result, the white heroine is not solely an object of sexism and racism in jungle movies (although, as such an object she is considered subordinate, in need of white male salvation, and likened to "inferior" people and animals). She is also the white man's object of desire, his romantic partner at the conclusion, and a painful reminder that white heterosexuality is never a given but has to be won under conditions that rarely guarantee its enduring success. The white heroine, whatever her other metaphorical functions, signifies the fragility of whiteness in general and white masculinity in particular. Heroes always get the opportunity to test their mettle in jungle films. But even when successful at slaying beasts and keeping the wilderness at bay, their heroism is often under threat from within or nearby. White women remind male leads that no matter how brave they are, or how well they save heroines from darker forces, white heroes are destined to fight an uphill battle against their own ineptitude, and against the imagined evolutionary pull that binds white women to blacks.

That white women serve interstitial roles in 1930s jungle films does not make these movies ideologically progressive. They are complicit with the larger mappings of racist attitudes that punctuated the era as a whole. However, the racial mobility of heroines suggests that dominant culture's investment in a racial hierarchy, in asserting the primacy of whiteness and the mastery of white masculinity, is also tenuous at best. By being both representatives of whiteness and passing for white, heroines highlight the precariousness of racial designations. These films inadvertently announce, by their very ambivalent convergences among race, gender, and monstrosity, that the insisted-upon supremacy of whites is itself the most elaborate ruse, the masquerade that keeps passing itself off as truth.

Afterword: The Horror of It All

In November 1935, *Vanity Fair* published a full-page cartoon with the following caption: "The horror boys in Hollywood." A sidebar commentary on the previous page, entitled "Torture as you like it," accompanied the drawing, which consists of a motley crew of monsters and madmen in various poses. The commentary offered the following profile of the fiends on display:

> Artist Steig has run up for us in his spare time a group portrait of the more popular monsters of the screen. These are the boys who, when it comes to terror, certainly know how to dish it out—and make it pay. At the extreme left, you see Boris "Frankenstein" Karloff lumbering off with a luscious armful, while directly behind him cringes Charles Laughton [Dr. Moreau], going pathological on us again. The gentlemen tinkering with the mummified corpse are easily recognizable as Warner Oland [Dr. Fu Manchu], and Peter Lorre [Dr. Gogol] in one of his sadist moods. Henry Hull is the attractive werewolf pouring himself a little snort of arsenic, while out of the doorway—Peekaboo!—jumps Bela Lugosi [Dracula], ready to have at him with that old Florentine dagger. If you peer sharply into the room behind him, you can spot John Barrymore [Maestro Svengali] acting carnal in a sinister way.[1] (figure 7.1)

Framed in a cramped, dark, and ominous space, the "horror boys" of Steig's cartoon wield weapons (a knife in the case of Dracula), and fondle women and patients (Frankenstein's monster holds a yielding woman in his arms, while Gogol rests a hand on the torso of a bandaged figure). The reader is provided with a humorous and detailed caricature of the standard model of classic horror—this is a family portrait, of sorts, a tableau that depicts horror as male terrain, and positions women as tortured, unconscious, or dead.

This image was published in *Vanity Fair* near the end of the first sound cycle of Hollywood horror, on the cusp of the genre's recycling of earlier films (such as the double-bill reissue of *Dracula* and *Frankenstein* in 1938), and years before horror's journey toward parody. The cartoon tries to encapsulate a financially lucrative genre— as the writer notes, the monsters "make it [terror] pay." And those who pay for it are, though rendered in vague terms, assumed to enjoy horror's male exploits—this is, after all, "Torture as *you* like it." Steig's

Figure 7.1. "The horror boys of Hollywood" are gathered together in this portrait of the genre's favorite male-coded fiends. *Copyright © 1935 Vanity Fair.*

drawing and the accompanying commentary, then, summarize the signifying field of Hollywood's classic horror cinema, pare it down to a single (if exaggerated) image, and, in the process, provide a short-hand version of the genre to the American public or, at the very least, to the readership of what Joshua Gramson calls the "elite-serving"[2] *Vanity Fair*.

As a form of generic synopsis, the image fails miserably—it mixes monsters' identities and narrative details at will (neither Fu Manchu nor Gogol operates on a bandaged patient in their respective movies, but Dr. Frankenstein, who is not depicted, does); it tells little of the representational nuances of horror films (such as the doubling of heroine with fiend); and it completely elides the role of heroes (especially the numerous failures of heroism). Yet, as cultural commentary, Steig's drawing is effective. For it details horror or, more specifically, monsters in three ways: first, and primarily, as male-coded creatures that torment helpless women (as illustrated by the exploits of Frankenstein's creation and Maestro Svengali); second, as male figures that attack other men (Dracula threatens to do away with the werewolf); and, finally, as male figures that are under threat from either tangible or vague forces (the werewolf seems about to poison himself unless Dracula gets to him first, and Moreau is portrayed as a lone madman who "cringes" at the gruesome acts performed around him).

My choice of the term *performed* is intentional, given my focus on the performative dimensions of the genre in the preceding chapters, and given the highly theatricalized setting for the *Vanity Fair* image. For not only are classic horror's most popular monsters placed in a proscenium-like setting that accommodates the frontally positioned and off-frame viewer's gaze, but the mise-en-scène itself underscores theatrical conventions, especially those pertaining to gender. "The unfortunate attached to the wall behind him [Svengali]," notes the anonymous reporter, "in addition to the pretty creature neatly pinned up behind Charles Laughton, are merely decorations" (42). This commentary, while it dubs one of the victims a "creature," concludes the sidebar description of Steig's drawing and casts two of the cartoon's three women as decorative elements of the mise-en-scène—they are a gruesome rendition of feminine wallpaper.

Yet the role of women in the image does not end here, for yet a third decorative female figure is presented—a faint heroine who, clutched in Karloff's monstrous arms, occupies the foreground to the left. With her gown clinging tightly to her body, her feminine curves are emphasized for the reader and contrast with Karloff's angular figure. The first two women—the wall "decorations," according to *Vanity Fair*—point to both the central as well as performative function of heroines in the genre (horror requires female victims, but they are put on display in rather heavy-handed ways), while the third woman under direct threat by a fiend, Karloff's "luscious armful," highlights the necessity of heroines as proof of male monstrosity.

In the final analysis, it is the lack of subtlety of the image, its insistence on both rewriting and streamlining the genre's "horror boys" that I find most fascinating. For while I have read some signifying complexity into the drawing—male monsters attack other males, male monsters experience terror, female victims are sometimes creatures and serve performative, if undervalued, roles—the overriding impression of the image is its correlation between maleness and monstrosity and between maleness and female victimization.

So, why bring this drawing of horror as male terrain to the fore in my conclusion, given that I have argued against precisely this generic identity throughout *Attack of the Leading Ladies*? I do so, first, to illustrate that the gender presumption that has guided so much criticism about classic horror cinema since the 1930s—its "maleness" as a genre—was promoted when the films were first released. But, more important, I have chosen to conclude with this image, and the meanings that circulate in it, to emphasize *Vanity Fair*'s particular brand of gendered promotion as a mode of cultural production imbued with ideological significance. In its very confirmation of conventional gender roles, not to mention normative (albeit sadistic) heterosexual relations, *Vanity Fair*'s illustration sidesteps horror's gender-bending forays and avoids the genre's alternations between convention and transgression.

On the one hand, such an oversight can be read as the magazine's disdain for the genre as a whole—this is a view of horror in toto as "boys' play," as a lesser genre populated by ridiculous creatures made that much more ridiculous in the cartoon's exaggeration of their devious exploits. In this way, *Vanity Fair* might be read as slightly ahead of its time, for but a decade later horror was perceived as lowbrow entertainment by most critics. On the other hand—and this is the perspective I favor—the drawing, and its accompanying prose, can be read as an effort to maintain conventional (although monstrous) gender dynamics at all costs, no matter what the films and publicity campaigns offered in the way of gender transgressions or gender play. For even though Laughton, for one, is pictured as a cringing male, the cartoon's cast of characters is described as boys who "know how to dish . . . out" terror; they are, therefore, neither males who know how to take it nor male-coded fiends that are likened to females in a significant way.

Given the portrait of classic horror that I have drawn throughout this book, *Vanity Fair's* cartoon looks more like an effort at gender revisionism than an attempt to carefully summarize the genre's most pronounced features. Yet, as a text that can be read in ideological terms, the illustration is in keeping with efforts, such as those exhibited by a number of reviewers, to chart the centrality of traditional gender roles in the genre. Whereas *Vanity Fair* portrays male monsters as repulsive creatures committed to torturing women, some reporters sought to provide readers with heroic males, even where none existed. One reporter for the *Christian Century*, for example, was so invested in providing a traditional hero for *Dracula's Daughter* in 1936 that he or she argued that the police and Dr. Garth arrived to save the heroine in the nick of time.[3] Granted, the *Christian Century* required its writers to practice brevity—most reviews are two or three sentences in length—but the result is a highly misleading synopsis of the film. For the vampire's assistant, not the police or hero, kills the female bloodsucker at the conclusion and, furthermore, she is murdered just as she is about to sink her teeth into Dr. Garth, not the heroine.

So, why the urge to portray Garth as a hero when the film itself tells another story? Why the decision to focus on horror's "boys" to the exclusion or reduction of its girls? I think there is a very simple answer to these questions, one that has to do with the ways in which American patriarchy constructs its favorite stories, such as its tale of traditional gender roles. The image of male monsters that do nothing more than victimize women and the conventional scenario of heroism can both be read as cultural wish-fulfillment—an urge on the part of *Vanity Fair* to maintain the maleness of horror and on the part of the *Christian Century* to make the ending heroic in spite of what actually happens in the movie. Powerful fiends have to be vanquished by heroes, so patriarchy would have it, and, whether as monsters or saviors, power always rests in male hands in these two accounts of classic horror.

What I am trying to describe is, of course, an ideological process, the means by which cultural conventions and myths are instituted and promoted at the expense of subtlety and complexity. For, as I noted in chapter 1, classic horror cinema has to be read as a representational terrain upon which competing ideologies do battle, with neither progressive nor conservative forces winning at the conclusion. Yet to represent that complexity, to give form to ideological contradiction, means sacrificing the simplistic benefits of stereotypes (and caricatures, for that matter) and abandoning some of American society's fondest assumptions—that monsters are always powerful male figures that cannot control their ravenous desires for women, that women are merely passive and decorative victims of male aggression, and that heroes always save the day and ensure that the animalistic side of maleness (represented by monsters) is tempered by a civilizing role.

The urge to read heroism into male ineptitude, the effort to represent male monsters as sadists that torment women, can be understood, then, not merely as mistaken or selective views on the genre respectively. Rather, those efforts need to be situated alongside the very similar perspectives on classic horror that have been produced by scholars for many years. For if classic horror is neither, or not solely, a conservative home to heinous misogynistic impulses nor a radical critique of patriarchy, then the genre has to be viewed (or reviewed as the case may be) as a site of ideological negotiation, a narrative (and marketing) space in which complex gender roles and rules are put on display, rejected, performed, and, in some instances, embraced. Classic horror represents these impulses simultaneously; it figures gender as a malleable feature of identity, as well as a stable role. To see it otherwise is to impose a familiar, but reductive, model of gender and genre relations.

Classic horror and jungle films, as I indicate in my final chapter, are malleable genres, making their way between the poles of convention and boundary crossings with regularity—the genres posit stable racial and sexual roles while they also test the limits of humanness and identity. The genres also share a focus on (white) women as the vehicles through which borders are crossed, such as the assumed divisions between human and nonhuman, male and female, attacker and victim, heterosexual and homosexual, black and white, masculine and feminine, and sexual and asexual. As she screams her way through films, or gazes at a mesmerizing fiend with a vacuous expression, the horror and jungle movie heroine both experiences and, sometimes, performs her terror with skill and enthusiasm—an enthusiasm often matched by her counterparts in the audience. *Vanity Fair* might be correct, then, to figure heroines as "decorations," in the sense that they serve very particular performative functions, but it is incorrect in assuming that they are "*merely* decorations" and nothing more (emphasis added).

But what of the audience, that group of men and women that watches the complex affective performances that appear on-screen? Strapped to their seats in the dark of the movie theater, viewers travel on an emotional roller coaster of shifting identifications and desires, a ride during which they oscillate between sadism and masochism, play the gender roles promoted by patriarchal culture with style, or throw them to the wayside in an effort to wear their spectatorship as a costume that offers temporary release from everyday identities.

"Treat all supernatural beings with respect," said Confucius, "but keep aloof of them." Fortunately, or unfortunately, classic horror is well beyond the wisdom of Confucius' warning—there is no way to keep aloof, no way to keep the boundaries between the monstrous and the nonmonstrous intact. In light of this collapse of boundaries, the best advice I can offer when it comes to classic horror and jungle cinema is to just sit back, scream your lungs out or bite your lower lip, and, above all else, enjoy the ride.

Notes

1. Introduction: Horror of Classic Horrors

1. While most fiends are constructed as male, the history of horror cinema has included a range of female monsters that have wrought havoc on the social fabric as well. A number of those female creatures are the subject of Barbara Creed's book, *The Monstrous-Feminine*. Creed's main argument is that female monsters represent male anxieties about femininity—specifically, anxieties linked to an archaic notion of the mother's abject body and, in turn, fears of maternal potency.

2. See, for example, Ivan Butler, Carlos Clarens, Les Daniels, Charles Derry, Alan Frank, Phil Hardy, David J. Hogan, Tom Hutchinson, Frank Manchel, S. S. Prawer, David J. Skal, David Soren, Andrew Tudor, James B. Twitchell, and Leonard Wolf.

3. James B. Twitchell describes this scenario when he writes of the spectator-text rapport for *Dracula* (Universal, 1931): "Essentially a young male is interested in the vampire saga because he sees in that scenario an 'acting out' of his own buried desire (i.e., that he may 'conquer' the special woman, the mother who is virginal to the boy, and command her attention so that he will be the only man in her life). . . . However, to a young woman in the audience, the female 'victim' in the story is her projected self. The female virgin is a willing, although not overly conscious, co-conspirator . . . who is carefully inducted into sexuality by the older man, the vampire, the father" ("*Frankenstein* and the Anatomy of Horror," p. 44). Despite the tenacity of Twitchell's schema, Carol J. Clover has recently argued against this scenario, at least in terms of male

sadism. For Clover, masochism is the primary psychic state assumed by male spectators. See note 4.

4. Clover, *Men, Women, and Chain Saws,* p. 46.

5. Williams, "When the Woman Looks," p. 88. One of the few other critics to remark upon the doubling of woman and monster is Bruce Kawin, who provides a looser framework for that alignment. In his discussion of Universal's 1941 production of *The Wolf Man,* Kawin asserts: "Although it can be said that *The Wolf Man* is the dream of the screenwriter . . . it could also be analyzed as Larry's dramatized dreamworld—or, taking a cue from *Beauty and the Beast,* as Gwen's projection of the two sides of her sexuality, werewolf and gatekeeper" ("The Mummy's Pool," pp. 9–10). Kawin allows for the heroine-monster doubling but sees it as merely one possibility among many.

6. Carroll, *Philosophy of Horror,* pp. 32–33.

7. Because monsters are not human, the conventional definitions of identity (and sexuality) that are usually applied to men and women have to be revised—instead of offering stable gender, sexual, and human identities, monsters explode categories of identity, rendering the divisions between male/female, heterosexual/homosexual, and living/dead, for example, unstable and mutable. In an effort to mark those category transgressions in the pages that follow, I will refer to monsters with gendered pronouns (Dracula is a "he," his daughter is a "she"). Yet I will also discuss these monsters in nonhuman terms (Dracula is a monster *that,* not *who,* attacks women).

8. Huss, "Almost Eve: The Creation Scene in *Bride of Frankenstein,*" p. 54.

9. Freund, and screenwriters P. J. Wolfson, John L. Balderston, and Guy Endore, also replicate the popular assumption of the 1930s and 1940s that women are responsible for deciding on leisure entertainment for couples and families.

10. Kane, "Beauties, Beasts, and Male Chauvinist Monsters," p. 8.

11. Throughout *Attack of the Leading Ladies,* I alternate between detailed summaries of horror movies and cursory mentions of plot points. To remedy that inconsistency in narrative detail, the reader will find a Filmography of film synopses at the end of this book.

12. Garber, *Vested Interests,* p. 49.

13. "Dracula," *Time,* p. 62.

14. Bige, "King Kong."

15. Examples of horror criticism that favor a rigid and traditional sexual division of labor (passive heroines, monstrous men, and male heroism) include Calvin T. Beck, David J. Hogan, Joe Kane, Richard Koszarski, Gerard Lenne, Edward Lowry and Richard de Cordova, S. S. Prawer, James B. Twitchell, and Dennis L. White.

16. Wood notes that horror's basic formula is as follows: "Normality is threatened by the Monster" ("An Introduction," p. 175). Normality—a cultural construct that privileges heterosexuality, matrimony, the family, monogamy, and social institutions such as the law—is challenged by a monster that represents the "return of the repressed." While Wood does not artic-

ulate it, implicit in his description of the monster is a belief in interstitiality. For in order to threaten the norm the monster must be a part of it—s/he must possess human traits, and s/he must be different (in being monstrous s/he is, in many ways, not-human). Wood's understanding of the monster is, then, akin to Carroll's. Yet Wood focuses on the pivotal role of sexuality in horror and, moreover, on the horror of sexual transgression. One of horror's primary terrors, Wood asserts, is that it represents sexualities that usually go unrepresented, such as bisexuality. While this is an important point, Wood overlooks the fact that horror cinema engages in the *sexualization* of culturally marginalized, though not-necessarily-sexual, aspects of Western society. For example, although the physical disabilities and racial differences (from Caucasian Christendom) that mark certain monsters and other characters are not explicitly sexual in nature, part of their threat to the stability of able-bodied white leads is that they are also signifiers of sexual depravity. This is true especially in jungle-horror narratives in which blackness is coded as sexually aggressive. For Wood, sexual repression returns as a monster marked by racial, economic, sexual, and/or ethnic Otherness. This is conceived as a progressive trait of the genre—the destruction of the status quo by a monster that enacts repressed desires is read as positive (although conservative eras, such as the 1980s horror film, are remarked upon by Wood). But it seems to me that one of horror's favored challenges is to ensure that variables such as racial, sexual, and/or ethnic Otherness—i.e., that which is *socially* repressed—return as sexualized monsters. Not only does this throw into question the primacy of sexual repression in readings of the genre, it also lays bare the fluidity of horror's representations and the inadequacy of noting an either/or progressive/conservative impulse.

17. "Dracula's Daughter," *Film Daily*; Scho, "Dracula's Daughter;" and Nugent, "Dracula's Daughter," *New York Times*.

18. James Wingate report to Will Hays, October to December 1932. MPAA files, Margaret Herrick Library, Los Angeles, Calif.

19. "Peter Lorre in 'Mad Love,'" *Film Daily*.

20. Skal, *The Monster Show*, p. 144.

21. Mordaunt Hall, writing for the *New York Times*, called the film a mystery ("Bram Stoker's Human Vampire"); Edward Churchill of the *Motion Picture Herald* said it was "weirdly unusual" ("Dracula"); and an anonymous reviewer at *Film Daily* thought it was a "fine melodrama" ("Dracula"). Richard Watts Jr. of the *New York Herald Tribune*, described it as "an absorbing adventure in morbid fantasy" ("'Dracula'—Roxy"); while *Time* concluded it was "an exciting melodrama" ("Dracula"). Although Marquis Busby noted in the *Los Angeles Examiner* that "Tod Browning's direction achieves the maximum of horror and spine-tickling thrills," he was commenting more on its impact on viewers than its generic membership ("'Dracula' Better Film Than Stage Play, at Orpheum").

22. For a brief summary and analysis of the traditional Gothic's portrayal of the heroine, see Modleski, *Loving with a Vengeance*.

23. *Dracula* (Universal, 1931) Pressbook. In *Dracula* (production background provided by Philip J. Riley), n. p.

24. Ibid.

25. Lugosi's self-proclaimed stature as a heartthrob of sorts is noted by Tino Balio, who remarks: "At the height of his popularity, he reputedly received as many letters as any romantic screen idol, almost all of which, he said, came from women" (*Grand Design*, p. 299).

26. Freund, who was director of photography for *Dracula* in 1931, directed *The Mummy* for Universal in 1932 and *Mad Love* for MGM in 1935. His German expressionist roots are evident in his role as cinematographer for *The Golem* (1921), *The Last Laugh* (1924), *Variety* (1925), and Fritz Lang's *Metropolis* (1926).

27. Ken Hanke asserts that Universal was most responsible for sparking the horror cycle of the early 1930s: "It was not until Universal started to produce its famous 1930s horror films that the horror series caught fire" (*Critical Guide to Horror Film Series*, p. xiii). The cycle's popularity received quite a bit of attention. For example, in 1931 Leo Meehan asserted that Rouben Mamoulian's *Dr. Jekyll and Mr. Hyde* was "a distinctive contribution to the present cycle of 'horror' thrillers which seems to be upon us" ("Dr. Jekyll and Mr. Hyde," pp. 27, 30). A year later, an anonymous critic for *Variety*'s daily publication thought that *Island of Lost Souls* failed as "A deliberate and mechanical attempt to cash in on the horror cycle" ("Island of Lost Souls"). The beginning of the cycle was mentioned in *News-Week*'s review of *Bride of Frankenstein* (Universal, 1935). Here, the reviewer referred to James Whale's 1931 adaptation of Mary Shelley's novel as "the harbinger of horror pictures" ("Frankenstein").

28. F. S. N., "At the Rialto and the Mayfair," p. 23.

29. In *Universal Horrors*, Michael Brunas, John Brunas, and Tom Weaver argue that Universal's classic films, which are in many ways synonymous with classic horror as a whole, ceased production in 1946.

30. Although there is some disagreement among critics as to the precise period denoted by the term *classic horror*, my choice of the 1931–1936 era is shared by Tino Balio, who cites the five years as the genre's "classic period" (*Grand Design*, p. 298). See note 27.

31. The influence of the Gothic novel on classic horror may extend beyond source material to suggest a market for female viewers in the 1930s. The Gothic traded in the victimization of heroines *and* relished gender-bending of sorts. Despite or because of those elements, it was a favorite among late eighteenth- and nineteenth-century female readers. Kate F. Ellis traces the Gothic's popularity in her book *The Contested Castle* and cites female readership as a response to the shifting social and sexual dynamics of the era. As she notes, "popular culture can be a site of resistance to ideological positions as well as a means of propagating them" (*Contested Castle*, p. vii). It is noteworthy that the Gothic novel, like horror, did both at once. For an

excellent overview of horror's roots in prior literary and artistic movements, see Carroll's, *The Philosophy of Horror*, especially pp. 4–7.

32. Although S. S. Prawer, for example, recognizes the literary and theatrical heritage of classic horror, he also claims that James Whale's *Frankenstein* (Universal, 1931) is a Depression film insofar as it emerged in "a world in which manipulations of the stock-market had recoiled on the manipulators; in which human creatures seemed to be abandoned by those who had called them into being and those who might have been thought responsible for their welfare; in which men were prevented from being men, from feeling themselves full and equal members of society, and were thereby filled with destructive rages such as those the poor monster gives way to after his taunting by the sadistic hunchback who is just a little better off than the monster himself" (*Caligari's Children*, pp. 22–23).

33. Twitchell, "*Frankenstein*," p. 43.

34. Twitchell, *Dreadful Pleasures*, p. 65.

35. Todorov, *The Fantastic*, p. 158.

36. In writing of the differential impact that Kong's demise might have on viewers, James Snead suggests the specificity of a black spectator's response: "Identifying with Kong would bring similar pleasures to black audiences as to white viewers, but it would be less easy for a black viewer, in most cases, to shrug off Kong's demise and death and to replace it with the image of the happy unified white couple" ("Spectatorship, *King Kong*," p. 66).

37. Hoffman, "Frankenstein Film."

38. "The Crime of Dr. Crespi" and "'The Crimes of Dr. Crespi' with Eric [sic] Von Stroheim."

39. Hall, "Frankenstein," p. 21.

40. Ibid., "Lionel Atwill," p. 17.

41. Ibid., "A Fantastic Film," p. 12.

42. Char, "Doctor X."

43. F. S. N., "At the Rialto," p. 23.

44. For a compelling analysis of *Dracula*'s homoerotic modus operandi in the original novel, I recommend Christopher Craft's "'Kiss Me with Those Red Lips,'" pp. 107–33.

45. Gilbert, "New Film at Rialto," p. 19.

46. Ibid.

47. Scho, "Dracula's Daughter."

48. Letter from Joseph I. Breen to Harry Zehner (Universal Studios), dated October 23, 1935. MPAA files, Margaret Herrick Library, Los Angeles, Calif.

49. Letter from E. M. Asher to Joseph I. Breen, dated January 14, 1936. MPAA files, Margaret Herrick Library, Los Angeles, Calif.

50. Letter from Joseph I. Breen to Harry Zehner, dated January 15, 1936. MPAA files, Margaret Herrick Library, Los Angeles, Calif.

51. GS memo to file, dated February 6, 1936. MPAA files, Margaret Herrick Library, Los Angeles, Calif.

52. Joseph I. Breen memo to file, dated October 13, 1936. Similar deletions were requested by the Ontario Censor Board (Joseph I. Breen memo to file, dated June 25, 1936). MPAA files, Margaret Herrick Library, Los Angeles, Calif.

53. Laqueur, *Making Sex*, p. 4.

54. Butler, *Gender Trouble*, p. 17.

55. As Heath remarks: "The production of a man or a woman is now understood as long, complex, and approximate (the standards of 'a man' or 'a woman' are cultural, not natural)" ("The Ethics of Sexual Difference," p. 139).

2. Spectatorship-as-Drag: Re-Dressing Classic Horror Cinema

1. *Supernatural* (Paramount, 1933) Pressbook, Library of Congress microfiche file, Washington, D.C.

2. Ibid.

3. While the role-playing theme is not nearly as explicit in other classic horror films at the narrative level, the advertising campaigns for a number of movies relied on it as a sales pitch. One section in the Pressbook for *The Crime of Dr. Crespi*, for example, a mad-doctor film that will be addressed in chapter 5, describes the eponymous character as follows: "Great Surgeon— or Inhuman Fiend?" (*The Crime of Dr. Crespi* [Republic, 1935] Pressbook, Library of Congress microfiche file, Washington, D.C.). The either/or phrasing, and the fact that the storyline suggests that he is both a great surgeon and inhuman fiend wrapped in one, puts role-play at the forefront of marketing. The publicity campaign for *Daughter of the Dragon* (1931), the third film in Paramount's Fu Manchu series about the monstrous evils of a Chinese doctor, employed similar signifiers of role-play and disguise: "Fu Manchu's Daughter, A Fascinating Beauty Whose Beauty Masks the Vengeful Heart of a Serpent About to Strike" (*Daughter of the Dragon* [Paramount, 1931] Pressbook, Library of Congress microfiche file, Washington, D.C.).

4. Dolan, "The Dynamics of Desire," pp. 156–74.

5. This is not to say, however, that gender and sexuality are only or always performances. But it is to say that, in the realm of classic horror spectatorship, viewers find themselves in a highly theatricalized social environment that fosters and invites a range of gender performances, some of which are promoted heavily in culture-at-large, while others transgress traditional mores.

6. Twitchell, *Dreadful Pleasures*, and Clover, *Men, Women, and Chain Saws*.

7. Hansen, *Babel and Babylon*. For a more detailed consideration of horror's relationship to sadistic and masochistic viewing patterns, as well as a revised reading of Freud's "A Child Is Being Beaten," please see my longer version of this chapter, "Spectatorship-as-Drag: The Act of Viewing and Classic Horror Cinema," in *Viewing Positions: Ways of Seeing Film*, ed. Linda Williams.

8. Mayne, *Cinema and Spectatorship*, p. 84.

9. Garber, *Vested Interests*, p. 10.

10. *Daughter of the Dragon* (Paramount, 1931) Pressbook, Library of Congress microfiche file, Washington, D.C.

11. The conflation of maleness with femaleness is not reserved for monsters in the genre, as the case of James Whale's *Old Dark House* (Universal, 1932) makes clear. Although composed primarily of men, the family who lives in the "old dark house" bears the surname "Femm," which signals the effete traits of the clan. The surname also throws into question the masculine and, ultimately, paternal status of the Femm patriarch, a 102 year-old father who lives locked away in a room in the upper reaches of the house. When the spectator finally meets Sir Roderick, he is a mysterious figure. Laying bare that mystery requires a little research and, finally, confirms the genre's propensity for the conflation and confusion of gender identities. Although the film's credits note that Sir Roderick is played by John Dudgeon, there is no record of an actor by that name. Instead, as James Curtis reveals in his biography of Whale, the part was played by an actress named Elspeth Dudgeon: " 'Jimmy couldn't find a male actor who looked old enough to suit him,' said David Lewis [Whale's longtime spouse]. 'So he finally used an old stage actress he knew called Elspeth Dudgeon. She looked a thousand'" (Lewis quoted in James Curtis, *James Whale*, p. 97).

12. Butler, "Imitation and Gender Insubordination," p. 22.

13. Although drag is defined as a gay male practice, that definition highlights the constructed components of this type of performance. When Esther Newton asked a female impersonator in the 1960s whether there are any heterosexual impersonators, he responded: "In practice there may be a few, but in theory there can't be any" (*Mother Camp*, p. 6). According to this performer's logic, the very act of transgressing gender roles and gender expectations defies heterosexuality; the latter is that which is transgressed and, therefore, cannot theoretically be that which does the transgressing.

14. Butler, *Bodies That Matter*, p. x.

15. An unlikely illustration of my arguments can be found in the film's Pressbook, which relied heavily on the conflation of wax models with real people. As one promotional story announced: "Impossible to Tell Human Figures from Wax Models in Film." And the story continued: "The wax figures were made from plaster models painted and colored to look *exactly* like the originals" (emphasis added) (*The Mystery of the Wax Museum* [Warner Bros., 1933] Pressbook, Library of Congress microfiche file, Washington, D.C.).

16. Ibid.

17. Modleski, *Women Who Knew Too Much*, p. 5.

18. Corber, "Reconstructing Homosexuality," p. 81.

19. Laplanche and Pontalis, *The Language of Psycho-Analysis*, p. 329.

20. Lee Edelman and Paul Willeman have made similar arguments for the importance of homosexuality. In his description of the primal scene from the case study of the Wolf Man, Edelman notes: " The primal scene as Freud

unpacks it presupposes the imaginary priority of a sort of proto-homosexual-ity, and it designates male heterosexuality, by contrast, as a later narcissistic compromise that only painfully and with difficulty represses its identification with the so-called 'passive' position in that scene" ("Seeing Things," p. 101). Willeman's valorization of proto-homosexuality appears in his discussion of fetishistic scopophilia. He notes that Laura Mulvey's definition of that process ignores its autoerotic origin: "Mulvey doesn't allow sufficient room for the fact that in patriarchy the direct object of scopophilic desire can also be male. If scopophilic pleasure relates primarily to the observation of one's sexual like . . . then the two looks distinguished by Mulvey are in fact varieties of one sin-gle mechanism: the repression of homosexuality" ("Voyeurism," pp. 212–13).

21. Hanson, "Undead," p. 328.

22. While psychoanalysis conceives of these identifications and desires by rewriting homosexual object-choices as displaced heterosexual ones—a les-bian may desire another woman insofar as that desire disguises and recasts her desire for men—subjects, as described by psychoanalysis, remain locked within the confines of sexual difference and heterosexuality.

23. A note of thanks is due to Anne Friedberg who listened to my qualms about the conventional theorizations of a one-to-one correspondence between viewers and their on-screen counterparts and offered the notion of "identifying against oneself" as a means of better conceptualizing spectator-ship. Although this concept has not been addressed in any detail in existing theories of spectatorship, it appears in an introductory form in Judith Mayne's *Cinema and Spectatorship* (see her fourth chapter, "Paradoxes of Spectatorship"), and in Anne Friedberg's book on the flâneuse, *Window Shopping.* As Friedberg writes: "Theories of spectatorship which imply a one-to-one correspondence between the spectator position and gender, race, or sexual identity . . . do not consider the pleasures of escaping this physically bound subjectivity. Isn't cinema spectatorship pleasurable precisely because new identities can be 'worn' and discarded?" (184–85). Carol J. Clover also introduces an identification-in-opposition motif, although she confines her analysis to gender: "No one who has read 'Red Riding Hood' to a small boy or attended a viewing of, say, *Deliverance* . . . or, more recently, *Alien* and *Aliens* . . . can doubt the phenomenon of cross-gender identification" (*Men, Women, and Chain Saws,* p. 46).

24. Clues to this component of spectatorship can be found in a number of historical accounts of movie-going. For example, Garth Jowett notes that the cinema provided early twentieth-century immigrants with "extra relief" amidst a difficult life of labor (*Film,* p. 39). According to both Jowett and Russell Merritt the fantasy elements of the movies were an escape from the drab and difficult conditions of the American immigrant's everyday reality (Merritt, "Nickelodeon Theaters 1905–1914," p. 88).

25. Mulvey, *Visual and Other Pleasures,* p. 33.

26. Doane, "Film and the Masquerade," p. 80. Reprinted in Doane, *Femmes Fatales.*

2. Spectatorship-as-Drag: Re-Dressing Classic Horror Cinema

27. In her article on Sheila McLaughlin's *She Must Be Seeing Things* (1987), Teresa de Lauretis makes the following claim: "The notions of masquerade, transvestitism, and cross-dressing have been recurrent figures of feminist discourse in the 1980s and in the theorization of female spectatorship in particular" ("Film and the Visible," p. 244). Focusing on Sue-Ellen Case's contribution to the field in "Towards a Butch-Femme Aesthetic," de Lauretis rejects the heterosexist theorizations of masquerade and transvestitism that have appeared thus far in feminist film studies (Sue-Ellen Case, "Towards a Butch-Femme Aesthetic," pp. 55–73). De Lauretis privileges lesbian subjectivity in butch and femme roles as modes of ideological resistance and political discourse. As my arguments in the forthcoming sections will indicate, I think it imprudent to align the transgressive spectatorial positions of drag solely with a homosexual subject.

28. For a critique of Doane's use of female bisexuality, see Patricia White, "Female Spectator."

29. Case, "Tracking the Vampire," p. 11.

30. Sedgwick, *Epistemology of the Closet*, pp. 159–60.

31. Although my focus is drag's impact on spectatorship in terms of gender and sexual orientation, the notions of identifying against oneself and performing identity also inflect the relationships between spectatorship and race and ethnicity, especially in classic horror cinema. For the genre is replete with monsters that, from the perspective of white America, are racial and ethnic Others—the fiend in *The Mummy* (Universal, 1932) is an Egyptian Arab, the eponymous monster in *The Mysterious Dr. Fu Manchu* (Paramount, 1929) is Chinese, and the over-grown ape in *King Kong* (RKO, 1933) is conflated with African natives. While these films may, in the end, ask viewers to disavow their identification with and desire for monsters, many horror narratives encourage spectators to bond with fiends through most of the films. Identification and desire may, therefore, take cross-racial or cross-ethnic form—a white viewer may identify with and desire Dr. Fu Manchu, or an Asian viewer may identify with and desire the mummy. As in the case of the vampiric gay gaze, the relationship between viewers of color and monsters may include a recognition of shared social status. While, on the one hand, this confirms the marginalization of viewers and monsters alike, the fact that monsters are often objects of fascination and attempt to disrupt American institutions of power also lends an unconventional element to those identifications and desires. Unfortunately, the performative dimensions of viewing in terms of race and ethnicity may be harder to pinpoint than gender (screaming, for example, is more readable as feminine than as a sign of a particular race or ethnic group).

32. Riviere "Womanliness as a Masquerade," p. 37.

33. The assertion that Riviere's masquerade allows for multiple identifications and orientations is an important one, especially since Doane does not address masquerade from this perspective. Both Judith Roof and Teresa de Lauretis complain of the heterosexism of Doane's model. According to de

Lauretis, Doane's masquerade is intended to "find a position in heterosexuality from which the woman (spectator) can see and signify her desire in her distance from the image" (248). Roof notes: "While masquerade could destabilize the essential genderment of viewing alignments if it shook up the certain heterosexual premises of desire—if, for example, it were admitted that no one's desire is strictly for the opposite sex—Doane's version of masquerade repeats the gender essentialism it tries to avoid" (*Lure of Knowledge*, p. 49). Although de Lauretis and Roof may be right that Doane's version of masquerade is heterosexist in its present articulation, the case study on which Doane's work is based allows for mobility.

34. Of the extensive writings on horror literature and film, only Christopher Craft's article, "Kiss Me With Those Red Lips," provides a sustained analysis of the homosexual components of Bram Stoker's original work. Although some film critics briefly note that Lambert Hillyer's sequel *Dracula's Daughter* (Universal, 1936), which followed five years after the Bela Lugosi classic, suggests lesbianism, male homosexuality, according to critical reviews, is absent from the classic vampire movies. Literary critic Elaine Showalter is one of the few scholars to assert the endurance of homosexual connotations in all film adaptations: "While most film versions of *Dracula* have been heterosexual, nevertheless, homosexuality is strongly represented in the films, coded into the script and images in indirect ways" (*Sexual Anarchy*, pp. 182–83).

35. "'When Will She Wake?' Rosy Asks Bridgeport," p. 91.

36. Mundorf, Weaver, and Zillman, "Effects of Gender Roles and Self Perceptions on Affective Reactions to Horror Films," pp. 656–57.

37. Critics have argued that masquerade is a female performance enacted for the benefit of men. Stephen Heath, for example, notes "the masquerade is the woman's thing, hers, but is also exactly *for* the man, a male presentation, as he would have her" (emphasis in original; "Joan Riviere and the Masquerade," p. 50). De Lauretis, who asserts the heterosexism of Doane's form of masquerade, argues: "it is not only inscribed within a male-defined and male-dominant heterosexual order, but more inexorably, in the current struggle for women's 'equal access' to pleasure in heterosexuality, the masquerade of femininity is bound to reproduce that order by addressing itself—its work, its effects, its plea—to heterosexual men" (249–50). While de Lauretis is correct to mention a limit point for heterosexually deployed versions of the masquerade within a broader cultural context, it is unclear to what degree the same rules apply in cinematic spectatorship. If one of the pleasures of viewing is identifying against one's identity, then the ideological effects de Lauretis speaks of may be that much more complex and, perhaps, that much less applicable to spectatorship.

38. When I question the concept that lesbians' objects of desire are not men, I want to suggest two variations on that statement. First, there are some lesbians who define their identities as a political or personal choice independent of and sometimes in spite of their sexual desires for men. Second,

a desire for men may be considered a component of *some* lesbian desires. As Butler notes of one femme's object of desire: "She likes her boys to be girls, meaning that 'being a girl' contextualizes and resignifies 'masculinity' in a butch identity. As a result that 'masculinity,' if it can be called that, is always brought into relief against a culturally intelligible 'female body'" (*Gender Trouble*, 123). By liking her boys to be girls, the femme's boys are unlike other boys. But, to a degree, a desire for boys who are girls brings a desire for masculinity into play.

39. By using the term *masquerade* to describe the feminine behavior of some lesbians and bisexual women, I do not mean to suggest that their feminine gender displays are always consciously mobilized or are not "normal" to those who experience them. Rather, I want to propose that in the example of a femme lesbian, especially a femme whose objects of desire are other femmes, the performative quality of sex-role behavior and object-choices is heightened, and masquerade functions as a means of disguising desires and identifications that run contrary to patriarchal culture. One of the other concepts that masquerade accommodates is that femininity may be donned as a mask for varying reasons, that the desires and identifications disguised behind the masquerade of womanliness are potentially unstable.

40. See Patricia White, *Uninvited*.

3. Horror for Sale: The Marketing and Reception of Classic Horror Cinema

1. Mitchell, "Mad Scientists."
2. There is a great deal of material available for anyone interested in horror's relationship to children, specifically, discussion by reviewers, reformers, and censors that horror was not appropriate for younger viewers. As McCarthy remarked of *Island of Lost Souls* in his review geared to exhibitors: "The picture should not be shown to children. It is too gruesome and its main plot too vividly sexy for juvenile consumption" ("Island of Lost Souls," p. 50). McCarthy's attitude was shared by industry reformers who found support for their disdain of horror in the Payne Fund Studies of 1933. As Fred Eastman maintained in "The Movies and Your Child's Health," which appeared in the *Christian Century*, "scenes of horror in the movies, if sufficiently strong, may be definitely, even permanently, injurious [to children's nerves]" (622). Surprisingly, after the Production Code Administration (PCA) was formed in 1934 and more stringent self-censorship efforts took place, some reporters shifted to a lighter attitude toward children and horror in reviews. Frank S. Nugent, for example, urged *New York Times* readers to make *Dracula's Daughter* a family outing: "Be sure and bring the kiddies" ("Dracula's Daughter," p. 14).
3. Staiger, *Interpreting Films*, p. 30.
4. Abel., "Old Dark House."
5. While *Attack of the Leading Ladies* is filled with references to original movie reviews, most of these reviews are either unsigned, signed by initials

only, or signed with pseudonyms. It is therefore impossible to determine whether these reviews were written by male or female reporters. As a result, what might have proven to be a compelling element of this book—addressing the ways in which male and female reviewers responded to the genre—must remain a good idea but one it is impossible to elaborate. I have therefore made some preliminary and brief comments—both in the text and the notes—when the reporter is a woman, and I assume that the rest of the reviewers (for example, Bige, Char, and McCarthy) will forever remain a mystery in gender terms. One of the other issues I was aware of when conducting my research was that of differentiating reviews that appeared in industry magazines from those geared toward the public at large. I initially assumed that industry reviews would be on the whole less critical than those appearing in general publications. I was wrong. Bad reviews for horror movies were as likely to appear in the *Hollywood Reporter, Film Daily,* and *Variety* as in the *Nation,* the *New York Times,* and the *New Yorker* (which was ruthless in its dismissals of 1930s horror). As a result, I have chosen to include reviews from different sources side by side. Although the intended readership of publications may have differed, each individual publication's overall attitude toward films remained consistent.

6. Hall, "Bram Stoker's Human Vampire," p. 21.

7. McCarthy, "Mark of the Vampire," p. 48.

8. Schallert, "'Frankenstein' a Hit."

9. Parsons, "Horror, Thrills and Suspense Fill Picture."

10. I found only one direct mention of horror's incompatibility with female patrons in my research, which appeared in a letter to the editor in the *Motion Picture Herald.* The letter reads as follows: "THEY HAVE OVERLOOKED THE WOMEN. The producers find that in some of the larger cities where their overhead is highest, horror pictures, weird and gruesome pictures . . . have taken their fair sized grosses. From this as a beginning they have figured that the whole country wants this type of film fare. In this they are very erroneous. . . . [T]he women have been almost entirely overlooked" (Letter to the Editor, signed F. M. A. Litchard, Morse Theatre, Franklin, Mass., *Motion Picture Herald* 111, no. 4 [April 22, 1933]: 50). The glut of horror and gangster films produced during the early 1930s were, according to Litchard, drawing "large numbers of unemployed men who have nothing to do." They were not pulling in the more important urban *and* rural patrons, namely women. Although Litchard's letter is the only direct complaint I located about horror's lack of appeal to women, the polarization of gender in viewership was commented on in a review for *Murders in the Zoo* (1933), a Paramount mystery film. As McCarthy noted in the *Motion Picture Herald*: " The men in the preview audience seemed to appreciate the ruthless Gorman and the comic Yates, with the animal element. The women, as could be expected did the gasping, and according to their comments, they seemed to agree that it was a little too brutal for feminine appreciation" ("Murders in the Zoo," p. 19). Of course, it is possible to read the responses of female

3. Horror for Sale: The Marketing and Reception of Classic Horror Cinema

patrons as ambiguous—their gasps may have indicated their appreciation of the film in line with gender norms, and their comments to the reviewer may have favored more conventional gender expectations.

11. Meehan, "Frankenstein," p. 40.

12. McCarthy, "Wax Museum," p. 23.

13. Thirer, "Doctor X."

14. "At the Roxy," p. 21.

15. "White Zombie."

16. Price and Turner, "*White Zombie*," p. 36.

17. Although Leo Handel's audience studies in the 1940s suggest that men liked horror more than women, the variance in preferences was less significant than might be expected, given popular assumptions about the relationship between gender and generic tastes. On the whole, the research reported by Handel for a 1942 study suggested that neither women nor men counted horror among their top four choices when they were asked to rank the story types they liked the most. Mystery and horror pictures were ranked as men's fifth favorite type, behind war pictures, adventure action pictures, musical comedies, and westerns. Women ranked mystery and horror movies (which were listed as a pair in the survey) as number seven out of a possible twenty-one options, after love stories, musical comedies, serious dramas, war pictures, sophisticated comedies, and historicals and biographies. It should be noted, however, that when ranking story types according to their dislikes, horror and mystery films ranked second behind westerns for women (and tied with G-men and gangster movies), while men rated the genre as the eighth most disliked (again, in a tie with G-men and gangster films). It is noteworthy that Handel's results also varied according to age—younger audiences from twelve to twenty-nine liked mystery and horror films far more than those viewers aged thirty to forty-four. (*Hollywood Looks at Its Audience*, p. 124.)

18. Rush, "Dracula."

19. *Motion Picture Herald* 102, no. 2 (January 10, 1931): 39.

20. Murphy, *Celluloid Vampire*, p. 21.

21. Frank, *Horror Movies*, p. 14.

22. Rush, "Frankenstein."

23. Charman, "Girls Want Mystery," p. 47.

24. Aaronson, "B. O. Explodes Idea," p. 24.

25. McCarthy, "The Mummy," p. 27.

26. McCarthy, "King Kong," pp. 37, 40.

27. *Motion Picture Herald* 105, no. 13 (December 26, 1931): 28.

28. Rush, "Dr. Jekyll and Mr. Hyde."

29. "Laby's Effective Lobby Display," p. 68.

30. "Don't Park Here," p. 82.

31. "Swinger Offers First Aid," p. 64.

32. Barry and Sargent, *Building Theatre Patronage*, p. 222. In her excellent study of early marketing stunts, "From Elephants to Lux Soap," Jane Gaines

mentions Barry and Sargent's ambulance ploy and adds: "The ambulance was also used threateningly to convey the message that audiences attended horror films at their own risk" (36). Since she only footnotes Barry and Sargent after this comment and since the exhibitors did not mention the usefulness of the ambulance for horror showings, my guess is that Gaines's reference points forward to the 1930s when ambulances and medical care became a promotional staple for the genre.

33. *Motion Picture Herald* 120, no. 1 (July 6, 1935): 99.

34. "Free Permanent Given for 'Invisible Ray'," p. 85.

35. Waldman, "From Midnight Shows to Marriage Vows," p. 41.

36. "'When Will She Wake?'" p. 91. The fainting female patron was, it seems, a fixture of classic horror stunts in the 1930s. In some cases, however, she may have been an unintended by-product of exhibitor efforts. According to Maury Foladare, one of *King Kong*'s publicists, a female patron in the Pacific Northwest was so distraught by a stunt that she fainted and sued for damages. As he noted many years later: "I got a big guy and rented an ape costume from Western Costume. I had the big ape walk into the Wenatchee (WA) Department Store. This one woman fainted. Later, she sued me and the studio (RKO) for $100,000." Eventually, the matter was settled without payment (Beyette, "Dean of Hollywood Publicists, 79, Keeps Plugging Away Honest").

37. Busby, "'Dracula.'"

38. In some instances it was less what women did than what they *did not* do vis-à-vis horror that was remarked upon. A reporter for the *New York World-Telegram* had the following to say about *Doctor X* in 1932: "As far as the eyes of this conscientious reporter could detect, not one woman in the audience fainted" (August 4, 1932).

39. "Louie Charnisky," p. 74.

40. Despite reviewer warnings that children and youth should not attend films, exhibitors encouraged their attendance quite enthusiastically by mid-decade.

41. "Emotion Test," p. 79.

42. *The Mystery of the Wax Museum* (Warner Bros., 1932) Pressbook, Library of Congress microfiche file, Washington, D.C.

43. "Dick and Ken," p. 78.

44. McCarthy, "Invisible Man," p. 37.

45. Kurt Singer, *The Laughton Story*, p. 105.

46. "Island of Lost Souls," p. 58.

47. *Island of Lost Souls* (Paramount, 1932) Pressbook, Library of Congress microfiche file, Washington, D.C.

48. Barry, "Such a Naughty Nero," pp. 46–47, 95–96.

49. *Photoplay* 43, no. 3 (February 1933): 4.

50. Whether or not *Svengali* is a horror film has been debated for a number of years. Phil Hardy does not include it in his *Encyclopedia of Horror*, but William K. Everson contextualized it in relation to Hollywood's horror cycle

3. Horror for Sale: The Marketing and Reception of Classic Horror Cinema

in "Svengali" in 1973. The film has a strong link to vampire and zombie films, with its hypnosis focus and the construction of the eponymous character as a fiend. *Svengali*'s status as a horror movie is merely assumed by Ellen Draper in an article on films in which fiends mesmerize heroines. According to Draper, *Svengali*, like the classic horror movie *White Zombie* (1932), depicts the victimization of women so well that it proves Laura Mulvey right about the sadistic male gaze. For Draper, however, *Svengali* and a number of other films go one step further: they overstate female suffering to the point that patriarchy's misogynistic machinations are laid bare. See Draper's "Zombie Women," pp. 52–62. As I will argue in chapter 4, the hypnosis film's visual dynamics cannot be reduced to the sadistic male gaze, even one that reveals its own power structures, as Draper would have it.

51. *Photoplay* 40, no. 2 (July 1931): 7.

52. Studlar, "The Perils of Pleasure?" p. 8.

53. *Photoplay*, 39, no. 6 (May 1931): 8.

54. "And Who Is This Girl?" p. 68.

55. "You Should See My Kid Sister," p. 31.

56. *Picture Play* (February 1931); (Fay Wray Collection, University of Southern California Cinema Archives; Fay Wray Scrapbook 1929–1933, p. 54.)

57. *Screenland* (February 1931); (Fay Wray Collection, University of Southern California Cinema Archives; Fay Wray Scrapbook 1929–1933, p. 55.)

58. *Photoplay* 39, no. 6 (May 1931): 18.

59. Her sweet reputation was reinforced by stories about her home life. For example, one New York paper painted an affectionate portrait of Wray's relationship with her husband, John Monk Saunders. According to the piece, her husband's "pet nickname for her is Goofy. She is very proper and merely calls him John" (Skolsky, "Tintypes," p. 82).

60. "What Power Can Save Them?" p. 30.

61. In one 1933 item from Wray's personal scrapbook, a reporter claimed: "She is one of the best girl athletes in pictures" ("No More Horror for Fay Wray," p. 22).

62. The Lux Toilet Soap advertisement appeared in the *Los Angeles Examiner* (March 27, 1933). Fay Wray Collection, University of Southern California Cinema Archives. Other horror starlets such as Mae Clarke, Marion Davies, Sidney Fox, Miriam Hopkins, Leila Hyams, Elsa Lanchester, Marian Marsh, and Lupe Velez graced *Photoplay*'s pages. Some modeled outfits, as was the case with Sidney Fox, star of *Murders in the Rue Morgue* (Universal, 1932), who looked "girlish" wearing a "boyish suit" in the April 1931 issue (*Photoplay* 39, no. 5 [April 1931]: 61). Mae Clarke, heroine of *Frankenstein*, was the subject of a rise-to-stardom piece by Harry Lang in 1932 ("'I'll Have Vanilla'," pp. 72, 115).

63. Ruth Rankin, "Meet the Monster!" p. 60.

64. *Photoplay* 43, no. 3 (February 1933): 27.

220

3. Horror for Sale: The Marketing and Reception of Classic Horror Cinema

65. *Photoplay* 41, no. 4 (March 1932): 8.
66. "Ask the Answer Man," p. 86.
67. *Photoplay* 41, no. 2 (January 1932): 58–9.
68. Letter from Jason S. Joy to Carl Laemmle Jr., dated August 18, 1931. MPAA files, Margaret Herrick Library Collection, Los Angeles, Calif.
69. James Fisher, report to file, dated January 14, 1931. MPAA files, Margaret Herrick Library, Los Angeles, Calif.
70. Jacobs, *Wages of Sin*, p. 27.
71. In his overview of the Payne Fund Studies, Fred Eastman summarized a 1930 project headed by Dr. Edgar Dale of Ohio State University: "What does your child see when he goes to the movies? To be sure, he sees some of the fine pictures already mentioned—but he sees much more. . . . [Dr. Dale] found that the shift in recent years has been away from love stories and toward sex and crime pictures, so that of the 500 features produced in 1930, 137 had crime as their major theme, 44 were primarily devoted to war, horror, and mystery . . . and 70 centered around sex" ("Your Child and the Movies," p. 592). The statistic regarding horror is interesting, given that the genre did not seem to exist in any consistent form until 1931. One of the questions that arises in relation to Dale's findings is what did he mean *exactly* by the term *horror*? Unfortunately, a response is not forthcoming.
72. Letter from Joseph I. Breen to Harry Zehner, dated July 24, 1934. MPAA files, Margaret Herrick Library Collection, Los Angeles, Calif.

4. Looks Could Kill: The Powers of the Gaze in Hypnosis Films

1. Hall, "Feminine Love of Horror," p. 33.
2. In the final chapter of her book *Men, Women, and Chain Saws*, Carol J. Clover explores contemporary horror's obsession with looking. As her opening sentence forewarns—"Eyes are everywhere in horror" (166)—Clover unravels the processes of looking employed in the genre's contemporary films. My description of an economy of looks for classic films in this chapter owes much to Clover's original study and her efforts to take horror's complex sight lines beyond eye-level.
3. Letter from Joseph I. Breen to Louis B. Mayer, dated December 28, 1934. MPAA files, Margaret Herrick Library, Los Angeles, Calif.
4. Given the heightened awareness of lesbian connotations at the PCA the following year when *Dracula's Daughter* was released, the avoidance of the topic in relation to *Mark of the Vampire* was probably the result of the film's surprise ending: the vampires are revealed to be members of a performance troupe hired to trap the murderer. Irena and Luna merely *acted* out an attack as part of their plan and did not, from the perspective of hindsight, express monstrous lesbian desire.
5. "Mark of the Vampire," *Film Daily*.
6. Char, "Mark of the Vampire."
7. "Mark of the Vampire," *Time*.
8. Ibid.

9. See Mulvey, "Visual Pleasure."

10. Gaines, "White Privilege and Looking Relations," p. 76. As the title of Gaines's article suggests, she explores cinematic looking relations from the double perspective of gender and race. This dual focus also has a role when it comes to hypnosis films, as I will suggest later in this chapter. Here, however, I want to note the importance of race to processes of looking in hypnosis movies and link that import to a film series that was the immediate precursor to the horror cycle that began with *Dracula* in 1931. As Ken Hanke remarks, "A horror series in the more accepted sense of a continuing story did not occur until Paramount's short-lived run of Fu Manchu thrillers in 1929, 1930, and 1931. This, however, was a rather limited success, and it was not until Universal started to produce its famous 1930s horror films that the horror series caught fire" (*A Critical Guide*, p. xiii). According to Hanke, the Fu Manchu series was a precursor to horror in general, but I think the films are best thought of as the direct ancestors of the hypnosis film. In each of the Fu Manchu movies, *The Mysterious Dr. Fu Manchu, The Return of Dr. Fu Manchu,* and *Daughter of the Dragon,* which starred Anna May Wong as a fiendish beauty, a white heroine in the first two films and an Asian heroine in the third are brought under a Chinese monster's sway and transformed into vapid and potentially destructive creatures. Race played a significant role in processes of looking—so much so, in fact, that promoters used Wong's Chinese identity as a selling ploy to publicize *Daughter of the Dragon*. One section in the Pressbook urged promoters that "Using Eye Slant" was the best strategy available. The Pressbook continued: "Any town big enough to have a Chinese laundry or a Chop Suey emporium is big enough to boost the grosses on 'Daughter of the Dragon' with a new kind of beauty contest" (*Daughter of the Dragon* [Paramount, 1931] Pressbook, Library of Congress microfiche file, Washington, D.C.). For a more detailed discussion of race and processes of looking in the Fu Manchu films, see my dissertation, *Attack of the Leading Ladies*. Race is also a significant element in *White Zombie* (1932), at least insofar as the title highlights matters of racial difference. The film is set in Haiti and a number of black zombies appear as background figures. Despite these allusions to race, *White Zombie* posits a white woman as the most significant victim in the film, and the white hypnotist, played by Bela Lugosi, is the movie's most compelling monster. Blackness remains important for signifying threats of miscegenation, and the potential terrors (to whites) of nonwhite environments and peoples, but the film's central concern is the way in which whiteness is absorbed into the dark traditions of Haitian culture, traditions manufactured through Hollywood's racist fantasies.

11. Altman, "Dickens, Griffith, and Film Theory Today," p. 327.

12. Altman's arguments, and their applicability to classic horror, echo Tom Gunning's claims that silent cinema until 1906–1907 is a "cinema of attractions," a mode of exhibition in which "theatrical display dominates narrative absorption, emphasizing the direct stimulation of shock or surprise at the expense of unfolding a story or creating a diegetic universe" ("Cinema

of Attractions," p. 59). Like the silent films of which Gunning writes, classic horror privileges the "direct stimulation of shock or surprise," but in consort with, not at the expense of, the unfolding story.

13. Leo Meehan, for example, called *King Kong* "one of the most thrilling and unusual melodramas ever produced" ("Bringing Them Together, p. 32). An anonymous reviewer for *Film Daily* stretched generic categories when it came to *White Zombie* and called the film a "weird melodrama" ("White Zombie").

14. As Abel remarked in 1932, "With the horror school . . . the audience seemingly doesn't expect coherence, and so everything goes by the boards" ("Old Dark House").

15. Linda Williams goes so far as to note that "A key moment in many horror films occurs when the monster displaces the woman as site of the spectacle" ("When the Woman Looks," p. 89).

16. Quoted in Balio, *Grand Design*, p. 301. Original source is cited as the *New York Times*, December 5, 1931.

17. J. C. M., "Gallipoli," p. 80.

18. Hoffman, "Karloff Thrill."

19. "Mummy," p. 19.

20. Hansen, *Babel and Babylon*, p. 272.

21. McConnell, "Rough Beasts Slouching," p. 26.

22. "More Pantomime, Less Dialog [sic] to Form Screen Techniques," p. 20.

23. Churchill, "Dracula," p. 74. Churchill both aligns Mina with monstrosity and provides a clue as to why horror has had the reputation of being a genre of heroic male leads. Churchill remarks that David Manners, who plays John Harker, saves the heroine. Yet that claim is patently false. Dracula is murdered by the older wise man in the film, Dr. Van Helsing, and not John. John may get Mina at the end—he literally lifts her into his arms and carries her up a staircase—but he does so only *after* Van Helsing dispatches the vampire. Churchill's insistence that John saves Mina might be read, then, as one reviewer's refusal to accept the failures of male heroism in classic horror, a form of denial repeated by other reporters in the 1930s.

24. *Dracula* (Universal, 1931) Pressbook. In *Dracula* (production background provided by Philip J. Riley), n. p.

25. "Mark of the Vampire," *Time*, p. 40.

26. L. N., "Beyond the Pale," p. 18.

27. Abel, "White Zombie," p. 15.

28. While George du Maurier's original novel *Trilby* was not of the horror genre, and while *Svengali*'s fiend defies the immortal status often associated with monsters, the movie was marketed like other classic horror films. As I argue in chapter 3, Svengali is a romantic object of desire and a terrifying figure. Furthermore, like other hypnosis fiends, his mesmerizing transformations of the heroine are both alluring and frightening, thereby bearing a striking similarity to the conventions deployed in vampire and mummy

movies. In the context of classic horror, Maestro Svengali is best viewed as a vampire without fangs.

29. Dijkstra, *Idols of Perversity*, p. 35.

30. Auerbach, *Woman and the Demon*, pp. 15–16.

31. Lucy is a fascinating case in Browning's film and yet another example of the genre's forays into narrative incoherence. Although Dracula attacks her and turns her into a vampire before he sets his sights on Mina, and although she is shown in one scene with a child-victim in her arms, she is never killed nor is she mentioned at the film's conclusion. She is a vampire that remains unaccounted for to this very day.

32. *White Zombie* (United Artists, 1932) Pressbook, Library of Congress microfiche file, Washington, D.C.

33. Source unknown (private collection of Ronald V. Borst, Los Angeles, Calif.).

34. *The Mummy* (Universal, 1932) Pressbook. In *The Mummy*, p. 52.

35. Musetto, "Mummy Zita Rises from the Past."

36. *Motion Picture Herald* 109, no. 12 (December 17, 1932): 28–9.

37. *The Mummy* (Universal, 1932) Pressbook. In *The Mummy*, p. 53.

38. *Motion Picture Herald* 103, no. 17 (June 6, 1931): 54.

39. "Svengali," p. 48.

40. Hall, "Trilby," p. 30.

41. J. C. M., no title, p. 70.

42. *Svengali* (Warner Bros., 1931) Pressbook, Warner Bros. Archives, University of Southern California Special Collections.

5. The Interpretation of Screams: Female Fear, Homosocial Desire, and Mad-Doctor Movies

1. Hall, "A Fantastic Film," p. 12.

2. Beck, *Scream Queens*, p. 18.

3. For a Gothic-focused discussion of the shift from female to male reproduction in the mad-doctor scenario, see Ellen Moers, "Female Gothic" and Mellor, "Possessing Nature."

4. The homoerotic impulses that mark classic mad-doctor movies do not make a neat historical leap from the 1930s to the 1970s; rather, they find representation in other decades as well. Harry Benshoff, for example, asserts that the teenage monster movies of the 1950s, such as *How to Make a Monster* (American International Pictures, 1958), depict a "monster and/or mad scientist [who] takes on a distinctly homosexual and pedophilic threat" ("Pedophiles, Pods, and Perverts").

5. Quoted in Gladys Hall, "Feminine Love of Horror," p. 86.

6. While Tracy may be heroic at one point in the film, his overall stature in the movie was less than impressive, at least according to *Time*'s reviewer who called him "a jittering reporter as usual" ("Doctor X," p. 20). The review in *Commonweal*, on the other hand, indicated that Tracy did a fine job: "There is, of course, the inquisitive reporter, who falls in love with Doctor

5. The Interpretation of Screams: Female Fear, Homosocial Desire, and Mad-Doctor Movies

Xavier's daughter, and manages in the end to rescue all concerned from a horrible predicament" ("Doctor X," p. 411).

7. The relationship between Joanne's fear and the shadowed actions of men is first established early in the film. After the police leave Xavier to his experiments, he goes to his library. Balanced on a ladder, he leafs through books. The dark does not seem to bother him or lessen his energetic research. The camera pans to the doorway where Joanne enters, looks at Atwill, and screams. He asks her what is wrong and Joanne turns on the light. She responds to his query: "Nothing. I just came in here to say good night to you." Joanne's comment suggests that she *knew* that the man in the dark was her father. In this brief sequence, Joanne's frightened responses do not so much disguise Xavier's actions as they establish the precariousness of her display of fear (she screams even though she knows the man in the dark is her father). Her screams also suggest that her father might be a worthwhile object of terror.

8. *Motion Picture Herald* 108, no. 13 (September 24, 1932): 58. The same phrase is also utilized in the Pressbook (*Doctor X* [Warner Bros., 1931] Pressbook [private collection of Ronald V. Borst, Los Angeles, Calif.]).

9. The source for this two-page advertisement is a Pressbook Herald, a promotional pamphlet handed out to spectators at theatrical screenings (private collection of Ronald V. Borst, Los Angeles, Calif.).

10. Sedgwick, *Between Men*, pp. 1–2.

11. Irigaray, *This Sex Which Is Not One*, p. 171.

12. Tudor, *Monsters and Mad Scientists*, p. 32.

13. Koszarski, "Mad Love," p. 26. While Koszarski is at pains to argue that the hero and Gogol are rivals for the heroine's attentions, he also (inadvertently, I would guess) indicates the degree to which *Mad Love* is a far from conventional tale of masculine prowess. By declaring that Gogol has to *wean* the heroine away from her husband, he feminizes the doctor, literally rendering him maternal.

14. Sedgwick, *Epistemology of the Closet*, p. 187.

15. *The Island of Dr. Moreau* was renamed *Island of Lost Souls*.

16. Staiger, *Interpreting Films*, p. 136.

17. Staiger mentions this phrase in her discussion of reviewer responses to von Stroheim in 1922 (132), and the same sentence flooded the Pressbook for *The Crime of Dr. Crespi* thirteen years later (*Crime of Dr. Crespi* [Republic, 1935] Pressbook, Library of Congress microfiche file, Washington, D.C.).

18. Despite producer efforts to harken back to the success of *Foolish Wives*, *The Crime of Dr. Crespi* was a box-office failure. Apparently, neither the multiple connotations promoted nor von Stroheim's fame were enough to pull crowds to the picture.

19. Homosocial desire and the construction of mad doctors as simultaneously attractive and repulsive can be found in Edgar G. Ulmer's *The Black Cat* (Universal, 1934) as well, a film that stars horror's favorite actors: Boris

5. The Interpretation of Screams: Female Fear, Homosocial Desire, and Mad-Doctor Movies

Karloff and Bela Lugosi. Here, Lugosi and Karloff interact as rivals for female attention, but their rivalry depends on intimate conversations, homo-erotic interactions with each other, and a near-seduction of the hero. *The Raven* (Universal, 1935) also offers a forum for Lugosi and Karloff to express homosocial desire.

20. Although Dr. Frankenstein's given name is Victor in both the novel and in Kenneth Branagh's most recent screen adaptation, *Mary Shelley's Frankenstein* (1994), screenwriter John L. Balderston calls him Henry in Whale's films. Perhaps Balderston's Henry is meant to be a composite character comprised of both Victor and Henry Clerval, Frankenstein's medical school-mate in the novel. If so, however, the decision to introduce a character named Victor (John Boles) into the film further confuses the choice of names.

21. Ken Hanke, unlike Twitchell, assumes that homosocial meanings are more overtly represented in James Whale's *Frankenstein* films. According to Hanke, the figure of the monster is a stand-in for both the mad doctor and Whale, a gay director whom I will address in greater detail shortly: "The Monster as Henry Frankenstein's alter ego being shut away in the laboratory dungeon once he becomes inconvenient makes a telling parallel to closeted homosexuality" (*A Critical Guide*, 34–35).

22. Hanke even goes so far as to suggest that Whale's casting of women may have also been motivated by gay associations. As he remarks of the casting of Elsa Lanchester as Mary Shelley and the Bride in *Bride of Frankenstein* (Universal, 1935): "Perhaps the mere casting of a woman [Lanchester] married to a homosexual [Charles Laughton] as Mary was sufficient [exploration of homosexual and illicit desire] in itself to those 'in the know'" (36). See note 37 for further discussion.

23. In his discussion of queer popular culture, Alexander Doty underscores the same link between Whale's sexual orientation and cinematic accomplishments that I am trying to suggest here: "It is . . . amazing that gay horror director James Whale has yet to receive full-scale queer auteurist considerations for films such as *Frankenstein* (the idea of men making the 'perfect' man), *The Bride of Frankenstein* (gay Dr. Preorius; queer Henry Frankenstein; the erotics between the blind man, the monster and Jesus on the cross; the overall campy atmosphere), *The Old Dark House* (a gay and lesbian brother and sister; a 103-year-old man in the attic who is actually a woman), and *The Invisible Man* (effete, mad genius Claude Rains spurns his fiancée, becomes invisible, tries to find a male partner in crime, and becomes *visible* only after he is killed by the police)" (emphasis in original, *Making Things Perfectly Queer*, pp. 14–15).

24. Ronald V. Borst, a collector and expert on horror cinema, matter of factly mentioned Clive's bisexuality during a conversation we had about Whale's first film. My guess is the rumor was passed on to him in a similar fashion (conversation with Ronald V. Borst, July 5, 1994, Los Angeles, Calif.).

25. Gleiberman, "Alive and, Well . . .," p. 48.

26. Wolf, *Horror*, p. 144.

27. Sheehan, "Revival Pick of the Week," and Russo, *Celluloid Closet*, p. 50.

28. Curtis, *James Whale*, p. 125.

29. *Motion Picture Herald* 105, no. 11 (December 12, 1931): 63.

30. *Motion Picture Herald* 105, no. 12 (December 19, 1931): 67.

31. The advertisement also suggests the voice of another mother who remains absent in the film: Frankenstein's mother. The unheard voice that narrates the advertisement, the one who utters the words, "I gave him life but he wanted love! Frankenstein," may well be the doctor's own lifegiver. Like her son's relationship to his creature in the film, the cutline suggests that Frankenstein's mother is a monstrous parent, one who gives birth but who cannot give love.

32. *Motion Picture Herald* 105, no. 13 (December 26, 1931): 59.

33. As Anne K. Mellor remarks of the doctor in the novel: "Frankenstein's most passionate relationships are with men rather than with women" ("Possessing Nature" 225).

34. Walter Evans also notes the importance of the Baron's mistaken assumption; however, he reaches different conclusions as to the significance of the point: "There is, of course, no other woman. The movie's horror is fundamentally based on the fact that the monster's life has come without benefit of a mother's womb" ("Monster Movies: A Sexual Theory," p. 359).

35. F. S. N., "At the Roxy," p. 21.

36. Ferguson, "Two Films," p. 75.

37. J. C. M., "Just a Few Snarls," p. 70. Lanchester's rendition of the Bride not only drew raves from contemporary critics, it also led at least one reporter to remark upon the actress's unconventional gender attributes. As *Time*'s reporter noted in April 1935: "In private life also Miss Lanchester is the wife of Henry VIII (Charles Laughton). Although he is noted for his plump effeminacy, she is mannish in dress" (quoted in Young, "Here Comes the Bride," p. 415). The inclusion of this seemingly superfluous comment in a review of Whale's film suggests that Ken Hanke may be correct to assume that the casting of Lanchester—a woman married to a homosexual, according to Hanke—was deliberate (see note 22). Furthermore, the remark indicates that Lanchester's Bride may from the start have been read by audiences as a signifier of "aberrant" femininity, given the supposed gender-bending associations attached to the actress, and given that the genre's gender play was recognized by critics at the time.

38. The relationship between monstrosity and Mary Shelley has been the subject of a number of works on *Frankenstein*. For example, Mellor asserts that the novel represents Shelley's analysis of sexist gender relations, in which the male is valued above the female: *Frankenstein* "supports a patriarchal denial of the value of women and female sexuality" ("Possessing Nature," p. 220).

39. In addition to the use of female fear as a disguise of male effeminacy, homosociality, female accomplishment, and female monstrosity, it also

serves a more general narrative function. In the figure of Minnie, Elizabeth's curious and shrieking maid, female terror is a comic device. It is *intended* to be seen as superficial by audiences at a number of moments. For example, although Minnie puts on a front of bravado—she offers to bind the creature when the townspeople first capture him—she also runs away in a fit of melo-dramatic hysteria when she accidentally bumps into the fiend.

40. By 1935, the year in which *Bride of Frankenstein* was released, the term *queer* was already popular slang for homosexual. Whale was more than likely aware of the dual meanings of the term—that is, odd and gay—and, no doubt, was instrumental in using the word to describe Pretorius, the film's most effeminate and stereotypically gay character.

41. Conger and Welsch, "The Comic and the Grotesque," p. 300.

42. As I mentioned in chapter 3, *Bride of Frankenstein* is instructive in terms of the ways in which the Production Code Administration (PCA) may have inadvertently created homosocial meanings in the very act of censorship. Here, Joseph Breen requested that any sexual connotations that might be read into the monster's relationship with the female creature be tempered by using neutral terminology, such as *companion*. In the end, Universal pre-ferred *friend* to the original word *mate*. Yet the vagueness of the term *friend* and the fact that the monster calls both Pretorius and the bride his friends, reinforces the film's homosocial charge. In Henry Frankenstein's world male and female "friends" have the same status as objects of desire and con-jugal partners.

43. "Bride of Frankenstein," p. 52.

44. Young, "Here comes the Bride," p. 404.

45. Wells, "Preface to *The Island of Dr. Moreau*," p. ix.

46. As this brief description already indicates, *Island of Lost Souls* crosses generic boundaries. While it is an excellent example of a mad-doctor movie, it is also a jungle-horror text, displaying many of the attributes that will be outlined in the next chapter. In fact, the homosocial connotations of *Island of Lost Souls* are remarkably similar to the representation of the evil fiend in Merian C. Cooper and Ernest B. Schoedsack's *The Most Dangerous Game* (RKO, 1932). In RKO's picture, Count Zaroff (Leslie Banks) is a maniacal hunter who turns his jungle island into a perverse animal reserve. While Zaroff refuses to hunt animals, less for humanitarian reasons than because he finds them boring game, he gets his thrills from chasing and then killing men. As McCarthy phrased it in the *Motion Picture Herald*, the film focuses on a "mad-man playing a heartless, relentless game of stalking his fellow men" ("Most Dangerous Game," p. 32). While the sexual connotations of the term *stalk-ing* are more pronounced in the 1990s than they were in the 1930s, McCarthy's word choice points unintentionally to the film's homosocial undercurrent. As if the act of hunting other men were not enough to mark Zaroff as a homosocial figure, Banks's performance choices add to the mix. Zaroff has an effete manner, signified in part by his odd way of holding a cig-arette. Instead of clutching the cigarette between his index and third finger,

Zaroff gently grasps the end with four poised fingertips. As one advertisement proclaimed, drawing upon the multiple connotations so dear to publicity ploys, "Cooper and Schoedsack . . . now plunge you into the strangest world of all—THE WORLD OF IMAGINATION—creating a picture that *hurls precedent out the door and ignores tradition* with thrill-charged *romance born of adventures never even dreamed of* 'til now" (emphasis added, *Variety* 108, no. 3 [September 27, 1932]: 12–13).

47. Leonard Wolf points to Laughton's homosocial proclivities when he notes that Moreau's "sexuality is very ambiguous" (121). As for the actor himself, Laughton's name appears in a number of gay publications that list famous homosexuals, such as a handout distributed by the Gay and Lesbian Public Awareness Project Speaker's Bureau. Despite his marriage to Elsa Lanchester, it was a well circulated Hollywood rumor that Laughton's sexual orientation was far from straight. By suggesting that Laughton's sexuality informed his performance as Moreau I do not mean to imply that he was a "bad" actor, that he could not separate his personal life from his performances. Instead, it is my belief that his extratextual experiences enhanced a role that called for the display of homosocial desire. Despite or, perhaps, because of the connotations attached to Laughton, the film's promotional machinery was primarily heterosexual in orientation. Of the numerous advertisements printed, only one Pressbook poster suggested homosocial desire, with Laughton's enlarged face peering around a corner to stare at Parker who holds Lota in his arms (*Island of Lost Souls* [Paramount, 1933] Pressbook, Library of Congress microfiche file, Washington, D.C.).

48. Another exception to the mad-doctor conventions developed in the preceding section is *The Ape* (1940) starring Boris Karloff as Dr. Adrian. William Knight's B-movie tells the story of a good doctor who wears an ape's skin in order to kill the film's "bad guys," e.g., the town moneylender who exploits his clients and cheats on his wife. Misunderstood by most of the townspeople except his young female patient, her mother, his housekeeper, and the pharmacist, Adrian kills in order to obtain serum to cure the heroine's paralysis. *The Ape* is a variation on the conventional mad-doctor movie, having most in common with *The Walking Dead*, in which the doctor is also constructed as good and not as an object of fear.

49. Wood, "Return of the Repressed," p. 27.

50. Hyde's sadism was so striking a departure from Stevenson's novella that *Time*'s reviewer mentioned it in 1932: "Director Rouben Mamoulian added to the story a few Freudian touches. He made Hyde an incarnation of primitive sadism rather than a London bogeyman who was bad without good reason" ("Dr. Jekyll and Mr. Hyde," p. 25).

51. Hall, "Fredric March," p. 14.

52. Though by no means explicit, some advertisements offered homoerotic images, as was true of the publicity surrounding *The Crime of Dr. Crespi* in 1935. But whereas von Stroheim's film included homosocial connotations, thus offering a parallel to the representation of ambiguous male sexu-

ality in posters, *Dr. Jekyll and Mr. Hyde* works against homosocial meanings at the textual level. In a two-page advertisement that was part of a twenty-four page insert by Paramount in the *Motion Picture Herald*, a triangular rapport consisting of Jekyll, Hyde, and Muriel is depicted. A huge photo of Jekyll facing the camera is coupled with a smaller image of Hyde in the upper-right on one page of the poster. Hyde grins and leans seductively and menacingly toward his doubled and respectable self. On the second page is an image of Jekyll leaning toward Muriel, appearing as if he is about to kiss her (*Motion Picture Herald* [January 16, 1932]). In the advertisement, the triangular relationships among characters are marked both by heterosexuality (Jekyll is embracing Muriel) and homosociality (Hyde is about to embrace Jekyll), but the heterosexual dynamic is strongest at the narrative level of the film, and the homosocial dynamic of the advertisement is reduced to one man's desire for his second self. Like Twitchell's notion of bisexuality, Mamoulian's Jekyll/Hyde is homosocial only in a narcissistic sense.

53. Although *Mad Love* is a standard mad-doctor movie, its marketing campaign tried to expand the film's appeal by aligning it with the hypnosis subgenre. For example, one poster had the following phrase printed across an image of Peter Lorre's bald head: "HIS HYPNOTIC EYE HOLDS WOMEN SPELLBOUND, FASCINATED" (private collection of Ronald V. Borst, Los Angeles, Calif.). While the film itself does little to suggest that the heroine is hypnotized by Lorre's character—in fact, there is one scene in which Lorre wears an elaborate disguise and seems to hypnotize the hero—MGM's publicity campaign tried to widen its generic appeal by drawing on the seductive connotations associated with vampire movies. See fig. 4.2.

54. "Mad Love," p. 30.

55. Sennwald, "Peter Lorre," p. 20. In spite of Sennwald's original description of Gogol as a complex and paradoxical figure in this sequence, critics continue to equate his response with sadistic satisfaction alone. As Andrew Tudor remarks in *Monsters and Mad Scientists*: "The first shot tracks in on his half-shadowed face as the torture begins, his one clearly visible eye focused with startling intensity on the woman stretched out on the torturer's frame. The second shot, at the performance's end, shows us that same eye slowly closing in a kind of orgiastic satisfaction as her screams of pain reverberate around the theatre" (189).

56. "Mad Love," p. 30.

57. Kawin, "Children of the Light," p. 17.

58. Here is the poetic context in which the phrase appears:
Yet each man kills the thing he loves,
By each let this be heard,
Some do it with a bitter look,
Some with a flattering word.
The coward does it with a kiss,
The brave man with a sword!
Oscar Wilde, "The Ballad of Reading Gaol," part I, stanza 7.

6. White Skin, White Masks: Race, Gender, and Monstrosity in Jungle-Horror Cinema

59. "Mad Love," p. 30.
60. Davy, "Fe/male Impersonation," p. 241.

6. White Skin, White Masks: Race, Gender, and Monstrosity in Jungle-Horror Cinema

1. Peary, "Missing Links," p. 42.
2. The MPAA file for *Ingagi* includes a number of memos regarding the MPPDA's discovery that the film was a fraud. For example, in a letter dated October 8, 1930 from John V. Wilson to Mr. Gabriel L. Hess, General Attorney for the MPPDA, Wilson notes: "After efforts covering a long period I have finally been able to induce the man who took the part of the gorilla in 'INGAGI' to . . . [sign an] affidavit to certain facts" (MPAA files, Margaret Herrick Library, Los Angeles, Calif.).
3. An article devoted to the Federal Trade Commission's investigation into *Ingagi* includes the following assertion about the film: "The native woman represented as being sacrificed by her tribe to the gorillas was a Los Angeles colored woman, while the people represented as 'strange creatures apparently half-human and half-ape' were actually colored people living in Los Angeles made up for the purpose of the picture" (Burt, "Officially 'Fake' Now"). Charles Gemora, the man who plays the ape in the film, confirmed the falsification: "One of these scenes which appeared in said picture, showed him [Gemora] dressed as a gorilla seizing and abducting a native woman represented by a colored actress of Los Angeles" ("Affidavit" [October 8, 1930], MPAA files, Margaret Herrick Library, Los Angeles, Calif.).
4. The Hays office was not alone in remarking upon the film's fakery. *Science* magazine ran an article about the protests against *Ingagi* mounted by the American Society of Mammalogists, an organization that took issue with the film's falsification of mammalian behavior ("The Gorilla Film 'Ingagi'"). *Nature* also ran a piece on the movie's lack of authenticity. Here, a sartorial inconsistency was remarked upon: "The woman alleged to have been put out for the gorillas wore one costume before the animal appeared, but in the next scene, she was differently arrayed" ("'Ingagi'—True or False?" p. 66).
5. "'Ingagi' Passes Censors," p. 34.
6. The conflation of nonwhite races with monstrosity is not limited to jungle movies. For example, at the end of the 1920s and beginning of the 1930s Paramount produced a series of Fu Manchu films that starred a Chinese doctor whose monstrosity and evil, as well as fascination, are linked to his race (*The Mysterious Dr. Fu Manchu* [1929], *The Return of Dr. Fu Manchu* [1930], and *Daughter of the Dragon* [1932]). For further discussion of this topic, see chapter 3 of my dissertation, *Attack of the Leading Ladies*.
7. Fanon, *Black Skin, White Masks*, p. 30.
8. *Ingagi* (Congo Pictures, 1930) Pressbook. Library of Congress microfiche file, Washington, D.C.
9. Ibid.

10. *Ingagi*'s conflation of black women with white women may be even more direct than the general use of the term *women* might suggest. For Gerald Peary notes that the actresses who portrayed the amazon women were in blackface (42). Yet in light of the findings reported by the MPAA, Peary's use of the term *black-face* is potentially misleading. Initially, I assumed that Peary meant that the women were white actresses in black-face (thus suggesting the combination of white and black womanhood through the use of makeup). However, as I indicate in note 3, the *Motion Picture Herald* ran an article claiming that the film's actresses were "colored women" from Los Angeles. Since Peary does not provide references for his source materials in his article, there is no way to determine whether white actresses were ever involved in the production, whether Peary merely mistook black actresses for white, or whether African-American actresses were "darkened" by extra makeup.

11. In the case of *Kongo*, a 1932 MGM jungle movie set in Africa, John S. Cohen Jr. reported the following in the *New York Sun*: "There are horror pictures and horror pictures, but 'Kongo' at the Rialto seems a bit more meaningless than most" ("'Kongo' Is Revived With New Terrors"). Despite the horror label, *Kongo* portrays no supernatural or scientifically manufactured monsters. Instead, characters are horrid in all too human terms.

12. McCarthy, "Most Dangerous Game," p. 32. More recent critics, such as Peter Haining, have assumed the film's status as a horror movie: "Not all the early horror films relied entirely on monsters and things that go bump in the night for their effect. Indeed as the genre grew more sophisticated, adventurous producers and directors started looking even further afield for subjects that terrorized by implication or frightened by tension. A distinguished example of this type of production is MOST DANGEROUS GAME" (Haining quoted in "Most Dangerous Game").

13. Marianna Torgovnick comments on this phenomenon of boundary transgression with reference to Edgar Rice Burroughs's *Tarzan* novels. As she remarks: "As the series develops, it increasingly affirms existing hierarchies, including the hierarchy of male over female, white over black, West over rest. But, especially in the opening volumes of the series (and intermittently thereafter), the Tarzan materials also expose the shaky basis of these hierarchies by showing how far from 'natural' they seem to Tarzan as a boy and young man and how subject they are to cultural variation" (*Gone Primitive*, p. 46).

14. *New York Times*, March 17, 1931. The second quotation is from an unknown source (April 16, 1930) and can be found in the clipping file at the Margaret Herrick Library, Los Angeles, Calif.

15. Bogdan, *Freak Show*, p. 192.

16. Both Fanon and historian George M. Fredrickson describe the popular links forged by whites between black male sexuality and fantasized violence against white women. For example, in his description of race writings in the early 1900s, Fredrickson describes the work of Charles Carroll who

claims: "The apelike Negro was the actual 'tempter of Eve,' and miscegenation was the greatest of all sins" (Carroll quoted in Fredrickson, *Black Image*, p. 277).

17. Hoch, *White Hero Black Beast*, p. 43.

18. As Valerie Smith notes: "Myths of black male and female sexual appetitiveness were constructed to enable certain white men during slavery to exert their rights over the bodies of black men and white and black women" ("Split Affinities," p. 272).

19. Davis, *Women, Race, and Class*, pp. 184–85.

20. Quoted in Carter, *Scottsboro*, p. 36.

21. My focus is on white heroines in this chapter. However, there are 1930s jungle films in which white heroes also cross the "color line," e.g., *Kongo* (MGM, 1932), *The Most Dangerous Game* (RKO, 1932), *Prestige* (RKO, 1932), and *White Woman* (Paramount, 1933). For further discussion of those films, please see chapter 6 of my dissertation, *Attack of the Leading Ladies*.

22. This scenario takes a slightly different form in the *Tarzan* films of the era, in which the white male vies for a mediative position with the white heroine, Jane. In this instance, the hero is a more successful negotiator in that his affinity with apes and black men is better developed than hers. Despite Tarzan's more direct association with the darker races, however, he serves a conventional role, often saving Jane *from* the (bad black) savages. Thus, like the heroines of other jungle films, Jane also occupies an important position between the white and black worlds: she is the object exchanged between white and black men.

23. As bell hooks wrote in 1984: "White women who dominate feminist discourse today rarely question whether or not their perspective on women's reality is true to the lived experiences of women as a collective group. Nor are they aware of the extent to which their perspectives reflect race and class biases, although there has been a greater awareness of biases in recent years. Racism abounds in the writings of white feminists, reinforcing white supremacy and negating the possibility that women will bond politically across ethnic and racial boundaries" (*Feminist Theory*, p. 3).

24. Doane, *Femmes Fatales*, p. 214.

25. Dyer "White," p. 45.

26. For readings on Kong as a black rapist see, for example, Gottesman and Geduld, eds., *Girl in the Hairy Paw*, and Hogan, *Dark Romance*. For analyses of Kong as a projection of white male virility see, for example, Ambrogio, "Fay Wray" and Chaikin, "King Kong."

27. The success of Lewis's biography was remarked upon by at least one film reviewer: "[*Trader Horn* is] a faithful reproduction of the life of the famous African trader whose life story has captured the imagination of millions of book lovers" ("Trader Horn," *Minneapolis Sunday Tribune*).

28. "Trader Horn," *Motion Picture Herald*, p. 71.

29. *Motion Picture Herald* 102, no. 8 (February 21, 1931): 70.

30. *Trader Horn* (MGM, 1931) Pressbook, Margaret Herrick Library, Los Angeles, Calif. In addition to the cruel goddess and romance themes, the Pressbook includes tie-ins to products that appear in stills from the film, such as Underwood Typewriters, Packard cars, Lipton Tea, Shell Motor Oil, and Singer Sewing Machines. At least one of the tie-ins adds some ambiguity to the white goddess character, played by Edwina Booth. According to the publicity, Booth chose the Coty perfume *L'Aimant* as her favorite, and took it with her on her jungle expedition. Thus, her character may be savage, but the actress who plays her, viewers were informed, is quite civilized.

31. In a sense, Peru and Nina are doubles in the film: as a Latin lover, a man whose very name signifies his geographical difference from a conventional white American hero, Peru begins the film akin to the savage world. His transformation into a man comfortable in the jungle, then, can be read as his acceptance of what might be assumed to be his supposed indigenous identity and not as a representation of heroism. This is true especially given that he facilitates Nina's escape from the jungle but leaves the battles against the jungle's savages to Horn and Renchero. His heroism is considerably less demanding than the feats of bravery faced by the other male leads, including one who is black.

32. Cohen Jr., "'Trader Horn.'"

33. Richard Watts Jr., "'Trader Horn.'"

34. Cohen Jr., "'Trader Horn.'"

35. Hall, "An Impressive Jungle Melodrama."

36. Murray, "Trader Horn." Only two out of the eleven reviews I located thought Booth less than credible as a savage. For example, Thornton Delehanty critiqued Booth's snow-white skin, which seems out of place given that she is supposed to have lived in the jungle for twenty years ("The New Film"). Julia Shawell, one of the few reviewers identified as female, is even more skeptical: "Edwina Booth . . . does not once suggest the white girl captured by man-eating natives at infancy and reared to practices more ruthless than her foster-people" ("Screen-views").

37. *Motion Picture Herald* 107, no. 5 (April 30, 1932): 41.

38. *Motion Picture Herald* 107, no. 9 (May 28, 1932): 101.

39. *Motion Picture Herald* 107, no. 13 (June 25, 1932): 55.

40. Rosen, "*King Kong*," p. 8.

41. *The Blonde Captive* (Capital Films, 1932) Pressbook, Library of Congress microfiche file, Washington, D.C.

42. "Blonde Captive."

43. Hall, "Strange Experiences," p. 21.

44. Ellis, *Visible Fictions*, p. 31.

45. Pizor, "Blonde Captive."

46. Hall, "Strange Expedition," p. 21. In addition, the MPAA file for *The Blonde Captive* includes a typed review of the film, signed by R. E. P., with the following to say: "To my mind the continuity of the story is a little too smooth to be true and especially around the eyes and upper part of the face the

woman seems to be made up" (review dated March 8, 1932, MPAA files, Margaret Herrick Library, Los Angeles, Calif.).

47. Although the film was never investigated on the basis of veracity, it came before the Production Code Administration in 1942, some ten years after its initial release, to receive a seal of approval. In an interesting historical twist, the legal counsel who authored the appeal to the PCA, resorted to antifascist rhetoric in order to critique the miscegenation elements of the code: "It is certainly the most reactionary stand for the most progressive institution to wit . . . to have within its code a prohibition which absolutely enunciates the racial barriers discriminatory in its inception and tends to sustain by analogy the theory of race problem advocated by Nazi Germany and against which we are today shedding the blood of our citizenry without any distinction to race, creed or color" ("Appellate's Brief," n.d., MPAA files, Margaret Herrick Library, Los Angeles, Calif.).

48. In *The Devil Finds Work*, James Baldwin mentions the appeal of Tarzan and Rudolph Valentino's character in *The Sheik* to white audiences: "Both the Sheik and Tarzan are white men who look and act like black men—act like black men, that is, according to the white imagination which has created them: one can eat one's cake without having it, or one can have one's cake without eating it" (38).

49. For an excellent discussion of Tarzan's race and gender dynamics in his literary role, see Torgovnick's second chapter, "Taking Tarzan Seriously," in *Gone Primitive*, pp. 42–72.

50. Unlike *The Blonde Captive* and *Trader Horn*, *The Savage Girl*, though it depicts interstitial qualities, was not popular with audiences or reviewers, as Chic's piece in the May 2, 1933 *Variety* suggests: "'Savage Girl' is strictly for the lowest brackets" ("Savage Girl").

51. *The Savage Girl* (Monarch Pictures, 1932) Pressbook, Margaret Herrick Library, Los Angeles, Calif.

52. Cooper quoted in Turner, "Hunting *The Most Dangerous Game*," pp. 41–42.

53. "Half breed" is the phrase used by James E. Mitchell, who described Carrillo's character thus: "Leo Carrillo, as a half breed, so inordinately proud of his English blood that he considers himself a white man, volunteers to lead them to a port, but loses his way the first day" ("'4 Frightened People'"). In another contemporary review, the preferred phrase is "half-caste" (Abel, "4 Frightened People"). In both examples, Carrillo's character is bestowed a liminal and inadequate racial status—he is half versus whole.

54. Haraway, *Primate Visions*, p. 20.

55. Parsons, "Horror, Thrills and Suspense Fill Picture."

56. Beck, *Scream Queens*, p. 84.

57. Ambrogio, "Fay Wray," p. 128.

58. Bige, "King Kong."

59. *Los Angeles Sunday Times*, September 11, 1932; Fay Wray Collection, University of Southern California Cinema Archives; Fay Wray Scrapbook 1929–1933, p. 119.

60. *Los Angeles Examiner,* March 27, 1933; ibid. n. p.

61. Carroll, "*King Kong,*" p. 233.

62. Snead, "Spectatorship and Capture in *King Kong,*" p. 60.

63. Wray cites other contradictory aspects of *King Kong* when she writes of the monster's ability to elicit sympathy from viewers. Using her own spectatorial response as a gauge, she remarks: "If Kong were purely a horrifying and horrible fellow, the sympathy he evokes when, finally, he is struck down, wouldn't exist. There is no doubt about such sympathy. Even I, seeing the film a year or so ago, felt a great lump in my throat on behalf of Kong" ("How Fay Wray Met Kong," p. 224).

64. Wray, *On the Other Hand,* pp. xi–xii.

65. Griffin, "Sympathy for the Werewolf," p. 84.

66. While Ann is ambivalent about Jack's overtures, Fay Wray was recently quite clear about her personal predilections in the film: "'Bruce Cabot, who played the love interest [Jack], was not the kind of person I would have been attracted to,' Wray admits today. 'Kong was more thrilling. . . . There was an elemental goodness and kindness in him, and a tenderness . . . it seemed so cruel to shoot him down. My throat hurts—*aches*—for him when I see that scene: I can believe it" (emphasis in original; Fay Wray quoted in Aronson, "Fay Wray," p. 163).

67. Fox, "Golden Age of Terror."

68. *King Kong* (RKO, 1942) Pressbook, Margaret Herrick Library, Los Angeles, Calif.

69. Krasniewicz and Blitz, "Review of *Primate Visions,*" p. 168.

Afterword: The Horror of It All

1. "Torture," p. 42.

2. Gramson, *Claims to Fame,* p. 28.

3. The full description was as follows: "'Dracula's Daughter' emerges from the grave at night, a beautiful woman seeking victims. Kills three, heroine next, but hero and police arrive in time" ("Dracula's Daughter," *Christian Century*).

Filmography

Compiled by Lia Hotchkiss

The Black Cat. 1934. *Director:* Edgar G. Ulmer. *Screenplay:* Edgar G. Ulmer and Peter Ruic. *Production/release:* Universal. Stranded in Austria, honeymooners (David Manners and Jacqueline Wells a.k.a. Julie Bishop) meet psychiatrist Dr. Vitus Werdergast (Bela Lugosi) and seek shelter in the mansion of his host, architect Hjalmar Poelzig (Boris Karloff). The mansion is built over the ruins of Fort Maramos, where Poelzig betrayed thousands of men in World War I and sent them to their deaths. As a result of this treachery, Werdergast spent fifteen years in a Russian prison and has now returned, seeking wife, daughter, and vengeance. Werdergast learns that his wife had died at the hands of Poelzig, and his daughter meets the same fate during the course of the narrative. In the end, Werdergast flays Poelzig alive, allows the young couple to escape, and then blows up the mansion, with Poelzig and himself in it.

The Blonde Captive. 1932. *Director:* Louis King. *Production/release:* Capital Films. This film records a 1929 expedition led by Dr. Paul C. Withington into northern Australia in search of the supposed descendants of the Neanderthals. It is a travelogue picture that offers footage of native peoples on a number of islands, including Hawaii and Bali. Near the conclusion, a blonde boy is discovered among a group of Aborigine children, and the viewer is offered a tale of a white woman who was shipwrecked many years before and who had had the child with an Aborigine man. In the end, she refuses to return to Europe with the explorers.

Bride of Frankenstein. 1935. *Director:* James Whale. *Screenplay:* William Hurlbut and John L. Balderston. *Production/release:* Universal. A thunderstorm rages around a castle as the camera cuts to Percy Bysshe Shelley (Douglas Walton), Mary Shelley (Elsa Lanchester), and Lord Byron (Gavin Gordon) recapping the plot of *Frankenstein* and prompting Mary Shelley to create a sequel. Cut to the burning windmill, where the movie *Frankenstein* left off, as Henry Frankenstein (Colin Clive) is carried to his father's castle. Dr. Septimus Pretorius (Ernest Thesiger) arrives at the Frankenstein castle and urges Henry to resume his work and to create a mate for the monster. The monster's (Boris Karloff) newly created bride (Elsa Lanchester), however, rejects Frankenstein's first creature. In response, the monster urges Henry and Elizabeth to escape, after which he blows up the laboratory, thus killing Pretorius, the monstrous bride, and himself.

The Crime of Dr. Crespi. 1935. *Director:* John Auer. *Screenplay:* Lewis Graham and Edwin Olmstead. *Production/release:* Republic/Liberty Pictures. A surgeon, Dr. Crespi (Erich von Stroheim), seeks revenge on Dr. Ross (John Bohn), the man who married the woman he loved (Harriet Russell). Crespi administers a drug to Ross, which induces a cataleptic trance that gives the impression that Ross has died in surgery. Crespi then buries his enemy alive. Two suspicious colleagues, however, free Ross, who then wanders the hospital corridors in a maddened state and drives the surgeon to commit suicide.

Daughter of the Dragon. 1931. *Director:* Lloyd Corrigan. *Screenplay:* Sidney Buchman. *Production/release:* Paramount. In the third of Paramount's series of Fu Manchu films, the dying Chinese patriarch (Warner Oland) tells his daughter Ling Moy (Anna May Wong) to carry out the murders of Sir John Petrie (Holmes Herbert) and his son Ronald (Bramwell Fletcher). The sleuth Ah Kee (Sessue Hayakawa) and Scotland Yard, however, frustrate her efforts. Ronald falls in love with Ling Moy, who shares his feelings but decides to fulfill her promise to her father and proceeds with plans to kill Ronald and Ah Kee, who is also attracted to her. In the end, however, Ling Moy is killed, together with Ah Kee.

Dr. Jekyll and Mr. Hyde. 1931. *Director:* Rouben Mamoulian. *Screenplay:* Samuel Hoffenstein and Percy Heath. *Production/release:* Paramount. Dr. Henry Jekyll (Fredric March) researches compounds that he claims release the buried half of human nature. Experimenting upon himself, Henry releases a devious second identity—Mr. Hyde (also Fredric March)—a monster that torments a barmaid named Ivy (Miriam Hopkins). In the meantime, Henry's fiancée returns from a trip with her father, and Henry resolves to give up his double life. His efforts to do so are in vain, however, since he no longer needs the elixir to transform into Hyde. As Hyde, Henry kills Ivy and threatens Jekyll's fiancée and her father. Police chase Hyde to Jekyll's home, where he is killed by the police.

Doctor X. 1931. *Director:* Michael Curtiz. *Screenplay:* Robert Tasker and Earl Baldwin. *Production/release:* First National/Warner Brothers. Police pursue a full-moon murderer who kills with a scalpel found only at Dr. Xavier's (Lionel Atwill) Academy of Surgical Research. Xavier proposes reenacting the crimes before his colleagues in order to catch the murderer, but his first reenactment ends in the death of one of his colleagues. He is assisted in a second staging of a murder scene by his daughter Joanne (Fay Wray). Xavier's one-armed colleague (Preston Foster) is revealed to be the fiend at the conclusion and is dispatched by a newspaper reporter, played by Lee Tracy, who, after a series of inept displays, redeems himself and saves the day.

Dracula. 1931. *Director:* Tod Browning. *Screenplay:* Garrett Fort. Based on the stage play by John L. Balderston and Hamilton Deane. *Production/release:* Universal. A British real estate agent, Renfield (Dwight Frye), travels to Transylvania to conclude a sale to Count Dracula (Bela Lugosi). Once there, he is bitten by the vampire, who then sails to England with his latest victim, now insane. In London, Renfield is committed at Dr. Seward's (Herbert Bunston) sanitarium, and the count meets Seward, his daughter Mina (Helen Chandler), her fiancé John Harker (David Manners), and their guest Lucy (Frances Dade) at the symphony. The count attacks Lucy, who dies that night, which eventually turns her into a vampire with a preference for young girls. Professor Van Helsing (Edward Van Sloan) is called in, recognizes the mark of the vampire, and, when Mina begins to suffer too, suspects the count. Eventually Dracula abducts Mina. Van Helsing and Harker follow to save the heroine, which Van Helsing does by staking the count in offscreen space.

Dracula's Daughter. 1936. *Director:* Lambert Hillyer. *Screenplay:* Garrett Fort. *Production/release:* Universal. In this sequel to Browning's *Dracula,* Scotland Yard finds the bodies of Renfield and Count Dracula at Carfax Abbey. Still on the scene, Dr. von Helsing (Edward Van Sloan; the character's name changes) confesses to the murders and is arrested. The investigating officer brings in a psychiatrist named Jeffrey Garth (Otto Kruger) to determine if von Helsing, who raves about vampires, is insane. As Garth is analyzing von Helsing, Dracula's body is stolen from the police by Countess Marya Zaleska (Gloria Holden), Dracula's daughter. In a dramatic scene, Zaleska burns her father's remains in the hopes that his demise will free her from his vampiric curse. But to no avail—she remains caught in Dracula's blood lust. Zaleska meets Garth at a party. He encourages her to overcome her desire for what plagues her, but she succumbs to her urges and bites a girl named Lili (Nan Grey). Dismayed to find that Garth is incapable of helping her, Zaleska kidnaps his secretary, Janet Blake (Marguerite Churchill), and escapes to Transylvania. Garth follows them and confronts Zaleska, who threatens to kill Janet unless Garth joins her as a vampire. He agrees, but her assistant (Irving Pichel) shoots a wooden arrow through her heart before Garth succumbs.

Four Frightened People. 1934. *Director:* Cecil B. DeMille. *Screenplay:* Bartlett Cormack and Lenore Coffee. *Production/release:* Paramount. Off the coast of Malaysia, cholera breaks out on a tramp steamer. Passengers Judith Jones (Claudette Colbert), a New England schoolteacher; the wealthy Mrs. Marsdick (Mary Boland); Stewart (William Gargan), a war correspondent and world traveler; and Arnold (Herbert Marshall) reach land in a small boat. They find a guide, played by Leo Carrillo, who offers to take them to a port, but he loses his way and they find themselves in the midst of adventures. The hapless guide is dispatched by a pygmy arrow, and the women, in turn, become increasingly sexually aggressive and independent as the group makes its way into the depths of the jungle. Boland's character enjoys an affair with a native chief and the gang eventually reaches "civilization."

Frankenstein. 1931. *Director:* James Whale. *Screenplay:* Garrett Fort, Francis Edwards Faragoh, John Russell (uncredited), and Robert Florey (uncredited). Based on the stage play by John L. Balderston. *Production/release:* Universal. Henry Frankenstein (Colin Clive) creates a monster (Boris Karloff) from parts of corpses. Hoping to persuade the obsessed medical student to desist, his fiancée, Elizabeth (Mae Clarke), friend Victor Moritz (John Boles), and former professor Dr. Waldman (Edward Van Sloan) arrive just in time to see the monster brought to life with a lightning bolt. When the monster kills the scientist's hunchbacked assistant, Fritz (Dwight Frye), Waldman persuades his student to resume his wedding plans and let him destroy the monster by dissection. As the professor prepares to do so, the monster comes out of sedation and strangles him. The escaped monster befriends and accidentally kills a young peasant girl (Marilyn Harris). After news of the additional murders, Henry and a search party track it down. The monster drags its creator to a decrepit windmill, which villagers set ablaze; the monster throws Henry's body down and, trapped in the flames, the fiend perishes (until the sequel, of course).

Ingagi. 1930. *Director:* William Campbell. *Production/release:* Congo Pictures. Compiled of footage gleaned from other jungle films and original footage shot in a studio soundstage, this film nonetheless claims in its opening titles to portray a two-year expedition into Africa, which began in 1926 and was led by Sir Hubert Winstead and Captain Swayne. Also suggested in the title, the film's draw is the supposed discovery of tribal women given as sacrifices to palliate the gorillas (the ingagi). The Pressbook calls the women "veritable amazons" and "wild women who live in trees" who, it is implied, have borne to the gorillas "creatures . . . half-ape, half-human."

Island of Lost Souls. 1932. *Director:* Erle C. Kenton. *Screenplay:* Waldemar Young and Philip Wylie. *Production/release:* Paramount. Edward Parker (Richard Arlen), shipwrecked in the Pacific, is rescued from his raft by a boat headed for an uncharted island. There, the ship drops off Montgomery (Arthur

Holt), an agent of Dr. Moreau (Charles Laughton), and a cargo of wild animals. Parker is dropped off as well and finds Moreau's island populated with strange beasts—the results of Moreau's experiments in turning animals into humans through surgery. Hoping to determine whether the bestial has completely receded from his most advanced creation, he nearly succeeds in involving Parker in an affair with sensuous Lota the Panther Woman (Kathleen Burke), who is given away at the last moment by her talonlike fingernails. Meanwhile, Parker's fiancée, Ruth Thomas (Leila Hyams), learns of his fate and sets out to rescue him. With Montgomery's assistance she succeeds, leaving Moreau to perish at the hands of the creatures he has tormented.

King Kong. 1933. *Director:* Merian C. Cooper and Ernest B. Schoedsack. *Screenplay:* James A. Creelman and Ruth Rose. *Production/release:* RKO. Promised money and adventure, Ann Darrow (Fay Wray) agrees to star in movie producer Carl Denham's (Robert Armstrong) film, which requires her to go on a voyage. Heavily stocked with ammunition, the ship follows a route marked on a primitive chart Denham has obtained from an old sea captain. He hopes to find something called a god on Skull Island. They arrive, and the native chief, fascinated with Ann's blonde hair, seeks to trade six native women for her. When rebuffed, the natives kidnap Ann to offer her as a sacrificial bride to the giant Kong, who takes the fainting Ann into the jungle. The crew, led by Jack Driscoll (Bruce Cabot), who has fallen in love with Ann, steals her away from Kong. The monster follows and walks into a trap prepared by Denham. On display in America, Kong is so infuriated by flashbulbs that he bursts out of his chains and wreaks havoc on New York City. After finding Ann, Kong climbs the Empire State Building; as he is shot down by planes, he gently sets Ann down upon a ledge and falls to his death.

Kongo. 1932. *Director:* William Cowen. *Screenplay:* Leon Gordon. *Production/release:* MGM. Flint (Walter Huston), a man who has lost the use of his legs, leads a band of ivory thieves in Africa. The latest victim of Flint's thievery, Gregg (C. Henry Gordon), had run off with Flint's wife years before and had kicked Flint's spine, thus paralyzing him. In revenge, Flint confines the couple's daughter Ann (Virginia Bruce) to a convent and subsequently sends her to a whorehouse in Zanzibar. An ill, desperate drunk, she now lives with the gang of thieves. A drug-addicted doctor named Kingsland (Conrad Nagel) appears to cure Flint's paralysis. Smitten with Ann, the doctor promises to save her but fails to do so. Ann's father comes down the river and reveals to Flint that he and Flint's wife had had no child; Ann is actually Flint's daughter. Attacked by natives acting on Flint's orders, Gregg dies, and Ann, whom everyone but Flint believes to be Gregg's daughter, faces the native custom that demands the sacrifice of a daughter at a father's funeral. Kingsland and Flint help Ann escape, and Flint perishes after helping to rescue her.

Mad Love. 1935. *Director:* Karl Freund. *Screenplay:* P. J. Wolfson, Guy Endore and John L. Balderston. *Production/release:* MGM. Dr. Gogol (Peter Lorre) is madly in love with the actress-wife of a concert pianist (Frances Drake and Colin Clive, respectively). When the latter's hands are irreparably damaged in a train wreck, the doctor grafts on the hands of a knife-thrower who had been guillotined for murder. To the pianist's horror, his new hands begin to exhibit their former owner's propensities. In an effort to drive the pianist insane, and attract his wife's affections in the process, the doctor impersonates the dead killer and torments Clive. About to strangle Drake, whom he believes to be a wax statuette brought to life by his own desire, Gogol is killed by the knife-throwing Clive.

Mark of the Vampire. 1935. *Director:* Tod Browning. *Screenplay:* Guy Endore and Bernard Schubert. *Production/release:* MGM. A police inspector (Lionel Atwill), with the aid of a hypnotist (Lionel Barrymore), constructs an ominous supernatural scene populated with vampires (a troupe of actors led by Bela Lugosi) in order to flush out a murderer from the suspects. The heroine, Irena (Elizabeth Allan), goes along with the ruse and feigns submission to a female vampire named Luna (Carol Borland). The villain (Jean Hersholt) relives his crime under the influence of the literally hypnotic scene, which is only revealed to the film audience as a sham late in the action.

The Most Dangerous Game. 1932. *Director:* Ernest B. Schoedsack and Merrian C. Cooper. *Screenplay:* James A. Creelman. *Production/release:* RKO. A renowned but jaded big-game hunter named Count Zaroff (Leslie Banks) owns an island in the Malay archipelago to which he attracts passing ships that then founder in the reefs. The people strong enough to escape the sharks and swim to shore become his prey. He describes his game to his latest victim, another famous hunter (Joel McCrea), and urges McCrea to join him in his sport. When McCrea is appalled, Zaroff decides to hunt the hunter. McCrea takes Eve (Fay Wray), Zaroff's other captive, with him to try to escape. Zaroff hunts them with bow and arrow. McCrea's crafty character wins the game.

The Mummy. 1932. *Director:* Karl Freund. *Screenplay:* John L. Balderston. *Production/release:* Universal. In 1921, the archaeologist Sir Joseph Whemple (Arthur Byron) discovers the mummy of the high priest Imhotep and an alabaster box with an inscription promising anyone who opens it eternal punishment. While Whemple and his friend Dr. Mueller (Edward van Sloan) debate whether to open the box, Whemple's assistant does so, reviving the mummy (Boris Karloff) in the process. Eleven years later, an Egyptian scholar named Ardath Bey (Boris Karloff) approaches Sir Joseph's son Frank (David Manners). Bey is actually Imhotep, who had been executed for trying to bring his beloved Princess Anck-es-en-Amon back from the dead. Bey hopes to try to revive her again, but discovers her reincarnated as Helen Grosvenor (Zita Johann), a patient of Dr. Mueller. Helen is torn between a growing love for Frank and the influence of Ardath Bey. Bey kills Sir Joseph and attempts to kill Frank. At the British Museum, Bey persuades Helen to sacrifice herself to him. Helen prays to a statue of Isis for help. The goddess sends forth a flash of light that destroys both the scroll and Bey.

Murders in the Rue Morgue. 1932. *Director:* Robert Florey. *Screenplay:* Tom Reed, Dale van Every, and John Huston. *Production/release:* Universal. At a Parisian carnival, Pierre Dupin (Leon Waycoff), his roommate Paul (Bert Roach) and girl friend Camille L'Espanaye (Sidney Fox) come across Dr. Mirakle (Bela Lugosi), who is exhibiting an ape named Erik. Afterwards, Mirakle abducts a woman from the streets and takes her to a laboratory, where he apparently has injected her with Erik's blood. She dies, the third such victim to be found that week. Pierre, a medical student, performs an autopsy and discovers that she died by injection. Warning Camille not to respond to an invitation from Dr. Mirakle, Pierre discovers the nature of the doctor's work. Dr. Mirakle sends Erik into Camille's room to abduct her. Just as the doctor is about to inject Camille, Erik strangles him, picks her up, and ascends to the roof. Pierre saves Camille by shooting Erik.

The Mysterious Dr. Fu Manchu. 1929. *Director:* Rowland V. Lee. *Screenplay:* Florence Ryerson and Lloyd Corrigan. *Production/release:* Paramount. The first in a series of Fu Manchu films, this movie opens during the Boxer Rebellion. A British man sends his daughter to Dr. Fu Manchu (Warner Oland), a Chinese man loyal to the British. Unfortunately, some Boxers take refuge in Fu Manchu's garden, and the British open fire, killing Fu Manchu's wife and child. He swears vengeance, using the British girl to obtain it. Years later, using the hypnotized white daughter, Lia Eltham (Jean Arthur), as his agent, Fu Manchu systematically murders the European officers who put down the rebellion. Eventually, Fu Manchu is discovered, fails to kill the Petrie family, his latest prey, takes the poison intended for one of the Petries, and dies (until the sequel).

The Mystery of the Wax Museum. 1933. *Director:* Michael Curtiz. *Screenplay:* Don Mullaly and Carl Erickson. *Production/release:* Warner Brothers. A renowned wax sculptor named Ivan (Lionel Atwill) goes insane when he and his wax figurines are badly burned in a fire. Inspired by the waxen mask he wears to cover his disfigured face, he kills people who resemble the historical figures he sculpts and encases them in wax. Researching the disappearance of a body from the morgue, a reporter (Glenda Farrell) solves the case.

Old Dark House. 1932. *Director:* James Whale. *Screenplay:* Benn W. Levy. *Additional Dialogue:* R. C. Schiff. *Production/release:* Universal. In this subtle burlesque of horror, Philip and Margaret Waverton (Raymond Massey and

Gloria Stuart) and Roger Penderel (Melvyn Douglas), travelers lost in a storm, seek refuge at an old stone house. They meet a sinister butler (Boris Karloff), are invited in by a creepy brother and sister named Horace and Rebecca Femm (Ernest Thesiger and Eva Moore), and are joined soon after by other travelers. Philip knocks the butler unconscious in a quarrel. He and Margaret discover the frail 102-year-old master of the house, who warns them of his insane elder son, who is determined to burn the house down. The aggrieved butler releases the son, who sets the upper bannister on fire. In an ensuing struggle the son dies. The storm subsides, and the travelers leave the unperturbed Femms.

The Raven. 1935. *Director:* Louis Friedlander. *Screenplay:* David Boehm and Jim Tully. *Production/release:* Universal. A brilliant surgeon, Dr. Vollin (Bela Lugosi), goes insane when rejected by a beautiful dancer (Irene Ware). When a killer (Boris Karloff) begs him to improve his appearance surgically, Vollin responds by making the man even uglier and transforming him into a criminal-servant bound to the surgeon's will. A fanatical Edgar Allen Poe aficionado, Vollin not only collects Poe's works and keeps a raven, he also builds replicas of the torture chambers Poe describes in his work. When persuaded to operate on the dancer, who has been scarred in a crash, he subjects her to torture. Karloff frees her and sacrifices himself to save her and kill Vollin.

The Return of Dr. Fu Manchu. 1930. *Director:* Rowland V. Lee. *Screenplay:* writer unknown. Based on the story by Sax Rohmer. *Production/release:* Paramount. The second film in the Paramount series opens with Fu Manchu's funeral. In the elaborate ceremony, however, he (Warner Oland)—very much alive— slips out of a trap door in his coffin. Lia Eltham (Jean Arthur), the adopted white daughter whom he hypnotized in the first film, and Jack Petrie (Neil Hamilton) prepare for their wedding. Fu Manchu abducts Lia, her Aunt Agatha (Evelyn Hall), and Inspector Smith (O.P. Heggie), whose mind the Chinese doctor plans to destroy with a drug. Fu Manchu agrees to release the captives in return for a guarantee of safety, but Smith's men attack, and Fu Manchu escapes with Lia and a policeman in tow. Through hypnosis, Fu Manchu gains control over the policeman and uses him to kidnap Jack so that the doctor can remove the bullet lodged at the base of Fu Manchu's skull that promises imminent paralysis. After the successful operation, Fu decides to blow them all up, but Smith pushes the Chinese doctor into the water, presumably killing Fu Manchu.

The Savage Girl. 1932. *Director:* Harry Fraser. *Screenplay:* N. Brewster Morse. *Production/release:* Monarch Pictures. Jim Franklyn (Walter Byron), an explorer, and Amos P. Stitch, a man who wishes to gather animals for his private zoo, are warned by their assistant in Africa, Erich Vernuth (Adolf Millar), that they are heading into dangerous country where the natives worship the

Jungle Goddess, a white woman lost in the wilds as an infant. As they travel, they are indeed quietly observed by a white woman (Rochelle Hudson) who can speak to the animals. They successfully trap the woman. Franklyn fires Vernuth after the latter demands that he "share" the woman. Franklyn frees her, but meanwhile Vernuth has reported to the tribal chief that a white man has stolen the Jungle Goddess. Attracted to Franklyn, she returns to his camp. He repels her advances. The natives kidnap him, planning to sacrifice him. Stitch rescues him. Vernuth tries to grab the Savage Girl, but a gorilla saves her. The film ends with Franklyn and the girl embracing.

Supernatural. 1933. *Director:* Victor Halperin. *Screenplay:* Harvey Thew and Brian Marlowe. *Production/release:* Paramount. Alan Dinehart plays a fake spiritualist who betrays his associate (Vivienne Osborne), a three-time murderess, to the police. Vowing revenge, she is executed. He inveigles a wealthy heiress (Carole Lombard) to participate in a séance by claiming to have contacted the spirit of her recently dead brother. Lombard's doctor (H. B. Warner) has obtained permission to use Osborne's body in his experiments with soul migration, and, in his laboratory, Osborne's spirit enters Lombard's body, and Lombard then attacks and kills Dinehart. After much aggressive behavior on the part of Lombard, Osborne's spirit departs and Lombard is reunited with her fiancé (Randolph Scott).

Svengali. 1931. *Director:* Archie Mayo. *Screenplay:* J. Grubb Alexander. *Production/release:* Warner Brothers. Svengali (John Barrymore) is a poverty-stricken voice teacher living in Paris who captivates women with his hypnotic gaze. He visits the studio of three English painters, where he meets Trilby (Marian Marsh), a beautiful milkmaid and part-time model. She and one of the artists, Little Billie (Bramwell Fletcher), fall in love, but they have a falling out after he finds her posing nude. She disappears with Svengali, who is able to cure her headaches through hypnosis. Later the three artists attend a concert given by the now famous Madame Svengali and discover, to their surprise, that the formerly tone-deaf Trilby sings enchantingly. Knowing that she has never loved him, Svengali fears that she will return to Little Billie and flees with her. As he suffers from heart disease and obsesses over losing her, their fortunes decline. Little Billie tracks them down to a seedy nightclub; Svengali suffers a heart attack, and the loss of his hypnotic control renders Trilby tone-deaf in mid-song.

Tarzan, the Ape Man. 1932. *Director:* W.S. Van Dyke. *Screenplay:* Cyril Hume and Ivor Novello. *Production/release:* MGM. In this first sound version of *Tarzan,* the title character (Johnny Weissmuller), a white man completely ignorant of civilization and living in the African jungle, comes upon a safari led by James Parker (C. Aubrey Smith). Tarzan accompanies the safari and uses his considerable strength and ability to communicate with animals, to defend the safari's members from wild beasts, and to rescue them from a hostile native village. He falls in love with Parker's daughter, Jane (Maureen O'Sullivan), and at the end of the film wants her to remain in the wild as his mate.

Trader Horn. 1931. *Director:* W. S. Van Dyke. *Screenplay:* Dale Van Every. *Production/release:* MGM. Trader Horn (Harry Carey), a famous African hunter and his young companion, Peru (Duncan Renaldo), encounter a friend of Horn's, a woman named Edith Trend (Olive Golden), while traveling on safari. She is looking for a woman the natives call a "white goddess," whom she believes is her daughter Nina, who disappeared as a child. Trend is killed, and Horn decides to continue her quest. After much scenic travel, he and Peru find Nina (Edwina Booth). After persuading her to come away, they escape with her. She speaks no English, but Peru falls in love with her and takes her to "civilization." After a bittersweet parting, Horn stays in the jungle.

The Vampire Bat. 1933. *Director:* Frank Strayer. *Screenplay:* Edward T. Lowe. *Production/release:* Majestic. Lionel Atwill plays a mad doctor who succeeds in creating living tissue that continually needs fresh blood in order to grow. Because his murder victims are drained of blood and the village has become infested with bats, the inhabitants of this Central East European village become suspicious of the village idiot's (Dwight Frye) fondness for bats and kill him in the fashion prescribed for vampires. They do this despite the police chief's (Melvyn Douglas) protestations that the killer is human. The murders continue, and one of Atwill's assistants (Fay Wray) discovers the truth. Atwill threatens her, but Douglas arrives to save the heroine, while Atwill's other assistant (played by Preston Foster) shoots the mad doctor and destroys the laboratory.

White Zombie. 1932. *Director:* Victor Halperin. *Screenplay:* Garnett Weston. *Production/release:* Amusement Securities/United Artists. Madeline (Madge Bellamy) arrives in Haiti to marry her fiancé (John Harron). A coach takes her past a furtive burial ceremony. By the side of the road, she meets Murder Legendre (Bela Lugosi), who steals her scarf. A zombie master who supplies zombie labor for the local mills, Legendre has been enlisted by one of Madeline's fellow travelers (Robert Frazer) to ensnare her as a zombie. After her wedding, Legendre turns her into a zombie, which makes her appear dead. She is buried in a tomb, while her mourning husband looks on, but Legendre retrieves her body later that night. Legendre and Frazer keep Madeline in Legendre's castle but begin fighting over her, and Legendre turns Frazer into a zombie. Madeline's husband, Neil, refuses to believe she is dead and, eventually, helps free her from Legendre's clutches, but not before she tries to kill Neil under Legendre's bidding.

Bibliography

Aaronson, Charles S. "B. O. Explodes Idea That Women Dislike War and Crook Pictures. Feminine Attendance at Four Productions Classed as Lacking in Love or Romantic Interest Averages 61 Per Cent of Total at Matinees and 59 Per Cent at Night." *Exhibitors Herald-World* 110, no. 10 (September 6, 1930).

Abel. "4 Frightened People." *Variety* (January 30, 1934).

——. "Old Dark House." *Variety* (November 1, 1932).

——. "White Zombie." *Variety* (August 2, 1932).

Altman, Rick. "Dickens, Griffith, and Film Theory Today." *South Atlantic Quarterly* 88, no. 2 (Spring 1989): 321–59.

Ambrogio, Anthony. "Fay Wray: Horror Films' First Sex Symbol." In *Eros in the Mind's Eye: Sexuality and the Fantastic in Art and Film*, ed. Donald Palumbo. New York: Greenwood, 1986, pp. 127–39.

"And Who Is This Girl?" *Photoplay* 39, no. 4 (March 1931): 68.

Aronson, Steven M. L. "Fay Wray: King Kong's Favorite Costar at Home in Los Angeles." *Architectural Digest* 51, no. 4 (April 1994): 160–63; 274–75.

"Ask the Answer Man." *Photoplay* 41, no. 4 (March 1932): 86.

"At the Roxy." *New York Times*, May 11, 1935.

Auerbach, Nina. *Woman and the Demon: The Life of a Victorian Myth.* Cambridge: Harvard University Press, 1982.

Baldwin, James. *The Devil Finds Work.* New York: Dial, 1976.

Balio, Tino. *Grand Design: Hollywood as a Modern Business Enterprise, 1930–1939.* New York: Scribner's, 1993.

Barry, Barbara. "Such a Naughty Nero." *Photoplay* 14, no. 3 (February 1933).

Barry, John F. and Epes W. Sargent. *Building Theatre Patronage: Management and Merchandising.* New York: Chalmers, 1927.

Beck, Calvin T. *Scream Queens: Heroines of the Horrors.* New York: MacMillan, 1978.

Benshoff, Harry. "Pedophiles, Pods, and Perverts: Homosexual Monsters in the 1950s." Paper read at the 1995 Society for Cinema Studies Conference, New York, N.Y.

Berenstein, Rhona. "Spectatorship-as-Drag: The Act of Viewing and Classic Horror Cinema." In *Viewing Positions: Ways of Seeing Film,* ed. Linda Williams. New Brunswick: Rutgers University Press, 1994.

——. *Attack of the Leading Ladies: The Masks of Gender, Sexuality, and Race in Classic Horror Cinema.* Ph.D. diss., University of California, Los Angeles, 1992.

Beyette, Beverly. "Dean of Hollywood Publicists, 79, Keeps Plugging Away Honest." *Los Angeles Examiner,* September 21, 1986.

Bige. "King Kong." *Variety* (March 7, 1933).

"Blonde Captive." *Variety* (March 1, 1932).

"The Blonde Captive." *Motion Picture Herald* 106, no. 10 (March 5, 1932).

Bogdan, Robert. *Freak Show: Presenting Human Oddities for Amusement and Profit.* Chicago: University of Chicago Press, 1988.

"The Bride of Frankenstein." *Time* (April 29, 1935).

Brunas, Michael, John Brunas, and Tom Weaver. *Universal Horrors: The Studio's Classic Films, 1931–1946.* Jefferson, N.C.: McFarland, 1990.

Burt, Francis L. "Officially 'Fake' Now." *Motion Picture Herald* 111, no. 7 (May 13, 1933).

Busby, Marquis. "'Dracula' Better Film Than Stage Play at Orpheum." *Los Angeles Examiner,* March 28, 1931.

Butler, Ivan. *Horror in the Cinema.* London: A. Zwimmer, 1970.

Butler, Judith. *Bodies That Matter: On the Discursive Limits of "Sex."* New York: Routledge, 1993.

——. "Imitation and Gender Insubordination." In *Inside/Out: Lesbian Theories, Gay Theories,* ed. Diana Fuss. New York: Routledge, 1991, pp. 13–31.

——. *Gender Trouble.* New York: Routledge, 1990.

Carroll, Noël. *The Philosophy of Horror or Paradoxes of the Heart.* New York: Routledge, 1990.

——. "*King Kong:* Ape and Essence." In *Planks of Reason,* ed. Barry Keith Grant. Metuchen, N.J.: Scarecrow, 1984, pp. 215–44.

Carter, Dan. *Scottsboro: An American Tragedy.* Baton Rouge: Louisiana State University Press, 1969.

Case, Sue-Ellen. "Tracking the Vampire." *Differences* 3, no. 2 (1992): 1–20.

——. "Towards a Butch-Femme Aesthetic." *Discourse* 11, no. 1 (1988–1989): 55–73.

Chaikin, Robert A. "King Kong—A Re-Assessment." *The Psychoanalytic Reader* 67, no. 2 (Summer 1980): 271–76.

Char. "Doctor X." *Variety* (August 9, 1932).

——"Mark of the Vampire." *Variety* (March 28, 1935).

Charman, Bernard. "Girls Want Mystery; Boys War Pictures." *Motion Picture Herald* 111, no. 4 (April 22, 1933).

Chic. "Savage Girl." *Variety* (May 2, 1933).

Churchill, Edward. "Dracula." *Motion Picture Herald* 102, no. 1 (January 3, 1931): 71, 74.

Clarens, Carlos. *Horror Movies: An Illustrated Survey.* New York: Capricorn, 1967.

Clover, Carol J. *Men, Women and Chain Saws: Gender in the Modern Horror Film.* Princeton, N.J.: Princeton University Press, 1992.

Cohen John S., Jr. "'Kongo' Is Revived With New Terrors." *New York Sun,* November 17, 1932.

——. "'Trader Horn,' or Thrills, Animals, and Sex in Darkest Africa." *New York Sun,* February 4, 1931.

Conger, Syndy M. and Janice R. Welsch. "The Comic and the Grotesque in James Whale's Frankenstein Films." In *Planks of Reason,* ed. Barry Keith Grant. Metuchen, N.J.: Scarecrow, 1984, pp. 290–306.

Corber, Robert J. "Reconstructing Homosexuality: Hitchcock and the Homoerotics of Spectatorial Pleasure." *Discourse* 13, no. 2 (Spring/Summer 1991): 58–82.

Craft, Christopher. "'Kiss Me with Those Red Lips': Gender and Inversion in Bram Stoker's *Dracula." Representations* 8 (Fall 1984): 107–33.

Creed, Barbara. *The Monstrous-Feminine: Film, Feminism, Psychoanalysis.* New York: Routledge, 1993.

"The Crime of Dr. Crespi." *Variety* (January 15, 1936).

"'The Crimes of Dr. Crespi,' with Eric [sic] Von Stroheim." *Film Daily,* September 24, 1935.

Curtis, James. *James Whale.* Metuchen, N.J.: Scarecrow, 1982.

Daniels, Les. *Living in Fear: A History of Horror in the Mass Media.* New York: Da Capo, 1975.

Davis, Angela Y. *Women, Race, and Class.* New York: Random House, 1981.

Davy, Kate. "Fe/male Impersonation: The Discourse of Camp." In *Critical Theory and Performance,* ed. Janelle G. Reinelt and Joseph R. Roach. Ann Arbor: University of Michigan Press, pp. 231–47.

De Lauretis, Teresa. "Film and the Visible." In *How Do I Look?: Queer Film and Video,* ed. Bad Object-Choices. Seattle: Bay, 1991, pp. 223–64.

Delehanty, Thornton. "The New Film." *New York Post,* February 4, 1931.

Derry, Charles. *Dark Dreams: A Psychological History of the Modern Horror Film.* London: Thomas Yoseloff, 1977.

Dettman, Bruce and Michael Bedford. *The Horror Factory: The Horror Films of Universal, 1931–1955.* New York: Gordon, 1976.

"Dick and Ken Speed Up on *Invisible Man." Motion Picture Herald* 114, no. 4 (January 20, 1934).

Dijkstra, Bram. *Idols of Perversity: Fantasies of Feminine Evil in Fin-de-Siècle Culture.* New York: Oxford University Press, 1986.

Doane, Mary Ann. *Femmes Fatales: Feminism, Film Theory, Psychoanalysis.* New York: Routledge, 1991.

——. *The Desire to Desire: The Woman's Film of the 1940s.* Bloomington: Indiana University Press, 1987.

——. "Film and the Masquerade: Theorising the Female Spectator." *Screen* 23, nos. 3–4 (Fall 1982): 74–87. Reprinted in *Femmes Fatales.*

"Dr. Jekyll and Mr. Hyde." *Time* (January 11, 1932).

"Doctor X." *New York World-Telegram,* August 4, 1932.

"Doctor X." *Time* (August 15, 1932).

"Doctor X." *The Commonweal* 16 (August 24, 1932).

Dolan, Jill. "The Dynamics of Desire: Sexuality and Gender in Pornography and Performance." *Theatre Journal* 39, no. 2 (May 1987): 156–74.

"Don't Park Here Says Caldwell on 'Frankenstein.'" *Motion Picture Herald* 120, no. 5 (August 3, 1935).

Doty, Alexander. *Making Things Perfectly Queer: Interpreting Mass Culture.* Minneapolis: University of Minnesota Press, 1993.

Dracula. Production Background by Philip J. Riley. Universal Filmscripts Series Classic Horror Films-Volume 13. Absecon, N.J.: Magicimage Filmbooks, 1990.

"Dracula." *Film Daily,* February 15, 1931.

"Dracula." *Time* (February 23, 1931).

"Dracula's Daughter." *Christian Century* (June 24, 1936).

"Dracula's Daughter." *Film Daily,* May 18, 1936.

Draper, Ellen. "Zombie Women: When the Gaze is Male." *Wide Angle* 10, no. 3 (1988): 52–62.

Du Maurier, George. *Trilby.* New York: Dutton, 1931.

Dyer, Peter John. "The Roots of Horror." In *International Film Annual 3,* ed. William Whitebait. New York: Taplinger, 1959, pp. 69–75.

Dyer, Richard. "White." *Screen* 29, no. 4 (Autumn 1988): 44–64.

Eastman, Fred. "The Movies and Your Child's Health." *Christian Century* (May 10, 1933).

——. "Your Child and the Movies." *Christian Century* (May 3, 1933).

Edelman, Lee. "Seeing Things: Representation, the Scene of Surveillance, and the Spectacle of Gay Male Sex." In *Inside/Out: Lesbian Theories, Gay Theories,* ed. Diana Fuss. New York: Routledge, 1991, pp. 93–116.

Ellis, John. *Visible Fictions: Cinema, Television, Video.* London: Routledge and Kegan Paul, 1982.

Ellis, Kate F. *The Contested Castle: Gothic Novels and the Subversion of Domestic Ideology.* Urbana: University of Illinois Press, 1989.

"Emotion Test Hits on 'Frankenstein.'" *Motion Picture Herald* 119, no. 7 (May 18, 1935).

Evans, Walter. "Monster Movies and the Rites of Initiation." *Journal of Popular Film* 4, no. 2 (Fall 1975): 124–42.

——. "Monster Movies: A Sexual Theory." *Journal of Popular Film* 2, no. 4 (Fall 1973): 353–65.

Everson, William K. "Svengali." *The New School Program Notes* (June 26, 1973).
——. "A Family Tree of Monsters." *Film Culture* 1, no. 1 (January 1955): 24–31.
Fanon, Frantz. *Black Skin, White Masks.* Translated by Charles Lam Markmann. New York: Grove, 1967.
Ferguson, Otis. "Two Films." *New Republic* 83, no. 1069 (May 29, 1935).
Fox, Julian. "The Golden Age of Terror." *Films and Filming* 22 (June 1976): 16–23; (July 1976): 18–24; (August 1976): 20–24; (September 1976): 20–25; (October 1976): 18–25.
Frank, Alan. *Horror Movies: Tales of Terror in the Cinema.* London: Octopus, 1974.
"Frankenstein: Movie Magic Revives The Monster and Provides a Bride." *News-Week* 5 (May 4, 1935).
Fredrickson, George. *The Black Image in the White Mind: The Debate on Afro-American Character and Destiny, 1817–1914.* New York: Harper and Row, 1971.
"Free Permanent Given for 'Invisible Ray,'" *Motion Picture Herald* 124, no. 3 (July 18, 1936).
Friedberg, Anne. *Window Shopping: Cinema and the Postmodern.* Los Angeles: University of California Press, 1993.
F. S. N. "At the Rialto and the Mayfair." *New York Times,* May 3, 1935.
——. "At the Roxy." *New York Times,* May 11, 1935.
Fuss, Diana, ed. *Inside/Out: Lesbian Theories, Gay Theories.* New York: Routledge, 1991.
Gaines, Jane. "From Elephants to Lux Soap: The Programming and 'Flow' of Early Motion Picture Exploitation." *The Velvet Light Trap* 25 (Spring 1990).
——. "White Privilege and Looking Relations: Race and Gender in Feminist Film Theory." *Cultural Critique* 4 (Fall 1986): 59–79.
Garber, Marjorie. *Vested Interests: Cross-Dressing and Cultural Anxiety.* New York: Routledge, 1992.
Gilbert, Douglas. "New Film at Rialto Produces Chills." *New York World-Telegram,* May 19, 1936.
Gleiberman, Owen. "Alive and, Well . . ." *Entertainment Weekly* 247 (November 4, 1994).
"The Gorilla Film 'Ingagi.'" *Science* 71, no. 10 (June 6, 1930).
Gottesman, Ronald and Harry Geduld, eds. *The Girl in the Hairy Paw: King Kong as Myth and Monster.* New York: Avon, 1976.
Gramson, Joshua. *Claims to Fame: Celebrity in Contemporary America.* Los Angeles: University of California Press, 1994.
Griffin, Andrew. "Sympathy for the Werewolf." *University Publishing* 6 (1979): 1–17.
Gunning, Tom. "The Cinema of Attractions: Early Film, Its Spectator, and the Avant-Garde." In *Early Cinema: Space, Frame, Narrative,* ed. Thomas Elsaesser with Adam Barker. London: BFI, 1990.
Hall, Gladys. "The Feminine Love of Horror." *Motion Picture Classic* (January 1931).

Hall, Mordaunt. "A Fantastic Film in Which a Monstrous Ape Uses Automobiles for Missiles and Climbs Skyscraper." *New York Times*, March 3, 1933.

——. "Lionel Atwill and Lee Tracy in Exciting Murder Mystery at Warners' Strand." *New York Times*, August 4, 1932.

——. "Fredric March in Splendidly Pictorial Version of 'Dr. Jekyll and Mr. Hyde.'" *New York Times*, June 2, 1932.

——. "Strange Experiences of an Expedition Into the Wilds of Northern Australia." *New York Times*, February 29, 1932.

——. "Frankenstein." *New York Times*, December 5, 1931.

——. "Trilby." *New York Times*, May 1, 1931.

——. "Bram Stoker's Human Vampire." *New York Times*, February 13, 1931.

——. "An Impressive Jungle Melodrama." *New York Times*, February 4, 1931.

Handel, Leo J. *Hollywood Looks at Its Audience: A Report of Film Audience Research.* Urbana: University of Illinois Press, 1950.

Hanke, Ken. *A Critical Guide to Horror Film Series.* New York: Garland, 1991.

Hansen, Miriam. *Babel and Babylon: Spectatorship in American Silent Film.* Cambridge: Harvard University Press: 1991.

Hanson, Ellis. "Undead." In *Inside/Out: Lesbian Theories, Gay Theories*, ed. Diana Fuss. New York: Routledge, 1991, pp. 324–40.

Haraway, Donna. *Primate Visions: Gender, Race, and Nature in the World of Modern Science.* New York: Routledge, 1989.

Hardy, Phil, ed. *The Encyclopedia of Horror.* New York: Harper and Row, 1986.

Heath, Stephen. "The Ethics of Sexual Difference." *Discourse* 12 (Spring/Summer 1990): 128–53.

——. "Joan Riviere and the Masquerade." In *Formations of Fantasy*, ed. Victor Burgin, James Donald, and Cora Kaplan. London: Methuen, 1986, pp. 45–61.

Hoch, Paul. *White Hero Black Beast: Racism, Sexism and the Mask of Masculinity.* London: Pluto, 1979.

Hoffman, Jerry. "Frankenstein Film Tells How Monster Got Mate." *Los Angeles Examiner*, April 22, 1935.

Hogan, David J. *Dark Romance: Sexuality in the Horror Film.* New York: McFarland, 1986.

hooks, bell. *Feminist Theory: From Margin to Center.* Boston: South End, 1984.

Huss, Roy. "Almost Eve: The Creation Scene in *Bride of Frankenstein*." In *Focus on the Horror Film*, ed. Roy Huss and T. J. Ross. Englewood Cliff, N.J.: Prentice-Hall, 1972.

Hutchinson, Tom. *Horror and Fantasy in the Cinema.* London: Studio Vista, 1974.

"'Ingagi' Passes Censors for Second Time in Ohio; Extended Runs For Some." *Exhibitors Herald-World* 100, no. 7 (August 6, 1930).

"'Ingagi'—True or False?" *Nature* 16 (July 1930).

Irigaray, Luce. *This Sex Which Is Not One.* Translated by Catherine Porter. Ithaca: Cornell University Press, 1985.

"Island of Lost Souls." *Photoplay* 43, no. 3 (February 1933).

"Island of Lost Souls." *Variety* (December 2, 1932).

Jacobs, Lea. *The Wages of Sin: Censorship and the Fallen Woman Film, 1928–1942*. Madison: University of Wisconsin Press, 1991.

J. C. M. "Just a Few Snarls." *The New Yorker* 11 (May 25, 1935).

——. No title. *The New Yorker* 7 (May 9, 1931).

Jowett, Garth. *Film: The Democratic Art*. Boston: Little, Brown, 1976.

Kane, Joe. "Beauties, Beasts, and Male Chauvinist Monsters." *Take One* 4, no. 4 (March-April 1973): 8–10.

Kawin, Bruce. "Children of the Light." In *Shadows of the Magic Lamp: Fantasy and Science Fiction in Film*, ed. George Slusser and Eric S. Rabkin. Carbondale: Southern Illinois University Press, 1985, pp. 14–29.

——. "The Mummy's Pool." In *Planks of Reason*, ed. Barry Keith Grant. Metuchen, N.J.: Scarecrow, 1984.

Kosofsky Sedgwick, Eve. *Epistemology of the Closet*. Berkeley: University of California Press, 1990.

——. *Between Men: English Literature and Male Homosocial Desire*. New York: Columbia University Press, 1985.

Koszarski, Richard. "*Mad Love*." *Film Heritage* 5 (Winter 1969–70): 24–29.

Krasniewicz, Louise and Michael Blitz. "Review of *Primate Visions* by Donna Haraway." *Discourse* 12, no. 2 (Spring/Summer 1990): 168–71.

"Laby's Effective Lobby Display." *Motion Picture Herald* 106, no. 5 (January 30, 1932).

Lang, Harry. "I'll Have Vanilla." *Photoplay* 41, no. 2 (January 1932): 72, 115.

Laplanche, J. and J.-B. Pontalis. *The Language of Psycho-Analysis*. Translated by Donald Nicholson-Smith. New York: Norton, 1973.

Laqueur, Thomas. *Making Sex: Body and Gender from the Greeks to Freud*. Cambridge: Harvard University Press, 1990.

Lenne, Gerard. "Monster and Victim." In *Sexual Stratagems: The World of Women in Film*, ed. Patricia Erens. Translated by Elayne Donenberg and Thomas Agabiti. New York: Horizon, 1979, pp. 31–40.

Levine, George. "The Ambiguous Heritage of Frankenstein." In *The Endurance of Frankenstein*, ed. George Levine and U. C. Knoepflmacher. Los Angeles: University of California Press, 1979, pp. 3–30.

L. N. "Beyond the Pale." *New York Times*, July 29, 1932.

Lowry, Edward and Richard de Cordova. "Enunciation and the Production of Horror in *White Zombie*." In *Planks of Reason*, ed. Barry Keith Grant. Metuchen, N.J.: Scarecrow, 1984, pp. 346–89.

"Louie Charnisky Stages Swell *Black Cat* Show." *Motion Picture Herald* 116, no. 2 (July 7, 1934).

"Mad Love." *Time* (July 22, 1935).

Manchel, Frank. *Terrors of the Screen*. Englewood Cliffs, N.J.: Prentice-Hall, 1970.

"Mark of the Vampire." *Time* (May 6, 1935).

"Mark of the Vampire." *Film Daily*, March 28, 1935.

Mayne, Judith. *Cinema and Spectatorship*. New York: Routledge, 1993.

——. "'King Kong' and the Ideology of Spectacle." *Quarterly Review of Film Studies* 1, no. 4 (1976): 373–87.

McCarthy. "Mark of the Vampire." *Motion Picture Herald* 191, no. 1 (April 6, 1935).

——. "The Invisible Man." *Motion Picture Herald* 113, no. 6 (November 4, 1933).

——. "Murders in the Zoo." *Motion Picture Herald* 110, no. 11 (March 11, 1933).

——. "King Kong." *Motion Picture Herald* 110, no. 9 (February 25, 1933).

——. "Wax Museum." *Motion Picture Herald* 110, no. 2 (January 7, 1933).

——. "Island of Lost Souls." *Motion Picture Herald* 109, no. 11 (December 10, 1932).

——. "The Mummy." *Motion Picture Herald* 109, no. 10 (December 3, 1932).

——. "The Most Dangerous Game." *Motion Picture Herald* 108, no. 5 (July 30, 1932).

McConnell, Frank. "Rough Beasts Slouching." In *Focus on the Horror Film*, ed. Roy Huss and T. J. Ross. Englewood, N.J.: Prentice-Hall, 1972, pp. 24–35.

Meehan, Leo. "Dr. Jekyll and Mr. Hyde." *Motion Picture Herald* 105, no. 13 (December 26, 1931).

——. "Frankenstein." *Motion Picture Herald* 105, no. 7 (November 14, 1931).

Mellor, Anne K. "Possessing Nature: The Female in *Frankenstein*." In *Romanticism and Feminism*, ed. Anne K. Mellor. Bloomington: Indiana University Press, 1988, pp. 220–32.

Merritt, Russell. "Nickelodeon Theaters, 1905–1914: Building an Audience for the Movies." In *The American Film Industry*, ed. Tino Balio. Madison: University of Wisconsin Press, 1985, pp. 83–102.

Mitchell, James E. "'4 Frightened People' Liked at Paramount." *Los Angeles Examiner*, January 26, 1934.

——. "Mad Scientists, Cannibalism, Bodies—Gosh!" *Los Angeles Examiner*, August 12, 1932.

Modleski, Tania. *The Women Who Knew Too Much: Hitchcock and Feminist Theory*. New York: Methuen, 1988.

——. *Loving with a Vengeance: Mass-Produced Fantasies for Women*. New York: Routledge, 1982.

Moers, Ellen. "Female Gothic." In *The Endurance of Frankenstein*, ed. George Levine and U. C. Knoepflmacher. Los Angeles: University of California Press, 1979, pp. 77–87.

"More Pantomime Less Dialog [sic] to Form Screen Techniques, Says Laemmle. Universal Production Chief Sees Need for Greater Use of Silent Film's Methods." *Exhibitors Herald-World* 100, no. 4 (July 26, 1930).

"The Most Dangerous Game." *Cinema Texas Program Notes* 21, no. 2 (November 18, 1981).

Mulvey, Laura. *Visual and Other Pleasures*. Bloomington: Indiana University Press, 1989.

——. "Afterthoughts on 'Visual Pleasure and Narrative Cinema' inspired by King Vidor's *Duel in the Sun* (1945)." *Framework* 15/16/17 (Summer 1981): 12–15. Reprinted in *Visual and Other Pleasures*. Bloomington: Indiana University Press, 1989, pp. 29–38.

——. "Visual Pleasure and Narrative Cinema." *Screen* 16, no. 3 (1975): 75–99. Reprinted in *Visual and Other Pleasures*. Bloomington: Indiana University Press, 1989, pp. 14–26.

The Mummy. Production background by Philip J. Riley. Universal Filmscripts Series Classic Horror Films-Volume 7. Absecon, N.J.: Magicimage Filmbooks, 1989.

"The Mummy." *Time* (January 16, 1933).

Mundorf, Norbert, James Weaver, and Dolf Zillman. "Effects of Gender Roles and Self Perceptions on Affective Reactions to Horror Films." *Sex Roles* 20, no. 11 (1989).

Murphy, Michael J. *The Celluloid Vampire: A History and Filmography, 1897–1979*. Ann Arbor, Mich.: Pierian, 1979.

Murray, Richard. "Trader Horn." *Standard Union*, February 4, 1931.

Musetto, V. A. "Mummy Zita Rises from the Past." *New York Post*, December 15, 1989.

Newton, Esther. *Mother Camp: Female Impersonators in America*. Englewood, N.J.: Prentice-Hall, 1972.

"No More Horror for Fay Wray." Source unknown. Fay Wray Collection, University of Southern California Cinema Archives. Fay Wray Scrapbook, 1929–1933, p. 22.

Nugent, Frank S. "Dracula's Daughter." *New York Times*, May 1936.

Parsons, Louella O. "Horror, Thrills and Suspense Fill Picture," *Los Angeles Examiner*, March 25, 1933.

Peary, Gerald. "Missing Links: The Jungle Origins of *King Kong*." In *The Girl in the Hairy Paw*, ed. Ronald Gottesman and Harry Geduld. New York: Avon, 1976, pp. 37–42.

Pendo, Stephen. "Universal's Golden Age of Horror: 1931–1941." *Films in Review* 26, no. 3 (March 1975): 155–60.

"Peter Lorre in 'Mad Love.'" *Film Daily*, July 1, 1935.

Pizor, William M. "The Blonde Captive." *Liberty* (April 9, 1932).

Prawer, S. S. *Caligari's Children: The Film as Tale of Terror*. New York: Da Capo, 1980.

Price, Michael and George Turner. "*White Zombie*—Today's Unlikely Classic." *American Cinematographer* (February 1988).

Rankin, Ruth. "Meet The Monster!" *Photoplay* 41, no. 4 (March 1932).

Rice, Anne. *Cry to Heaven*. New York: Ballantine, 1982.

Rich, Adrienne. *Poems: Selected and New, 1950–1974*. New York: Norton, 1975.

Riviere, Joan. "Womanliness as a Masquerade." In *Formations of Fantasy*, ed. Victor Burgin, James Donald, and Cora Kaplan. London: Methuen, 1986, pp. 35–44.

Roof, Judith. *A Lure of Knowledge: Lesbian Sexuality and Theory*. New York: Columbia University Press, 1991.

Rosen, David N. *"King Kong:* Race, Sex, and Rebellion." *Jump Cut* 6 (March/April 1975): 8–10.

Rush. "Dr. Jekyll and Mr. Hyde." *Variety* (January 5, 1932).

——. "Frankenstein." *Variety* (December 8, 1931).

——. "Dracula." *Variety* (February 18, 1931).

Russo, Vito. *The Celluloid Closet: Homosexuality in the Movies*. New York: Harper and Row, 1985.

Schallert, Edwin. " 'Frankenstein' a Hit." *Los Angeles Times*, January 4, 1932.

Scho, "Dracula's Daughter." *Variety* (May 20, 1936).

Sennwald, Andre. "Peter Lorre in His First American Photoplay, 'Mad Love' on View at the Roxy Theatre." *New York Times*, August 5, 1935.

Shawell, Julia. "Screen-Views." *Graphic* (February 4, 1931).

Sheehan, Henry. "Revival Pick of the Week: The Bride of Frankenstein." *LA Weekly* (October 18, 1991).

Showalter, Elaine. *Sexual Anarchy: Gender and Culture at the Fin de Siècle*. New York: Penguin, 1990.

Singer, Kurt. *The Laughton Story: An Intimate Story of Charles Laughton*. Philadelphia: John C. Winston, 1954.

Skal, David J. *The Monster Show: A Cultural History of Horror*. New York: Norton, 1993.

Skolsky, Sidney. "Tintypes." *New York News*, October 19, 1931. Fay Wray Collection, University of South California Cinema Archives. Fay Wray Scrapbook, 1929–1933, p. 82.

Smith, Valerie. "Split Affinities: The Case of Interracial Rape." In *Conflicts in Feminism*, ed. Marianne Hirsch and Evelyn Fox Keller. New York: Routledge, 1990.

Snead, James. "Spectatorship and Capture in *King Kong:* The Guilty Look." *Critical Quarterly* 33, no. 1 (Spring 1991).

Soren, David. *The Rise and Fall of the Horror Film: An Art Historical Approach to Fantasy Cinema*. Columbia, Mo.: Lucas, 1977.

Staiger, Janet. *Interpreting Films: Studies in the Historical Reception of American Cinema*. Princeton, N.J.: Princeton University Press, 1992.

Studlar, Gaylyn. "The Perils of Pleasure? Fan Magazine Discourse as Women's Commodified Culture in the 1920s." *Wide Angle* 13, no. 1 (January 1991): 6–33.

"Svengali." *Time* (May 11, 1961).

"Swinger Offers First Aid." *Motion Picture Herald* 120, no. 11 (September 14, 1935).

Thirer, Irene. "Doctor X." *New York Daily News*, August 4, 1932. Fay Wray Collection, University of Southern California Cinema Archives.

Todorov, Tzvetan. *The Fantastic: A Structural Approach to a Literary Genre*. Translated by Richard Howard. Ithaca: Cornell University Press, 1975.

Torgovnick, Marianna. *Gone Primitive: Savage Intellects, Modern Lives.* Chicago: University of Chicago Press, 1990.

"Torture As You Like It." *Vanity Fair* 45, no. 3 (November 1935).

"Trader Horn." *Motion Picture Herald* 102, no. 1 (January 3, 1931).

"Trader Horn." *Minneapolis Sunday Tribune,* June 21, 1931.

Tudor, Andrew. *Monsters and Mad Scientists: A Cultural History of the Horror Movie.* Oxford: Basil Blackwell, 1989.

Turner, George. "Hunting *The Most Dangerous Game.*" *American Cinematographer* (September 1987).

Twitchell, James B. *Dreadful Pleasures: An Anatomy of Modern Horror.* New York: Oxford University Press, 1985.

——. "*Frankenstein* and the Anatomy of Horror." *Georgia Review* 37, no. 1 (Spring 1983): 41–78.

Ursini, J. and A. Silver. *The Vampire Film.* New York: Barnes, 1975.

Waldman, Diane. "From Midnight Shows to Marriage Vows: Women, Exploitation, and Exhibition." *Wide Angle* 6, no. 2 (1984): 40–49.

Watts, Richard Jr. "'Dracula'—Roxy." *New York Herald Tribune,* February 13, 1931.

——. "'Trader Horn,'" *New York Herald Tribune,* February 4, 1931.

Wells, H. G. "Preface to *The Island of Dr. Moreau.*" *The Works of H. G. Wells.* New York: Atlantic Edition, 1924.

"What Power Can Save Them?" *Photoplay* 43, no. 5 (April 1933).

"'When Will She Wake?' Rosy Asks Bridgeport." *Motion Picture Herald* 119, no. 13 (June 29, 1935).

White, Dennis L. "The Poetics of Horror: More Than Meets the Eye." *Cinema Journal* 10, no. 2 (Spring 1971): 1–18.

White, Patricia. *The Uninvited: Cinema and the Conditions of Lesbian Representability.* Ph.D. diss., University of California, Santa Cruz, 1993.

——. "Female Spectator, Lesbian Specter: *The Haunting.*" In *Inside/Out: Lesbian Theories, Gay Theories,* ed. Diana Fuss. New York: Routledge, 1991.

"White Zombie." *Time* (August 8, 1932).

Willeman, Paul. "Voyeurism, The Look, and Dwoskin." In *Narrative, Apparatus, Ideology: A Film Theory Reader,* ed Philip Rosen. New York: Columbia University Press, 1986, pp. 210–18.

Williams, Linda. "When the Woman Looks." In *Re-Vision: Essays in Feminist Film Criticism,* ed. Mary Ann Doane, Patricia Mellencamp, and Linda Williams. Frederick, Md.: AFI Monograph Series, University Publications of America, 1984, pp. 83–99.

Wolf, Leonard. *Horror: A Connoisseur's Guide to Literature and Film.* New York: Facts on File, 1989.

Wood, Robin. "Beauty Bests the Beast." *American Film* 8, no. 10 (September 1983): 63–65.

——. "An Introduction to the American Horror Film." *American Nightmares: Essays on the Horror Film.* Toronto: Festival of Festivals, 1979, pp. 7–28.

Reprinted in *Planks of Reason*, ed. Barry K. Grant. Metuchen, N.J.: Scarecrow, 1984, pp. 164–200.

——. "Return of the Repressed." *Film Comment* 14, no. 4 (July/August 1978): 25–32.

Wray, Fay. *On the Other Hand: A Life Story*. New York: St. Martin's, 1989.

——. "How Fay Wray Met Kong, or the Scream that Shook the World." In *The Girl in the Hairy Paw*, ed. Ronald Gottesman and Harry Geduld. New York: Avon, 1976, pp. 223–25.

Young, Elizabeth. "Here Comes the Bride: Wedding Gender and Race in *Bride of Frankenstein*." *Feminist Studies* 17, no. 3 (1991): 403–37.

"You Should See My Kid Sister." *Photoplay* 39, no. 5 (April 1931): 31.

Index